ORDNANCE SURVEY MEMOIRS OF IRELAND

Volume Twenty-one

PARISHES OF COUNTY ANTRIM VII
1832–8

Published 1993.
The Institute of Irish Studies,
The Queen's University of Belfast,
Belfast.
In association with
The Royal Irish Academy,
Dawson Street,
Dublin.

Grateful acknowledgement is made to the Economic and Social Research Council and the Department of Education for Northern Ireland for their financial assistance at different stages of this publication programme.

Copyright 1993.

All rights reserved. No part of this publication may be reproduced, stored in a retrieval system or transmitted, in any form or by any means, electronic, mechanical, photocopying, recording or otherwise, without the prior permission of the publisher.

British Library Cataloguing-in-Publication Data.
A catalogue record for this book is available from the British Library.

Paperback ISBN 0 85389 462 0
Hardback ISBN 0 85389 461 2

Printed in Ireland by SPRINT-print Ltd

Ordnance Survey Memoirs of Ireland
VOLUME TWENTY-ONE

Parishes of County Antrim VII
1832–8

South Antrim

Edited by Angélique Day and Patrick McWilliams.

The Institute of Irish Studies
in association with
The Royal Irish Academy

EDITORIAL BOARD

Angélique Day (General Editor)
Patrick S. McWilliams (Executive Editor)
Nóirín Dobson (Assistant Editor)
Dr B.M. Walker (Publishing Director)
Professor R.H. Buchanan (Chairman)

CONTENTS

	Page
Introduction	ix
Brief history of the Irish Ordnance Survey and Memoirs	ix
Definition of terms used	x
Note on Memoirs of County Antrim	x

Parishes in County Antrim

Aghagallon	1
Aghalee	26
Ballinderry	41
Camlin	60
Glenavy	77
Lough Neagh	92
Magheragall	98
Magheramesk	112
Tullyrusk	131

List of selected maps and drawings

County Antrim, with parish boundaries	vi
County Antrim, 1837, by Samuel Lewis	viii
Old church of Camlin	61

List of O.S. maps, 1830s

Aghagallon	2
Aghalee	27
Lower Ballinderry	42
Crumlin	65
Glenavy	78

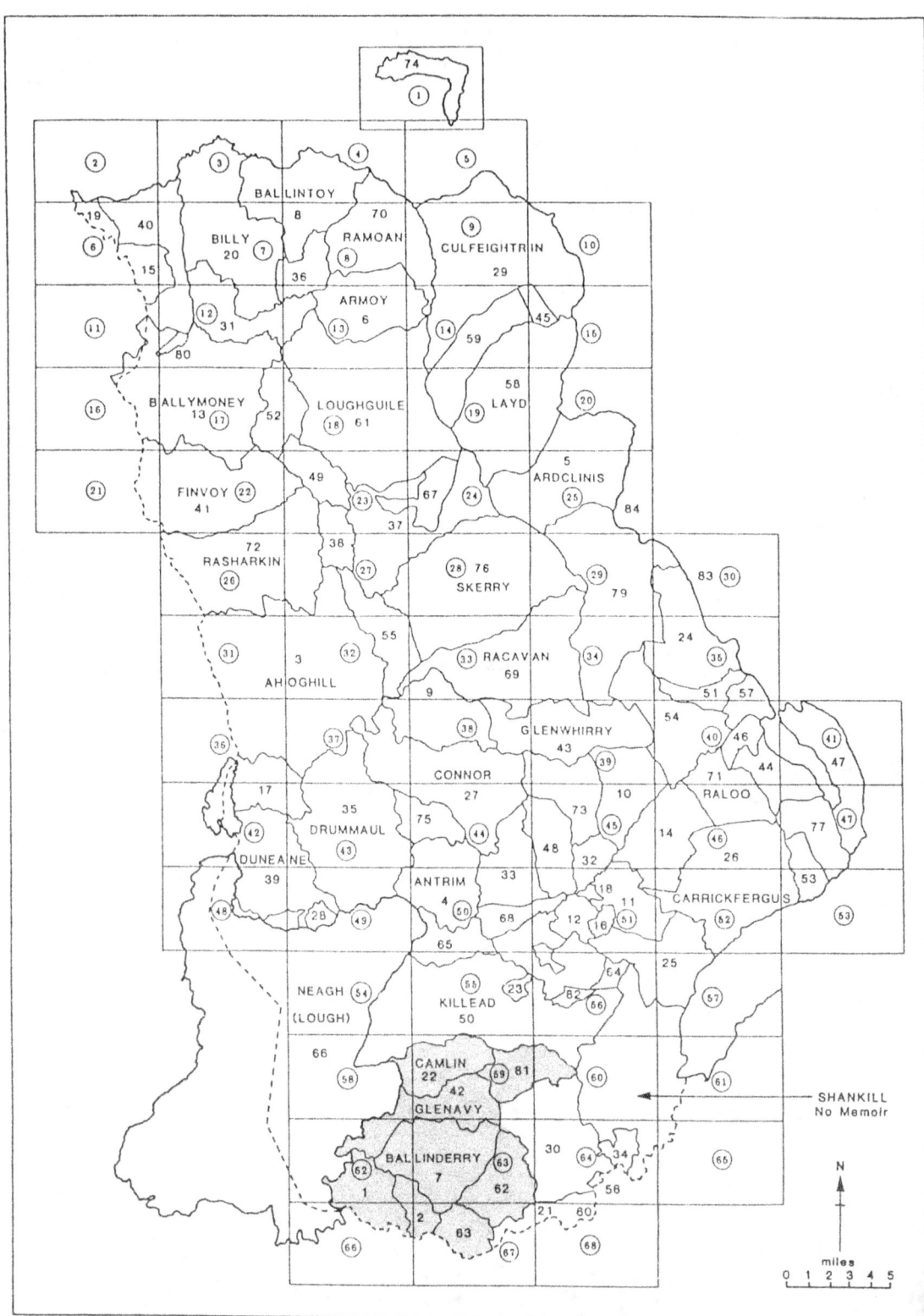

ACKNOWLEDGEMENTS

During the course of the transcription and publication project many have advised and encouraged us in this gigantic task. Thanks must first be given to the Royal Irish Academy, particularly former librarian Mrs Brigid Dolan and her staff, for making the original manuscripts available to us. We are also indebted to Siobhán O'Rafferty for her continuing help in deciphering indistinct passages of manuscript. For this particular volume we wish to thank Professor Brian Scott of Queen's for guidance on Latin texts.

We should like to acknowledge the following individuals for their special contributions. Dr Brian Trainor led the way with his edition of the Antrim Memoir and provided vital help on the steering committee. Dr Ann Hamlin also provided valuable support, especially during the most trying stages of the project. Professor R.H. Buchanan's unfailing encouragment has been instrumental in the development of the project to the present. Without Dr Kieran Devine the initial stages of the transcription and the computerising work would never have been completed successfully: the project owes a great deal to his constant help and advice. Dr Kay Muhr's continuing contribution to the work of the transcription project is deeply appreciated. Mr W.C. Kerr's interest and expertise have been invaluable. Professor Anne Crookshank and Dr Edward McParland were most generous with practical help and advice concerning the drawings amongst the Memoir manuscripts. We would like to thank the Director of the Ordnance Survey, Dublin and the keepers of the fire-proof store, among them Leonard Hines. Finally, all students of the nineteenth century Ordnance Survey of Ireland owe a great deal to the pioneering work of Professor J.H. Andrews, and his kind help in the first days of the project is gratefully recorded.

The essential task of inputting the texts from audio tapes was done by Miss Eileen Kingan, Mrs Christine Robertson, Miss Eilis Smyth, Miss Lynn Murray, and, most importantly, Miss Maureen Carr.

We are grateful to the Linen Hall Library for lending us their copies of the first edition 6" Ordnance Survey Maps: also to Ms Maura Pringle of QUB Cartography Department for the index maps showing the parish boundaries. For providing financial assistance at crucial times for the maintenance of the project, we would like to take this opportunity of thanking the trustees of the Esme Mitchell trust and The Public Record Office of Northern Ireland.

Left:

Map of parishes of County Antrim. The area described in this volume, the parishes of South Antrim, has been shaded to highlight its location. The square grids represent the 1830s 6" Ordnance Survey maps. The encircled numbers relate to the map numbers as presented in the bound volumes of maps for the county. The parishes have been numbered in all cases and named in full where possible, except those in the following list: Aghagallon 1, Aghalee 2, Ballyclug 9, Ballycor 10, Ballylinny 11, Ballynure 14, Ballyrashane 15, Grange of Ballyscullion 17, Ballywillin 19, Blaris and Lisburn 21 & 60, Grange of Carmavy 23, Carncastle 24, Cranfield 28, Derryaghy 30, Derrykeighan 31, Grange of Doagh 32, Donegore 33, Drumbeg 34, Grange of Drumtullagh 36, Dunaghy 37, Grange of Dundermot 38, Dunluce 40, Glynn 44, Inver 46, Island Magee 47, Kilbride 48, Killagan 49, Grange of Killyglen 51, Kilraghts 52, Kilroot 53, Kilwaughter 54, Kirkinriola 55, Lambeg 56, Larne 57, Granges of Layd and Inispollan 59 & 45, Magheragall 62, Magheramesk 63, Grange of Muckamore 65, Newtown Crommelin 67, Grange of Nilteen 68, Rashee 73, Rathlin Island 74, Grange of Shilvodan 75, Templecorran 77, Templepatrick 78, Tickmacrevan 79, Tullyrusk 81, Umgall 82.

Map of County Antrim, from Samuel Lewis' *Atlas of the counties of Ireland* (London, 1837)

INTRODUCTION AND GUIDE TO THE PUBLICATION OF THE ORDNANCE SURVEY MEMOIRS

The following text of the Ordnance Survey Memoirs was first transcribed by a team working in the Institute of Irish Studies at The Queen's University of Belfast, on a computerised index of the material. For this publication programme the text has been further edited: spellings have been modernised in most cases, although where the original spelling was thought to be of any interest it has been retained and is indicated by angle brackets in the text. Variant spellings for townland and lesser place-names have been preserved, although parish and major place-names have been standardised and the original spelling given in angle brackets. Names of prominent people, for instance landlords, have been standardised where possible, but original spellings of names in lists of informants, emigration tables and on tombstones have been retained. We have not altered the Memoir writers' anglicisation of names and words in Irish.

Punctuation has been modernised and is the responsibility of the editors. Editorial additions are indicated by square brackets: a question mark before and after a word indicates a queried reading and tentatively inserted information respectively. Original drawings are referred to in the text, and some have been reproduced. Manuscript page references have been omitted from this series. Because of the huge variation in size of Memoirs for different counties, the following editorial policy has been adopted: where there are numerous duplicating and overlapping accounts, the most complete and finished account, normally the Memoir proper, has been presented, with additional unique information from other accounts like the Fair Sheets entered into a separate section, clearly titled and identified; where the Memoir material is less, nothing has been omitted. To achieve standard volume size, parishes have been associated on the basis of propinquity.

There are considerable differences in the volume of information recorded for different areas: counties Antrim and Londonderry are exceptionally well covered, while the other counties do not have quite the same detail. This series is the first systematic publication of the parish Memoirs, although individual parishes have been published by pioneering local history societies. The entire transcriptions of the Memoirs made in the course of the indexing project can be consulted in the Public Record Office of Northern Ireland and the library at the Queen's University of Belfast. The manuscripts of the Ordnance Survey Memoirs are in the Royal Irish Academy, Dublin.

Brief history of the Irish Ordnance Survey in the nineteenth century and the writing of the Ordnance Survey Memoirs

In 1824 a House of Commons committee recommended a townland survey of Ireland with maps at the scale of 6", to facilitate a uniform valuation for local taxation. The Duke of Wellington, then prime minister, authorised this, the first Ordnance Survey of Ireland. The survey was directed by Colonel Thomas Colby, who had under his command officers of the Royal Engineers and three companies of sappers and miners. In addition to this, civil assistants were recruited to help with sketching, drawing and engraving of maps, and eventually, in the 1830s, the writing of the Memoirs.

The Memoirs were written descriptions intended to accompany the maps, containing information which could not be fitted on to them. Colonel Colby always considered additional information to be necessary to clarify place-names and other distinctive features of each parish; this was to be written up in reports by the officers. Much information about parishes resulted from research into place-names and was used in the writing of the Memoirs. The term "Memoir" comes from the abbreviation of the word "Aide-Memoire". It was also used in the 18th century to describe topographical descriptions accompanying maps.

In 1833 Colby's assistant, Lieutenant Thomas Larcom, developed the scope of the officers' reports by stipulating the headings or "Heads of Inquiry" under which information was to be reported, and including topics of social as well as economic interest. By this time civil assistants were writing some of the Memoirs under the supervision of the officers, as well as collecting information in the Fair Sheets.

The first "Memoirs" are officers' reports covering Antrim in 1830, and work continued on the Antrim parishes right through the decade, with special activity in 1838 and 1839. Counties Down and Tyrone were written up from 1833 to 1837, with both officers and civil assistants working on Memoirs. In Londonderry and Fermanagh research and writing started in 1834. Armagh was worked on in 1835, 1837 and 1838. Much labour was expended in the Londonderry parishes. The plans to publish the Memoirs commenced with the parish of Templemore, containing the city and liberties of Derry, which came out in 1837 after a great deal of expense and effort.

Between 1839 and 1840 the Memoir scheme collapsed. Sir Robert Peel's government could not countenance the expenditure of money and time on such an exercise; despite a parliamentary commission favouring the continuation of the writing of the Memoirs, the scheme was halted before the southern half of the country was covered. The manuscripts remained unpublished and most were removed to the Royal Irish Academy, Dublin from the Ordnance Survey, Phoenix Park. Other records of the Ordnance Survey, including some residual material from the Memoir scheme, have recently been transferred to the National Archives, Bishop Street, Dublin.

The Memoirs are a uniquely detailed source for the history of the northern half of Ireland immediately before the Great Famine. They document the landscape and situation, buildings and antiquities, land-holdings and population, employment and livelihood of the parishes. They act as a nineteenth century Domesday book and are essential to the understanding of the cultural heritage of our communities. It is planned to produce a volume of evaluative essays to put the material in its full context, with information on other sources and on the writers of the Memoirs.

Definition of descriptive terms

Memoir (sometimes Statistical Memoir): an account of a parish written according to the prescribed form outlined in the instructions known as "Heads of Inquiry", and normally divided into three sections: Natural Features and History, Modern and Ancient Topography, Social and Productive Economy.

Fair Sheets: "information gathered for the Memoirs", an original title describing paragraphs of information following no particular order, often with marginal headings, signed and dated by the civil assistant responsible.

Statistical Remarks/Accounts: both titles are employed by the Engineer officers in their descriptions of the parish with marginal headings, often similar in layout to the Memoir.

Office Copies: these are copies of early drafts, generally officers' accounts and must have been made for office purposes.

Ordnance Survey Memoirs for County Antrim

This volume describes eight parishes on the eastern side of Lough Neagh, including an account of the lough itself, which provides an interesting comparison to those described in volume 19. There are early officers' accounts which complement the unusually detailed parish descriptions by civil assistants James Boyle, T.C.

Hannyngton and George Scott, as well as the fascinating but idiosyncratic Fair Sheets by Thomas Fagan.

The report for Lough Neagh provides detailed information on the natural history of the lough, including names and descriptions of fish, from a manuscript by John Templeton. The Latin nomenclature is given as in the original but some spellings have been corrected here in accordance with current usage; where the variation in spelling is considerable, the original appears in angle brackets. The petrifying power of the lough is also discussed. This is illustrated with a Latin quotation from the 9th century writer, Nennius, from *De Mirabilibus Hiberniae* which is not part of his *Historia Brittonum* but is regularly found in addition to it. See A. Schultz, *Nennius und Gildas*, Berlin 1844, and Henrich Zimmer, *Nennius Vindicatus*, Berlin 1893.

The local economy is particularly well described, showing the wide diversity of occupations and products of the parishes: for instance, basket and mat making, as well as the usual fishing and farming activities, and the orchards of Glenavy and Camlin supplying the Belfast market with apples. In addition to this, there was a fine linen weaving tradition in the area and some cotton weaving; other than spinning, which was in decline, the women earned money by flowering muslin. There is also unusual allusion to domestic produce, the manufacture of cheese for home consumption in Glenavy. This attention to domestic detail also gives us some fine descriptions of housing, furnishings and clothing of the local people and their pastimes. There are references to hunting in Tullyrusk and Magheragall, as well as bullet play and common play.

Unusually for the Memoirs, politico-economic events in the past are touched on: there are some accounts by Fagan of the agrarian unrest experienced in the area at the end of the eighteenth century, of the troubles brought into the parishes by Rackers and Break-of-Day Men, as well as an account of the settlement of the boglands of the Montiaghs by dispossessed Catholic smallholders, and some reference to past disturbances such as the burning of the Catholic chapels in Aghagallon and Aghalee. Generally such topics were passed over by the Memoir writers, probably for the reason that these issues were too sensitive to discuss.

In the Memoir for Ballinderry there is a most interesting account of stations performed near Portmore at the beginning of August which incorporate Lughnasa rites. James Boyle makes some candid remarks about illegitimacy rates in this area, but for the most part he is full of admiration for the scenery and husbandry of these districts, frequently described as English, which may reflect a particular preference or a common perception of the times. In the report on Camlin, special mention is made of the land inheritance patterns where a single heir was chosen rather than the more common practice of subdivision among members of a family.

To assist readers, some of the material, particularly the Fair Sheets, has been rearranged to conform more closely with the Heads of Inquiry, but only insofar as it does not disturb the narrative.

Drawings in the Memoir papers are listed below and are cross-referenced in the text; some are illustrated. The manuscript material is to be found in Boxes 1, 3, 6, 11, 14, 15 and 16 of the Royal Irish Academy's collection of Ordnance Survey Memoirs, and section references are given beside each parish below in their printed order.

Aghagallon	Box	1	II	4, 5, 2 and 1.
Aghalee	Box	1	III	4 and 3, 2, 1.
Ballinderry	Box	3	I	4, 2, 3, 1.
Camlin	Box	6	I	2b, 2a, 4, 3, 1.
Glenavy	Box	11	II	4, 3, 2, 1.
Lough Neagh	Box	15	I	1.
Magheragall	Box	14	VI	2, VII 3, VI 1.
Magheramesk	Box	14	VII	4 and 3, 2 and 1.
Tullyrusk	Box	16	IX	4, 1 and 3, 2 and 5.

Drawings

Aghagallon (section 2):

Outline of stone hatchets found in Montiagh bog, full size.

Black glass bottle, view and full size of diameter at base; flint arrowheads, full size [all by T. Fagan].

Aghalee (section 2):

Bronze hatchet, full size [by T. Fagan].

Camlin (section 2a):

Interior of old church of Camlin, showing gravestones and arches.

Old church of Camlin, ground plan with dimensions; details of window, niche and style of masonry, with dimensions [illustrated].

Old church of Camlin, ground plan with dimensions.

Window of old church of Camlin, showing masonry detail with dimensions.

Glendarragh, showing mill, water wheel and mill-run.

5 circular objects, possibly forts, with dimensions.

Ground plans of ring forts: 5 in Ballydonaghy, 5 in Ballyshanaghill, 7 in Ballyvolan, 1 in Ballymacrevan, 1 in Aghnadarnagh.

Ground plans of 10 forts with annotations [all by J. Boyle].

Glenavy (section 2):

Outline of chalice.

Numbered forts, ground plans, 2 complete, 4 incomplete.

Standing stone in townland of [?] Lisnaree, with dimensions.

Ground plans of forts: 2 at Ballynacoy, 3 at Tullynewbank.

Magheramesk (section 2):

2 stone hatchets, 5 arrowheads, 2 ancient beads, part of a carved urn from Creenagh townland, full size.

Stone ornament from Lisnabilla Fort, full size.

Curious stone from Magheramesk townland, 2 views, full size.

Minute ground plan of Trummery ancient church and round tower.

Stone hatchet, copper coin, 3 flint arrowheads, oak plank with dimensions, from Inisloughlin Fort.

8 flint arrowheads, brass battleaxe, brass antique, 2 views of brass sword hilt, 2 views of copper saucer, from Inisloughlin Fort and other places.

2 flint arrowheads [all by T. Fagan].

Tullyrusk (section 5):

Ground plan of fort.

Stone hatchet.

Metal spearhead with dimensions.

13 forts, numbered.

3 forts in Tullyrusk.

Parish of Aghagallon, County Antrim

Statistical Remarks by Lieutenant George Boscawen, August 1832

GEOGRAPHY OR NATURAL STATE

Name, Situation and Boundaries

Aghagallon is the ancient and present name of this parish. It is situated in the barony of Upper Massereene, county of Antrim and province of Ulster. It is bounded on the north by the parishes of Glenavy and Ballinderry, on the east by the parish of Aghalee, on the west by Lough Neagh and on the south by the parishes of Shankill and Moira.

Ecclesiastical Union

It is a vicarage in the diocese of Connor and archdiocese of Armagh, and is united to the parishes of Aghalee and Magheramesk. It is a lay impropriation in the gift of the Marquis of Hertford, the proprietor of the estate. The patron receives the rectorial tithes. The present incumbent (the Reverend John Corken) receives the vicarial tithes and has made an agreement for 5 years at a moderate rate of 8d ha'penny per acre. There is but one church in the union, which is at Soldierstown in the parish of Aghalee.

NATURAL FEATURES

Surface and Soil

The highest ground in Aghagallon parish is 208 feet above the sea and the hills are of less elevation on approaching Lough Neagh, which is 50 feet above the same level. Except the Montyaghs, its surface may be termed gently undulating. The low grounds in Derryhirk and Drumaleet are subject to floods but produce good meadow and pasture.

About two-thirds of this parish is under cultivation and the soil is capable of producing the finest crops, the mode of culture being the same as in the adjacent parishes. The following would be considered a fair average produce per acre: barley 14 cwts, wheat and oats 18 cwts, and potatoes 250 bushels.

PRODUCTIVE ECONOMY

Turbary and Manures

On the north side of the Belfast Canal there are very extensive tracts of peat bog affording an abundant supply of fuel to this and the adjacent parishes. The farmers on this estate usually rent a bank, which is paid for according to its value, or the turf may be purchased by the load or stack varying in size: one of 10 yards by 3 and 30 rows high, average 1 pound 10s. Trunks of trees are found embedded and "moss fir" which, being imbued with resin, affords both fuel and light to the poor.

The manures are lime, gravel and the produce of the farmyard. There is no limestone in this part of the union, but it may be obtained at Soldierstown. The prices on the spot are 6d or 8d a load containing about 15 cwts; or where burned at the quarry, it is sold at 9d or 10d a barrel.

MODERN TOPOGRAPHY

Roads

The direct road from Lurgan to Antrim passes through the parish from Haney's bridge and leaves it a short distance south west of the village of Aghalee. It is otherwise well intersected with by-roads branching off to Moira and Lough Neagh.

Villages

None! The nearest markets are at Lisburn and Lurgan.

NATURAL FEATURES AND NATURAL HISTORY

Streams

There are a few nameless streams intersecting the parish. The principal ones are those that cross the road from Lurgan to Antrim at Haney's bridge, at Bullick's and at Gilbert's bridge.

Geology

The constituent rock is basalt. It is not quarried in any part of the parish. It is used for building and repairing roads. Besides the Lough Neagh pebble found on and near the shore, the only minerals are detailed portions of quartz and sandstones of mica and felspar.

ANCIENT TOPOGRAPHY

Antiquities

There are the ruins of 2 churches in this part of the union, one at Maghernagaw in Derrymore

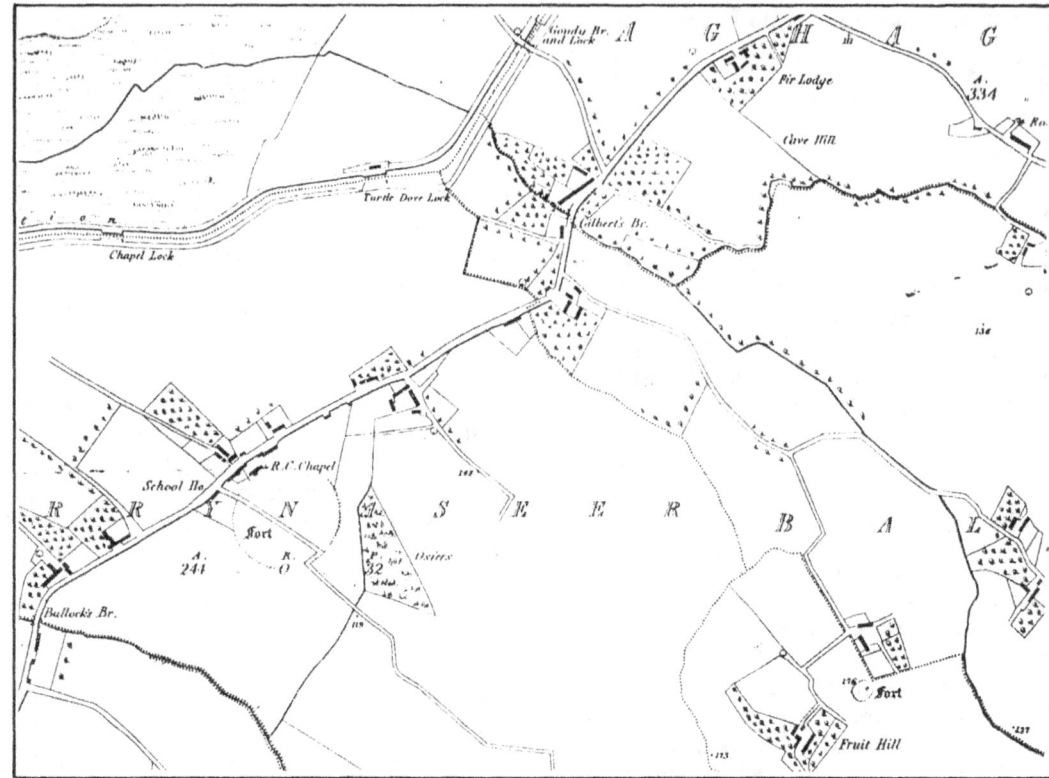

Map of Aghagallon from the first 6" O.S. maps, 1830s

townland and the other in Aghagallon townland. There are several old forts; the most remarkable one is the Chapel Fort in Derrynaseer, on the road from Lurgan to Aghalee; and at Shanport, buried in the shore, a boat was dug up a few years since, about 25 feet long and 5 feet breadth. It was made out of a single oak and is said to have been ornamented with curious carving.

SOCIAL AND PRODUCTIVE ECONOMY

Chapel and Schools

There is one Roman Catholic chapel, situated in the townland of Derrynaseer.

It contains 3 permanent schools, situated in Derrymore, Derrynaseer and Aghadrumglasney townlands. The last-mentioned has hitherto received a grant from the Kildare Street Society. The rate of tuition is from 2s to 3s per quarter.

Fishery of Lough Neagh

The Marquis of Donegall claims the right of the fishing of Lough Neagh and wished to restrain the fishermen to certain periods in the year. His claims, however, were resisted. From 20 to 25 men constantly employ themselves in fishing in this parish. There are 10 boats, these and the tackle being the property of the fishermen. There is one bank, called the Reedy flat, to the north of Lurgan bay which is adjacent to this parish; very well stocked with fish. The shore round Derryclone is rocky, but at Bartin's bay the beach is sandy and affords a good landing place for nets.

The fish which abound in the Lough Neagh are the salmon, trout, pike, tench, bream, eel and the pollen. The latter is said to be peculiar to this lake and forms a large portion of the food of the poorer class in this parish, and considerable portions are sent to the neighbouring markets, viz. Lisburn, Lurgan and Belfast.

Trade and Manufacture

Though it contain no collective manufactory, yet about 200 families are employed in trade and manufactories, which they combine with agriculture. The number of weavers in the parish is estimated at 209, and almost all the women spin. The chief manufacture is of cambric, in quality varying from 14 to 20 hundreds and seven-eighths wide. The prices obtained for this and the yarn are not remunerating. Some advantage is derived

Parish of Aghagallon

from the osier beds, the strongest of them being made in firkin hoops and the second size into baskets. Besides what has been mentioned, the only trade consists in the produce of the land and, by means of the canal, from Lough Neagh to Belfast, the produce can be readily exported to that market.

Population

This parish appears to be very thickly peopled and there is a great degree of comfort in all the farmhouses and cottages. The population by a census taken in 1831 is estimated at 3,567, viz. 1,736 males and 1,831 females.

Table of Townlands

Proprietor the Marquis of Hertford.

1, Aghadrimglasney, 404 acres 1 rood 39 perches, 34 families, 93 males, 86 females, total population 179.

2, Aghagallon, 334 acres 2 roods 26 perches, 40 families, 114 males, 103 females, total population 217.

3, Ballykeel, 220 acres 3 roods, 23 families, 60 males, 69 females, total population 129.

4, Ballymacilreny, 325 acres 2 roods 29 perches, 39 families, 94 males, 109 females, total population 203.

5, Ballycairn, 473 acres 2 roods 32 perches, 77 families, 190 males, 193 females, total population 383.

6, Drumaleet, 351 acres 1 rood 23 perches, 63 families, 123 males, 168 females, total population 291.

7, Derrynaseer, 244 acres 38 perches, 21 families, 61 males, 63 females, total population 124.

8, Derryhirk, 230 acres 8 perches, 31 families, 69 males, 76 females, total population 145.

9, Derryclone, 413 acres 2 roods 1 perch, 58 families, 171 males, 156 females, total population 327.

10, Derrymore, 457 acres 1 rood 21 perches, 93 families, 216 males, 225 females, total population 441.

11, Montyaghs, 1,543 acres 3 roods 34 perches, 124 families, 320 males, 367 females, total population 687.

12, Tiscallen, 323 acres 3 roods 38 perches, 61 families, 178 males, 172 females, total population 350.

13, Tamnyvane, 146 acres 3 roods 13 perches, 16 families, 47 males, 44 females, total population 91.

Area of the parish 5,470 acres 2 roods 22 perches: 680 families, 1,736 males, 1,831 females, total population 3,567.

[Signed] George Boscawen, Lieutenant Royal Engineers, 8th August 1832.

Draft Memoir by T.C. Hannyngton, March 1835

NATURAL FEATURES

Hills

This parish is not large. It is nearly all bog studded with numerous groups of small oval-shaped hills, having the most abrupt sides towards the south. They are all gravel and sand. The highest point on the parish is only 136 feet above the level of the sea. The average height of the hills throughout the parish might be taken at 70 feet above the sea. The small groups of hills are called islands by the inhabitants.

Lakes

Lough Neagh forms the western boundary of the parish. In the centre of the parish there is a small stretch of water called Lough Mona. It hardly deserves the name: it is nearly a fen or quagmire about 200 yards in breadth; in the summer it is dry. At the present time (March 1835) the whole of the parish to the north of the Lagan Canal is under water with the exception of the small hills.

Rivers

There are no rivers of importance, merely a few tributary streams flowing from the high ground beyond the eastern boundary of the parish.

Bogs

Nearly the whole plain of this parish is bog. It is of a light spongy nature full of fibres <fibers>. It is about 54 feet above the level of the sea and about 6 feet above the level of Lough Neagh. In the winter it is generally under water. The average depth of the bog is 8 feet, the substratum blue clay and sand. It contains numerous islands not formed by artificial means, but they are gradually increasing in size as cultivation extends. There is not much timber found in the bog, comparatively speaking. It is found promiscuously scattered as if it had been deposited by turbulent waters.

One part of the bog called Derryclone is famed by the inhabitants for the beauty of the oak found there. Derryclone is a kind of peninsula formed of a long gravel hill. The isthmus which joins it to the mainland is formed of bog. In this the oak is deposited. It may have grown here but it is much more probable that it was driftwood thrown in by chance. Bark is also found in small quantities. The only species of tree now growing in the parish is a kind of willow, some of very considerable dimensions.

Woods

There are no natural woods in the parish or any decided evidence of their having existed within any recent date.

Coast

The coast of this parish is flat throughout, with principally a sandy beach. There are some good pebbles found on it. It has one small bay called Bartin's bay. The water is shallow along the shores.

Climate

The climate of this parish is peculiarly damp, proceeding from its swampiness and also from its being so near the lake. In the mornings it is frequently covered with mist long after all the surrounding country has cleared, and at sunset again the fogs begin to rise from the marshes. It is peculiarly well adapted for the growth of osiers, which is a great speculation with the inhabitants. They make a vast number of baskets.

NATURAL HISTORY

Zoology

The fish on the coast of this parish are trout, pullens and perch. The fens are remarkably well stored with wild duck and widgeon. Seagulls are also numerous; they are the small white gull. They perch in the ploughed lands as well as on the water.

MODERN TOPOGRAPHY

Public Buildings

The only public building in the parish is a new Roman Catholic chapel not yet completed, situated in Derrynaseer. The cost cannot be ascertained as the accounts are not yet made up. The house is 78 feet by 35, the style of the building rather tasteful.

    Gentlemen's seats: none.

    Towns: none. There is neither town or village in the parish. The people live much within themselves. Small shops are established at different parts of the parish where tea, tobacco, sugar, candles, bread, flour and oatmeal are sold. These hucksters sell tea at the rate of the weight of a shilling for a ha'penny. They seldom have weights; they use round stones which they call lbs and half lbs. Pootheen is by no means a scarce spirit in the parish. They generally get the bread from carts which ply from the surrounding towns twice a week.

Mills

None: the parish has not a sufficient fall for the erection of a mill.

Communications

A mile and a quarter of the road from Crumlin to Lurgan is the only leading road in the parish; it is in good repair. There are an immense number of roads intersecting the bogs. They are quite impassable in a wheeled vehicle in the winter. They are generally a kind of causeway without fences of any kind.

PRODUCTIVE ECONOMY

Uses made of the Bogs

The bogs of this parish are used nearly altogether for fuel. Occasionally farmers draw a little to the uplands for manure but as it is the only bog for miles round, the demand for turf is very great. They are brought in boats to the parishes of Killead, Glenavy and Camlin and in cars to the inland parishes. They are a bad description of turf. They burn quick and do not throw out much heat. They produce white ashes, as light as feathers. There is very little sulphur contained in them.

Drainage

Numerous drains are cut through the bogs of this parish on purpose, to carry off the water from the bog banks previous to the commencement of the turf-cutting season.

Fishing

In this parish people do not follow fishing as a trade: they merely satisfy their own wants. Pullens are the principal object of their exertions. When salted, they are a good winter's provision for the poor cotters. When champed up with potato, they are an excellent dish.

Parish of Aghagallon

Lagan Canal

2 miles of the Lagan Canal pass through this parish. There are 8 locks within its boundary. This canal was cut at enormous expense, to judge from the replies of the people on its banks. They say it cost as many guineas as would extend from Belfast to the lough, supposing them to be laid in a row touching each other. What was the real cost I cannot find out.

Vessels of from 25 to 30 tons trade up the canal. The charge is 5s per ton for potatoes, oats etc. They bring timber from Belfast to the Tyrone and Armagh coasts, also slates, iron, sugar, coals and tar; in fact, anything that will fit in their boat. They have no objection to the dues paid by the boats at the locks: is 5d for the opening of each floodgate or 2 pounds 10s for the whole voyage. For detailed information, see pamphlet on *Inland navigation of Ireland*.

SOCIAL ECONOMY

Habits of the People

The people of this parish, generally speaking, are inferior in point of wealth to the adjoining parishes. Their houses are not as clean or as tasteful. It may be put down as a general rule that where fuel is plenty, the poorer class will always flock. From their want of horses they cannot draw fuel. Consequently they come to the bog edges. The beauty and richness of the parishes of Killead and Camlin may be attributed to the want of bog. The people build their houses on the islands through the bog and cultivate the hill on which they live. They rear a good number of geese which they sell to merchants who trade to Belfast. The parish is well adapted to this as the geese are turned loose at an early age and are only brought into the yard when winter sets in.

MODERN TOPOGRAPHY

General Appearance and Scenery

Little can be said for the beauty of this parish. It presents no object of art and nature has been very sparing. The lake is seen to advantage particularly when the Tyrone and Armagh shores are visible, but the parish of Aghagallon itself presents not one pleasing object.

ANCIENT TOPOGRAPHY

Antiquities

The only antique remains in the parish are the ruins of Magheranagow old church. Part of the west gable is all that now remains. This is built of round unhewn stones. It [is] almost impossible to distinguish the stones, they are so covered with mottled ivy. The ruins are 42 feet by 24 feet. There are no inscriptions or carving about the ruins.

SOCIAL ECONOMY

Table of Schools

[Table contains the following headings: townland, number of pupils subdivided by religion and sex, how supported].

Tascallon townland, 15 Protestants, 16 Catholics, 2 Quakers, 24 males, 8 females, 32 total; supported solely by the scholars.

Tascallon townland, 16 Protestants, 28 Catholics, 16 males, 28 females, 48 total; supported by the scholars.

Aghadrumglasny townland, 35 Protestants, 25 Catholics, 48 males, 12 females, 60 total; under the National Board of Education. [Signed] T.C. Hannyngton, Templecormac, March 1835.

Fair Sheets by Thomas Fagan, January and February 1838

NATURAL FEATURES

Native Wood

In Ballymacilrany, and holding of Henry Shillington, there stands about 1 and a half acre of remains of native wood but at present reduced to a mere scrag and occupied in pasture.

MODERN TOPOGRAPHY

Canal

The canal from Lisburn to Lough Neagh was opened between the latter places, for the access of boats and lighters, on the first day of January 1792. This canal was made by the Marquis of Donegall and others. The workmanship of sinking, building of locks and bridges on the line was superintended by the late Richard Owen, engineer. Informants Neal McStravoge, Owen McCann, John Magee and many others. 16th and 17th February 1838.

Canal Locks and Accommodating Dock

Sheerins lock, on the canal and situated at Sheerins bridge near the village of Aghalee, measures 70 and a half feet in length between the floodgates, 16 and a half feet wide and the fall of the water 7 feet 2 inches. The sluices are situated in the side walls near the entrance gate and the sill <scill> half-circle.

Bradley's lock on the same line measures 70 and a half feet between the floodgates, 16 and a half feet wide and the fall of the water 7 feet 2 inches. The sill and sluices are situated in this lock the same as above stated.

Between the latter and the following lock, on the south side of the canal, stands a dock several yards in length and constructed at the making of the canal, for the accommodation of lighters or boats detained under casual circumstances.

Cairn lock on the same line measures 70 and a half feet in length between the floodgates, 16 and a half feet wide and the fall of the water 7 feet 2 inches. The sill and sluices are situated in this lock the same as above stated.

Prospect lock on the same line measures 17 and a half feet in length between the floodgates, 16 and a half feet wide and the fall of the water 7 feet 2 inches. The sill and sluices in this lock is situated the same as above described.

Gowdy's lock on the canal, and situated on the Gowdy bridge, measures 70 and a half feet in length between the floodgates, 16 and a half feet wide and the fall of the water 7 feet 2 inches. The sluices are situated in the side walls near the entrance gate and the sill half-circle. 30th January 1838.

Canal Locks

Turtle Dove lock on the canal, west of the latter bridge, is situated at the lock-house; measures 70 and a half feet in length between the floodgates, 16 and a half feet wide and the fall of the water 7 feet 2 inches. The sill and sluices are situated in this lock the same as above described.

Chapel lock on the canal, west of the lock-house before mentioned, and the last lock on the canal within the above county, between the village of Aghalee and Lough Neagh: this lock measures 70 and a half feet in length between the floodgates, 16 and a half feet wide and the fall of the water 7 feet 2 inches. The sluices are situated in the side walls near the entrance gate and the sill half-circle.

The 7 locks now described are all situated within the above parish and stand on about one mile distance. They average 70 and a half feet by 16 and a half feet between the floodgates each, and the fall of the water from 7 feet 1 inch to 7 feet 2 inches in each, leaving only a difference of 1 inch in the whole. Any difference occurring in the length or breadth of the locks was occasioned merely by the setting in of the gates, as they were designed to be one and the same dimensions in every respect. However, the difference in any case does not exceed 6 by 3 inches. They are built of cut freestone and at present in good order. The sluices, being situated in the side walls and the sills half-circle in all these locks, are said to be of much safety to the boats and lighters but much more tedious on filling the locks than those sluices situated on the floodgates in the neighbourhood of Lisburn. Information from Arthur Richey and Edward Creaner, lock-keepers. 31st January 1838.

Sheerins Bridge

That bridge across the canal, west of and contiguous to the village of Aghalee on the leading road from the latter place to Lurgan, has one half-circle arch: span 16 foot 6 inches, breadth of the road on the bridge 19 feet 6 inches, breadth at the east end of the bridge 36 feet, breadth at the west end of the bridge 28 feet, average height of parapets on bridge 4 feet 3 inches, thickness of parapets on bridge 1 foot 8 inches, length of parapets on either side of the road 56 yards. Detached on one side of the above arch stands a half-circle arch, span 3 foot 9 inches. This arch accommodates a horse track on one side of the canal. Both these arches are turned with cut freestone and the parapets built of blackish quarry stones, all in good repair. It was built by the canal company above 40 years back. Informants Edward Fletcher and William Ferris.

Gowdy Bridge

The Gowdy bridge, across the canal and accommodating a by-road from the Lurgan road to the Montiagh bogs, has one half-circle arch: span 16 foot 6 inches, breadth of the road on the bridge 13 feet, breadth of the road at each end 26 feet, average height of the parapets 3 feet 9 inches, thickness of the parapets 1 foot 8 inches, length of parapet on either side of the road 50 yards. Detached on one side of the above arch stands a small half-circle arch to accommodate a horse track along the canal; span of this arch 3 feet 9 inches. These arches are turned with cut freestone and the parapets built of land and quarry stones. They are partially dilapidated. This bridge was built by the canal company above 40 years back.

Heaney's Bridge

Heaney's bridge, on the leading road between the village of Aghalee and Lurgan, and situated over a small river dividing the counties of Antrim and

Parish of Aghagallon

Down, has one half-circle arch: span 6 feet, breadth of the road on the bridge 21 feet 6 inches, average height of parapets 2 foot 6 inches, thickness of parapets 1 foot 6 inches, length of parapets on either side of the road 11 yards, and all in good repair.

Cranagh Bridge

The Cranagh bridge across the canal, on a leading road between White Hall on the Lurgan road and Crumlin etc., and passing by the old church of Maghernagah, has 1 arch approaching to half-circle: span 23 foot, breadth of the road on the bridge 16 foot 6 inches, breadth of the road at both ends of the bridge 29 foot, average height of parapets on bridge 3 foot 6 inches, thickness of parapets on bridge 1 foot 8 inches, length of parapets on either side of the road 60 yards. This arch accommodates a horse-track 6 and a half feet wide. It is turned with cut freestone and the parapets built of rough land and quarry stones, and partially dilapidated on top. On the east side of the bridge, adjoining the canal, stands a small basin to answer for boats detained under casual circumstances.

This bridge, as well as all the other bridges and locks situated on the canal within the above parish, were built by the canal company above 40 years back, engineer the late Richard Owen. The above is the last bridge situated on the canal, on the Lough Neagh direction, within the county of Antrim. A short distance west of the bridge the counties of Antrim and Down are divided on that line by wooden tunnels passing under the canal and accommodating the county drain. Along the canal, and situated in the above parish, are also several tunnels of stone and lime work accommodating small rivers and streams passing under the canal. Informants Arthur Richey, Edward Creaner and many others.

Roads

That line of by-road leading between Lower Ballinderry and the Montiagh bogs averages 17 feet wide clear of banks and fences and is kept up by presentments.

Chief road communications in the parish: 1, the main leading road between Antrim and Lurgan passes through the parish from east to west; averages 21 feet wide and is kept up under the new contract.

2, the Big Moss Loanen, a line of road joining the Lurgan road near the village of Aghalee and leading to Gawleys Gate at Lough Neagh. Also a line leading from Gawleys Gate along the lough banks by Maghernagah or Derrymore old church, and joining the Lurgan road at White Hall near the west end of the parish. These 2 roads open a communication from the lough shores to the east end of the parish near Aghalee, and the west end near the county mearing, on the Lurgan road.

3, a line opens from the Lurgan road near the west end of the parish and leads in a southern direction through Tiscallen, Aghadrumglasny to Soldierstown, or otherwise Aghalee church. These latter 3 lines open from the Lurgan road above mentioned and constitute the principal leading road. They average from 19 to 21 feet wide and are kept up by presentments.

Few parishes [are] perhaps better dissected with public leading and by-roads than the above. Besides those described on the last page, there are branching from them, into the different townlands and more particularly into those townlands locally denominated the Montiaghs, and the bogs situated in that part, various lines of by-roads, all which are kept up by presentments too and vary from 14 to 18 feet wide clear of banks or fences. There are also branching from some of these public leading and public by-roads, private lanes partly kept up from court leet grants, partly by the farmers whom they accommodate, as they are situated in backward portions of townlands where public roads do not extend.

Road Contracts

That portion of the main leading road from Antrim to Lurgan, and situated in the above parish, averages 21 feet wide clear of banks or fences and is to be kept in repair for 5 years, at 1s per perch per annum, by Edward Fletcher and Richard Welsh.

That line of road leading between the villages of Aghalee and Gawley's Gate at Lough Neagh, and locally called the Big Moss Loanen, averages 19 feet wide clear of banks or fences and is kept up by presentments.

General Communications

The canal enters the parish near the village of Aghalee and leads through the parish to the mearing of the counties of Antrim and Down near Shanport on the banks of Lough Neagh. Taking into account the aforesaid road, the canal and Lough Neagh which bounds the parish on the north west, it is well situated as regards road and water communications. Information obtained from William Ferris, Timothy Kelly and many others. 9th February 1838.

Aghagallon Chapel

Aghagallon Roman Catholic chapel is situated in the townland of Derrynaseer, on the leading road from Lurgan to Antrim and about the centre of the above parish. This is a splendid and spacious country edifice, 1-storey high and slated. It stands nearly east and west, with a handsome aisle attached to the front or north side. Entrance by 2 large doors, Gothic shape, one of which stands on the east side and the other on the west side of the above aisle. The body of the house measures 78 feet 8 inches by 35 feet 3 inches in the clear, and the aisle 20 and a half feet in breadth and 14 feet 3 inches in length in clear. Also the floors are made of clay. The walls are built of whinstone and blackish quarry stone 2 feet 2 inches thick, and the side walls 22 feet high in the clear and designed to accommodate galleries, which are not yet erected. The altar stands to the south side wall and in the middle of the house. Over it stands an ornamental Gothic arch, also a representation of Christ nailed to the cross. Detached from the east end of the altar, and elevated some feet above the floor, stands a very neat pulpit erected in the modern style and all enclosed by a handsome timber railing.

The interior of the chapel is spacious and well lit by 4 large Gothic windows in front, 4 similarly in the rear, and on each gable a large arch window at the proper height affords light to the intended galleries. On the aisle gable, and immediately opposite the altar, stands a fine Gothic window measuring 22 by 8 feet, and the top part ornamented by stained glass and affording a well-executed emblem of the cross. This window, together with being an ornament to the front of the chapel, will also afford light to the aisle gallery. Attached to the west end of the chapel stands a neat vestry 1-storey high and slated, and measuring 12 by 12 feet inside. It is lit by 2 square windows. Ventilation is afforded by lattices in the windows of the chapel.

Exterior of Chapel

The exterior of the chapel is in good order and the front corners of the body of the chapel, as well as of the aisle, strengthened by handsome square abutments running up to the roof and topped by handsome pinnacles of cut stone. Over the east and west gables stands 2 handsome stone crosses. On the aisle gable in the front of the chapel also stands a third stone cross with the date of erection, 1833, cut in the case stone at its foot. This edifice, if finished, will be one of the handsomest structures situated in a country parish, perhaps in the above or many other other counties. The yard is small and do not admit burial grounds. It is enclosed partly by a good stone and lime wall and partly by houses situated on the site and a good iron gate to the entrance.

Site of Chapel and Inscriptions

Aghagallon Roman Catholic chapel is situated on part of the site of one of the largest forts known in the north, but has been destroyed many years back.

Within the vestry attached to the chapel, and in the south side wall, stands a neat corniced cut stone bearing the following inscription: "This chapel was built by the Revd Felix O'Donnell, Arthur McHenry and the rest of the parish in the year 1748." Over this inscription, and composed of the same stone, is a representation of Christ nailed to the cross and on the top of the cross, the letters INRI. On either side of the cross, and made of the same stone, is a beast. These 2 beasts are situated at the foot of the cross, well executed and looking in opposite directions to each other. This stone stood in the original chapel, which was a small thatched house.

In the north side of the vestry also stands a very neat corniced stone bearing the following inscription: "Rebuilt AD 1834 by the Revd Daniel McGary P.P."

Congregation and Erection of Chapel

Divine service in the above chapel Sundays at 12 noon and Fridays at 10, morning. Average attendance in the summer from 700 to 800 persons; the chapel is not yet seated.

Collections are made in Aghagallon chapel on Sundays, the proceeds of which goes to liquidate debts due on the chapel and also to relieve distressed poor. The chapel was built or finished 1834, cost about [blank] pounds, this sum raised by liberal subscriptions from different persons of all religious denominations in the parish and surrounding neighbourhood. The congregation quarried the stones and sand and otherwise assisted in its erection by horse and manual labour, free of expense. The quarries was given gratis by different persons. The site or chapel ground was first granted about 90 years ago by the late Thomas Clarke, a farmer, and lastly granted and enlarged by Lancilet Turtle, a farmer, who occupies the farm on which the chapel is situated.

Parish Priest

The Revd James Denvir is parish priest of

Parish of Aghagallon

Aghagallon and a portion of Ballinderry annexed <annext> to it, and gets average annual income from the charge [blank] pounds.

ANCIENT TOPOGRAPHY

Chapel Fire

The original chapel of Aghagallon, which was a thatched house, was maliciously consumed by fire immediately after the rebellion of 1798, as was also the late Revd William Dawson's house, which stood contiguous to the chapel, and he himself robbed and left for dead. He was then parish priest of the above parish. The chapel at some after period was again roofed and slated and remained so till the present one was begun. Informants Marcus McKeavney, William Magee and others. 22nd January 1838.

Ancient Church of Aghagallon

Aghagallon ancient church stands in the townland of Aghagallon and is situated on an eminence about 1 mile south west of Aghalee old church, already described. This old edifice stood 61 by 23 and a half feet in the interior. The walls were built of grey and whinstone and bound together by grouted mortar <morter>, similar to other ancient buildings. As near as can be judged from their present dilapidated state, their original thickness was about 3 feet. The chief part of the stones with which they were built remain in their natural and rude shape. The mortar too is of a rough <ruff> quality but profusely used in the bowels of the walls. The chief part of the east gable and a small portion of the west gable and of both side walls is all that now remains. These too are greatly disfigured in consequence of such of the surface stones being taken off the walls as seemed useful for modern buildings in the neighbourhood. Yet the existing ruins are closely mantled over with ivy, which give them a handsome and venerable appearance.

On the east gable, and at a height of some feet above the surface, there is the ruins of a long but very narrow window, now nearly closed up by ivy. The body of the church is occupied by enclosures and burials. 18th January 1838.

Tradition regarding Church

Local tradition says that Aghagallon ancient church was destroyed by Oliver Cromwell and that it was roofed with oak timber and shingles.

Graveyard

The graveyard is large and well occupied by burials. It was enclosed about 100 years back by a quickset fence, and a good iron gate put on the entrance at a subsequent period.

The following are amongst the Christian names and surnames on tombs and headstones in the graveyard. Names of males: Alexander, Arthur, Arther, Barnard, Brice, Daniel, Edward, Fergus, George, Hugh, Henry, Henderson, James, John, Jonathan, Matthew, Moses, Nely, Owen, Pierce, Robert, Samuel, Tole, William, Thomas. Names of females: Ann, Anne, Bridget, Catherine, Cisley, Elizabeth, Elenor, Isabella, Jean, Katherine, Mary, Margaret, Marget, Sarah. A contrast in spelling these names will be seen.

Surnames on the tombs and headstones: Armstrong, Bell, Best, Blair, Bunton, Bullock, McCann, Crasly, Carter, Doyle, McDonald, Elliot, Gilbert, Gallagher, Hillis, McKenby, Kelly, Lownsdale, Lavery, Fallon, Faloon, Kearns, Forsyth, Magill, Macoum, Mulholland, Money, McQuillan, Walker, Thompson, McVeagh, McRorey.

Epitaph on Headstone

Epitaph on the late Revd William Dawson's headstone, who was formerly parish priest of the above parish: [small diagram with words surrounding figure of the cross: "Memento Mori, INRI"]. "Here lies the dust of Revd W.D., who ruled this congregation, now the 36th year and enters into the 70th year of his age, 2nd February 1809. My friends in faith and charity, I leave you bound to pray for me departed, 3rd December, 1814."

Further remarks on epitaph: Dawson had the above stone cut 5 years before his demise, as may be seen by the above epitaph. His grave is situated, similar to those of laymen, in the aforesaid graveyard and at variance with the common rule of priest's graves, as, in most cases, they lie contrary to the lay people. There are many stones defaced and many families who bury there but who have neither tombs nor headstones. 23rd January 1838.

Ancient Headstones

In Aghagallon old graveyard, and at the head of a grave at the south side of the church, stands a stone of rather rude shape and bearing on its side the following letters and date 1680: [coffin shape] R.B.M.K.S. The above represents the coffin. The letters and figures are rudely cut. It would appear from the shape of the stone that it was a pedestal that formerly supported a cross or some other relic belonging to the old church, and to be secured on the top of the above stone by a pivot.

Fount Stone

In the graveyard, and at the Revd Mr Dawson's headstone, also lies one half of a small fount stone of very hard quality. It is at present much disfigured, but would seem to have been circular, 12 inches in diameter and 6 inches thick. The fount too was circular, 4 and a half inches in diameter and 4 inches in depth. The other half of this fount stone lies among the other stones but cannot be found.

Observations

The oldest stones legible in the graveyard are 1680 and 1737, and the greatest age of the person in either tomb or headstone 93 years. All religious denominations still continue to bury in this old graveyard and some instances of the Irish cry accompanying Roman Catholic funerals coming to it up to 1830. Informants Hugh McCurry, John O'Neill, John McKeavney and many others. 23rd January 1838.

Maghernagah Ancient Church

Maghernagah ancient church is situated on a leading road by the Montiaghs from Antrim to Lurgan, about 11 miles north west of Lisburn and 14 miles north of Moira. It is surrounded to a great extent by bog. This edifice stood 50 feet 3 inches by 20 feet 3 inches in the clear; thickness of the side walls 2 and half feet and of the gables 3 feet. They were built of grey land stones, which remain in their natural state of irregular shape, but bound together by grouted mortar of a superior quality. A large portion of both gables and of the north side wall are yet standing and 13 feet long of the west end of the south side wall also, but no traces of doors or windows now visible on either. These walls are partially covered over with ivy. Oliver Cromwell is said to be the destroyer of this as well as of many other ancient edifices.

The graveyard is enclosed by a quickset fence and a good iron gate to the entrance. It is sheltered by ash, board-tree and other forest timber. This graveyard, though still small, was enlarged on the east side about 22 years back. It is occupied chiefly by Roman Catholics but very limited in headstones. 24th January 1838.

Burial Ground

The following are amongst the surnames on headstones in Maghernagah ancient burial ground.

Christian names of males: Arthur, Barnard, Hugh, John, Neal, Oliver, Patrick, Robert.

Christian names of females: Isabella, Ann.

Surnames: Byrns, Creainey, McCrory, McStea, McStravoge, Lavery.

The oldest headstone in the graveyard was erected within the last century and the greatest age on any headstone does not exceed 78 years.

Saints Bed

Within a few yards of the east end of the old church, and lying in the form of a tombstone, lies a long flat stone locally called the Saints Bed. It is partly covered with soil. However, on one end of this stone are a few irregular and detached holes said to be prints left by St Patrick's knees and elbows while performing a station or some ceremony of prayer on the stone. It is also said by some that the above prints were left in the aforesaid manner by St Colman, or Congall, but locally called St Culin, who is said to be the founder of the above and Aghagallon ancient churches. However, the prints in the Saints Bed before alluded to seem rather to be the work of nature than otherwise caused.

At this bed lay for centuries 2 stones of moderate size, with the prints of the thumb and 4 fingers on the surface of each and locally said to be left on them by some of the aforesaid saints, who held one of them in each hand and alternatively struck their breasts by them while praying at the above bed. It was a general feeling throughout the neighbourhood if one of those stones were at any time removed or taken away from the Saints Bed, that it would be found again on the following day or some short period in its proper place in the bed, and to be brought back by a miraculous or supernatural power. However, for experiment's sake, or perhaps contempt, a late Thomas Elliot of Moira brought one of the stones to his own house in the above town, where it was kept for some time. The result was that Elliot died, together with his family, having experienced much calamity in other respects, all in the space of a few days after the taking away of the aforesaid stone. In the meantime, his widow caused the stone to be left back at the Saints Bed.

About 60 years back a Rawden Studdert Esquire of Moira cast one of these stones into a small lake in the neighbourhood called Lough Money, but on the following day it was found again lying <lieing> in the Saints Bed. But these stones now altogether disappear, nor is there any account of what became of them.

Parish of Aghagallon

It is very generally believed that the saint who founded Maghernagah and Aghagallon old churches is buried beneath the aforesaid Saints Bed in Maghernagah. It is likewise said that Maghernagah old church was the first church built and was the original parish church of Aghagallon, and that Aghagallon old church, which is much larger in length and breadth, was built at a subsequent period as a chapel of ease.

Maghernagah old burial ground is said to have been much larger at a former period than it is at present. For, in labouring and sinking fences in surrounding grounds about 52 years back, there was coffin boards and a quantity of human bones lifted a considerable distance from the present enclosed burial grounds. These were again buried. The church is said to have been roofed with oak timber and shingles.

Spring Well

Contiguous to Aghagallon old church, and on the west side, stands a very ancient spring well and an old thorn-bush. This well is considered to have been attached to the old church but is not known by any ancient name. Informants Neal and Patrick McStravoge, William Magee and many others. 24th and 25th January 1838.

Ancient Cairns

In the townland of Aghagallon, and contiguous to the ancient spring well mentioned [above], there stood a large ancient cairn of stones. It was destroyed some years back but nothing of interest found about its ruins. Nothing now remains to denote its existence at any period but an ancient thorn-bush that stands on the site with a pile of stones round its roots.

In the townland of Ballycairn also stood an ancient cairn of stones locally called Cairnmall, by which name the portion of the above townland on which it was situated is called and known to the present day. This cairn was destroyed many years back. There is no account of any antiques having been found in demolishing it. In its neighbourhood stood an ancient fence, which was locally called a Danes' cast. This fence has also been destroyed at some former period.

Forts in Ballycairn

In the above townland also stood 2 Danish forts. These two were destroyed several years back and a number of flints, Danes' pipes and some stone hatchets found in and about their ruins. Some of these antiques were given to John Rogan, an antiquarian in the neighbourhood, and others lost. Informants Henry Welsh, Marcus McKeavney and many others. 26th January 1838.

Brass Battleaxe

Patrick McStravoge, in cutting turf in the Montiaghs, 1820, got, several feet beneath the surface of the bog, a brass battleaxe having 2 small lugs and a socket to embrace a handle. It was about 5 inches long, in a good state of preservation and the edge sharp. It was given in to Lord Hertford's office at Lisburn, subsequent to the above period.

Danes' Mill

In the Montiaghs was also found about 60 years back, at a considerable depth beneath the remains of a bog, a mill-stead supposed to have been the ruins of a Danes' mill, as there was found with it a large quantity of heath ground or cut very fine and locally conjectured to have been so manufactured for ale brewing. It is a general tradition amongst the principal inhabitants of almost all parishes that the Danes, when in this country, made all their ale out of heather. However, the above ruins was composed of an oak frame of considerable dimensions and well bound together by mortices and wooden pins. The frame was tolerably sound when discovered, but greatly disfigured in lifting it. The timber etc. of which it was composed was subsequently converted to other uses. Informants Patt and Neal McStravoge and many others. 27th January 1838.

Old Butter

In 1810 there was discovered in the Montiaghs, about 12 feet beneath the surface of a solid bog, 2 circular wooden vessels of the moderate size and containing each a quantity of old butter. It was quite hard and in colour resembled that of tallow, but when dissolved was found to be useful for cart grease and rush candles. The vessels were constructed out of a solid piece of oak timber, but quite decayed when discovered and crumbled down when a short time exposed to the air.

In 1820 there was found, a considerable depth beneath the surface of the above bog, another cask of old butter, in quality and usefulness as above described but the vessel made of thick and rude-shaped staves bound by thick wooden hoops. This vessel was also decayed and has subsequently fallen to ruin.

There was also found in the same bog a stone pitcher (a curious earthen vessel with a handle on one side and commonly used by poor people for carrying milk and water) containing a quantity of old butter. The butter was used as above stated, but the pitcher was broken by the turf spade.

Flints

On sundry occasions <occations> of cutting turf in the above bogs, and a considerable depth beneath the surface, was found together parcels of half-dressed flint arrowheads. Informants John Magee, Peter Magill, Felix Corry and others. 29th January 1838.

Wooden Box

Henry Welsh, in cutting turf in the Montiaghs about 1809, found, about 7 feet beneath the surface of the bog, a wooden case or box about 3 feet long, 2 feet broad and 12 feet deep, and containing, as he supposed, the entrails of some animal in a decomposed or congealed state. The box formed on one end a sort of half-circle. It was joined together by mortices but in a very decayed state when discovered. It was disjointed by the turf spade in lifting out of the bog and was subsequently broken into small pieces by little boys. The contents above mentioned was again buried in a bog pit.

Hazel Stakes

There have been invariably discovered, at different depths beneath the surface of the above bog, standing perpendicular both in the bog and in some instances in the sand, clay or subsoil beneath the bog, rows of sharp-pointed hazel stakes, varying in length and thickness, and forming in some instances oblong, square and circular enclosures. They are in all cases found to be brought to the small point in which they appear, by some sharp-edged tool. Many are the local conjectures respecting these stakes, but their original use seldom arrived at. Though they retain the bark when discovered, they are quite decayed and are consequently used for fuel or cast into the bog pits. Informants Henry Welsh, Felix Corry, John Magee and others.

Singular Discovery

Patrick McStravoge, in sinking a pump on the townland of Derryhirk in 1837, discovered, between 40 and 50 feet beneath the surface of a hard slaty soil, a piece of oak timber in rather a decayed state. Of its shape or dimension no idea could be formed, as it was only bored through, similar to the top and subsoil, in sinking the pump. Information from Patrick McStravoge and many others.

Island and Artificial Wooden Road

In draining a small lake in the Montiaghs locally called Lough Mooney about 25 years back, there was discovered, about the centre of the lake, an island composed of earth and stones, approaching to circular shape and about 70 yards in diameter. About 21 yards distant from this island was also discovered an oblong frame of oak beams, duffed at each end one over the other. The above distance of 21 yards intervening between the island and frame was laid with oak beams laid together in a temporary manner and forming a road or passage 4 feet wide. On either side of this road was sunk in the subsoil a row of oak and hazel stakes forming a paling or sort of parapet to the road. The stakes were brought to a small point by a sharp-edged tool and varied from 6 to 8 feet in length each. They were much decayed when found. Some of the beams and stakes were lifted out and more left undisturbed. The ruins are now grown over with bog and soil.

Old Butter

James McGarvil, in reclaiming the remains of bog in Drumaleet in 1818, got, at some depth beneath the surface, a parcel of old butter contained in the bark of a tree. The butter was found to be of great relief to persons afflicted with bodily pains and was all carried away by different persons for that purpose. Informants Patt McStravoge, James Mallon and Bryan Campbell. 1st February 1838.

Fort, Quern and Grinding Stone

John Bullock, in demolishing a fort in his holding in Drumaleet about 1808, found, a considerable depth beneath the surface of the fort, an ancient quern in a perfect state. It is of freestone and supported on 3 feet formed of the same stone. It is circular, 10 inches in diameter and 5 inches high, including the feet. It forms a hoop on the top, in which the runner or grinding stone is situated. This runner is also circular, 7 and a half inches in diameter and turned by a handle. In the centre of it stands a circular hole 2 inches in diameter, to admit the grain. This hole passes through the under or frame-stone also. On one side of the frame-stone also stands a stone to let the ground meal through. The perfect state of this antique, together with the art displayed in its construction, might render it worthy of further notice.

At Mr Bullock's house also stands a grinding stone, circular shape, 8 inches in diameter and 3 and a half inches thick. It is also of freestone, and at its centre a circular hole to admit a handle to work it by. This grinding stone was found in the remains of the above fort about 20 years back. Some small irons used in the securing of the handle was found in the stone but in a very decayed state. The above fort is now totally destroyed. Informant John Bullock, 19th January 1838.

Forts

In the townland of Tiscallen, and holding of James Corry, there stood a fort which is now destroyed and the site under tillage.

In the last-mentioned townland, and holding of John Lavery, there stood a fort which is also destroyed and the site under tillage.

Fort in Derrynaseer

The ruins of that large fort situated in the townland of Derrynaseer, and now partly occupied by the chapel grounds and a bridle road, is said to occupy 5 English acres and to have stood 1 mile in circumference. It formed nearly a circle. For the last 40 years [it] has undergone much alteration in shape and dilapidation, though a large portion of the parapet, which was composed of earth and stones, still remains and averages 4 feet high and from 4 to 8 feet thick. The interior is partly occupied by the chapel grounds and bridle road, and the remainder under pasture.

Races in Aghagallon

This fort was for a series of time the scene of great horse-racing, which was annually held in the latter part of autumn. The racecourse was situated round the fort and said to be a distance of 1 Irish mile. The assemblages on this occasion were very large and collected from different counties. The races lasted for 4 days each year and were well attended by vendors of liquor, confectionery and fruit etc. These races were abolished about the last rebellion of Ireland. They were called the Aghagallon races.

Ancient Boat

Mr Henry Bell found, at some depth beneath the sandy surface on the verge of Lough Neagh between the counties of Antrim and Down, in 1826, an ancient oak canoe boat about 40 foot long, 5 foot broad and a considerable depth. It was constructed out of a solid oak tree and said to be in a sound state when discovered, and has been since cut up for house roofing, for which purpose it was found perfectly useful. The neighbourhood of the above lough in which this ancient boat was found is commonly called Shanport.

Pleasure Patterns in Derryclone

In the last-mentioned townland, and holding of Timothy Kelly, there stands the ruins of a fruit plantation which was time immemorial the scene of large pleasure patterns held for 3 successive Sundays in August of each year. The assemblages on the occasions were very large and collected from different districts of Antrim, Armagh and Down counties, and enjoyed themselves at fruit, confectionery, bread and liquors, all which were abundantly supplied from different parts of the surrounding neighbourhood. These patterns were abolished 1837 by the Roman Catholic clergy. Informants Timothy Kelly, Patt Lavery and many others. 2nd February 1838.

Ancient Wooden Road

In cutting from time to time within the last 50 years a tract of bog intervening between the townlands of Derrymore and Derryclone, there was discovered in a straight line, and about 3 feet beneath the surface, an ancient wooden road composed of oak planks measuring about 6 feet long, 2 feet broad and 7 inches thick each, and duffed up on the end of each other in succession and fastened by alder spikes or pins; the latter much decayed but the planks sound and found useful for various purposes. The road was found to extend about 1 mile distance and a portion of its remains lifted out, 1836-1837. Informants Henry Cory, Henry Campbell, Patrick Cory and others.

Old Corn Mill

In Ballymacilrany, and holding of Robert Usher, there stands the walls of an old corn mill which measures 33 and a half by 19 feet on the outside. They are of stone and lime. This mill was erected by the late John Usher Esquire, who held a farm about a 100 English acres in the above townland. The mill was changed to a flax mill about 30 years back, in consequence of the supply of water having been reduced. To assist the canal, however, about 1826 the flax mill too had to be altogether relinquished for want of a sufficient supply of water, it being withdrawn from the old race, under the aforesaid circumstances.

Old Farmhouse and Tanyard

The late Mr Usher above mentioned erected on the above farm a good 2-storey house, which was originally roofed with shingles but is at present thatched and occupied by the above Robert Usher.

On the premises also stood a good tanyard founded by the said late John Usher Esquire, and the business by him extensively carried on for a series of time. This tanyard fell to ruin many years back. The pits are at present closed up. Informants Robert Usher and others. 8th February 1838.

Ancient Dishes and Butter

Hugh Lavery, in cutting turf in Derryclone bog in 1812, got about 12 feet beneath the surface of the bog 3 circular wooden dishes varying in size, the largest 13 inches in diameter and the others smaller in proportion. They were situated one within the other when found. Each was supported on 3 feet of the same wood and each foot about 3 inches in length. The whole was rather of a rude construction and in a complete <compleat> state of decay when discovered, and, though destroyed by the turf spade in lifting them out, yet created much interest amongst the local inhabitants, whose belief is that the dishes must have remained there since the Deluge.

William Glover, in cutting turf in the above bog in 1825, got about 4 feet beneath the surface of the bog a cask of old butter. The cask was circular, made of oak staves of rude shape and bound by wooden hoops. The butter, when rendered, made good cart grease and candles but the vessel was decayed and since neglected.

Fort and Ancient Coin

In Tamnyvane, and holding of John Mooney, there stood a fort which is now destroyed and the site under tillage. In demolishing this fort in 1804 there was found in it a circular piece of very ancient silver coin about the size of an old 5s piece. It was subsequently given to the Lord Bishop of Dromore.

Fort, Brass Plate and Brass Tube

Edward Magee of Ballycairn, in demolishing a fort in his holding in the latter townland in 1828, found about 12 feet beneath the surface of the parapet an ancient brass plate, oval shape, about 12 by 8 inches, and on its surface devices of different kinds. It was divided into small squares attached by hinges. It would appear, according to description, to have been part of a coat of mail. However, it was subsequently broken up and part given to a John Rogan, an antiquarian in the neighbourhood, and a part given to other persons for various uses.

In the above fort also stood, or was found, a brass tube or pipe about 3 feet long and wide at one end and narrow at the other. It was also broken up and used for different purposes.

Old Butter and Ancient Tools

James Matchett of Ballycairn, in demolishing a fort in his holding in 1830, got about 2 feet beneath the surface in the moat 2 circular wooden vessels constructed out of a solid piece of timber and each containing a quantity of old butter. They would contain about 1 and a half gallons each, but was quite decayed when found and has subsequently fallen down. The butter was, when dissolved, useful for cart grease.

There was also found with the above butter a quantity of different kinds of carpenter's tools of ancient construction. They have since been wrought up for other uses.

Ancient Wooden Vessel

The late John Branken of the above townland found in the Montiagh bog at some former period an ancient wooden vessel resembling a water jug, and would hold about 2 Irish quarts. It was rudely made, had 2 long handles and was supposed to be constructed out of a solid piece of timber. This curious old vessel created much interest but has been lost after the death of the above Branken about 20 years back.

Fire Hearth

John Lavery, in cutting turf in his holding in Ballymacilrany in 1837, got about 6 feet beneath the surface a paved fire hearth, timber cinders and about 1 peck of nut shells. Information obtained from John Lavery, James Matchett and others. 15th February 1838.

Stone Hatchets, Fort and Flints

The stone hatchets, of which the above drafts [2 drawings] is the shape and size, was found 1 foot beneath the surface in the Montiagh bog and are at present in John Lavery's house, townland of Ballymacilrany.

In the last-mentioned townland, and holding of John Lavery, there stands the ruins of a fort now occupied under fruit trees. The parapet was of earth and stones.

Parish of Aghagallon

The above John Lavery got, 1 foot beneath the surface of a bog in the last-mentioned townland in 1824, a quantity of well shaped flints lying together. Informants John Lavery and others.

Sand Strata in Ballymacilrany

John Lavery, in cutting turf in his farm in the above townland in 1835, found about 10 feet beneath the original surface a strata of white sand and fish shells, the depth of which could not be explored. It is supposed to be a continuation of the sandy shore of Lough Neagh, though the site in which it was discovered stands about three-quarters of a mile north west of the above lough and two-fourths of a mile south of Lough Beg.

Ancient Fire Hearth

George Dobson, in cutting turf in the Montiagh bog in 1828, got about 3 feet beneath the surface of the bog a paved fire hearth covered with timber cinders and a wash staff such as is commonly used in farmhouses for beetling linen.

Fire Hearth

Patrick McConaghy, in cutting turf in the Montiagh bog 1824, got about 16 feet under the bog a paved fire hearth, cinders and a Danes' pipe. Informant Patt McConaghy. 20th February 1838.

Timber

Richard Blair of Derrymore, in cutting turf in the Montiagh bog, found at a considerable depth beneath the bog, and situated under a large oak block or root, an oak stick 26 feet in length, which he has at present in his possession. He also on many occasions found sticks of various lengths lodged over each other in different directions, and situated on the top of those ledges, 1 or perhaps 2 roots standing perpendicular one above another, as if grown and decayed in that order; and in other instances sticks of sundry lengths, found lodged as above stated, 1 or perhaps 2 roots, in various instances the top part of the root, as well as the sticks, partly burned or singed by fire.

He found in the same bog several rows of sharp-pointed stakes of birch and alder, standing perpendicular both in the bog and the subsoil beneath the bog, but all in a decayed state. They varied from 2 to 6 feet in length each.

He likewise found at about 4 feet beneath the surface several oak planks of different lengths, and situated as if designed for footpaths. Part of one of these planks lies near Blair's house at present. It measures 4 and a half feet long, 1 foot broad and 3 inches thick, and brought to that shape by an edged tool. He also found on the subsoil under the bog an oblong stone of a whitish hard quality and concave on the one side, as if caused by grinding purposes. It measures 20 inches long, 13 inches broad and 5 inches thick. Informants Richard Blair and others.

Ancient Bottle, Arrowheads and Road

Ancient black glass bottle found beneath the surface of a bog in 1818 [outline and view]. The ancient black bottle above represented was found a considerable depth beneath the surface of the Montiagh bog in 1818. The circle denotes its diameter at the bottom, 6 inches, and concave shape. The neck was about 3 inches long, but at present [?] inferred. It was full of liquid and corked when found, and contains 1 quart. It is at present in my possession [signed] T. Fagan.

The 2 flint arrowheads here represented [drawings], as well as the glass bottle, were found in the above bog by my informant Anthony Kearney of Derrymore.

Anthony Kearney also found, a considerable depth beneath the surface of the above bog, a paved road 6 feet wide and made of moderate-sized stones. It led from north to south but length not explored. Informant as above.

Bog Timber

Oak and fir sticks from 50 to 60 feet in length and from 4 to 10 feet in circumference have been frequently found in the Montiagh bogs. These and the shorter timber were observed to lie indiscriminately and to have fallen in different directions, but chiefly from the east, south and south west. They are in many instances found lodged over each other in a disorderly state, also lying over roots, and in other cases the roots situated over the sticks. In many instances oak sticks and roots are found situated over fir roots and sticks, and in other instances fir roots and sticks situated over oak of the above description. The windfalls vary from 4 to 14 feet in length and are found to lie indiscriminately in the bog and all qualities and description of timber found, bearing in many cases the appearance of being fired. The oak is the principal timber found in the north side of the bogs and lies chiefly near the subsoil in the exterior, along the shores or arable land. But the large sticks, or most valuable part, are generally found to lie some feet above the clay.

In the bog soil the fir timber is more frequently

found in the interior than in the exterior of the bogs and at different depths, but generally situated higher in the bog than the oak. These 2 qualities of timber found embedded in the above bogs are chiefly used in roofing and joisting <joiceing> of dwelling and office houses, as well as in mill works and other machinery. Informants Arthur Moore, Richard Blair, John Finn and others.

Knockanroe and Discoveries

Knockanroe is an island situated in the Montiagh bog and townland of Drumaleet, and at present occupied by Arthur McQuillan, a farmer, who many years back erected on it a dwelling and office houses, fruit gardens. This island, containing about 4 and a half acres, was first discovered in the cutting of the turf about 50 years ago, when the discovery created much interest in the neighbourhood. As its summit stands much higher than the surface of the surrounding bog, the nearest point of dry land stands 2 furlongs distant on the island, accessible by boats only during the winter floods. The original bog is said to have stood 28 feet above the present surface of the island.

However, singular to remark, the above McQuillan, in reclaiming it from time to time, discovered all over the clay or subsoil a light strata of burnt soil, as if the island had been fired before the formation of the bog over it. He also discovered in sinking a well at his house, situated about the middle of the island, a strata of limestone 21 feet beneath the present surface which, together with the 28 feet of turf previously cut off, would, over the original surface of the bog, stand about 50 feet above this strata of limestone.

Brass Battleaxe

In the reclaiming of the island he also discovered at some depth beneath the surface a brass battleaxe, an iron chain and pot-hooks, all of rude shape, also a half-dressed hide, in a torn and decayed state and in a great measure resembling torn leather breeches. A quantity of Danes' smoking pipes was also found through the soil in labouring the island. Along its borders, and [a] considerable depth beneath the bog, was likewise found several well dressed oak planks varying from 4 to 8 feet long, 9 inches wide and 2 to 3 inches thick, situated in succession as if designed for footpaths through the bog.

Old Butter

In the island he also found, some feet under the surface of the bog, a parcel of old butter contained in a circular birch vessel. This vessel was quite decayed and resembled the bark of a tree. The butter was also decayed but subsequently used by different persons for the cure of bodily pain and candle grease. When rendered, it was found to be thickly mixed with cattle hairs of various colours.

He found in the same place an ancient well shaped brick about 9 inches in length and of a much harder quality than the modern brick. All the aforesaid articles were discovered at sundry periods; some of them were used for different purposes and others cast away as useless.

Ancient Roads

Beneath the surface of the surrounding bog the above McQuillan and others discovered, at sundry periods and in different parts of the bog, patches of ancient causeway composed of clay and stones, but have been destroyed by the cutting of turf on the lines. Informants Arthur and William McQuillan and others. 21st February 1838.

Dane's Causey

On the surface of the tract of bog that intervened between Courtney's Island, Drumaleet and Maghernagah old graveyard in Derrymore there stood an ancient line of road locally called the Danes' Causey. It was about 4 furlongs in length, ledged or buried underneath the sandstone and clay of which it was composed, with the heath and brambles. It was from 7 to 9 feet wide and a tolerable depth. The sand, clay and stones of which it was formed is locally said to have been carried from Lough Neagh shore in bags, as the materials correspond with those of the above shore and could not be brought to the site of this road by any other conveyance than in bags, on men or horses, as the surrounding neighbourhood of the road was chiefly a flow bog or morass. This road has been destroyed in cutting turf on the site from time to time. Information obtained from Patrick McCory, William McQuillan and others.

Ancient Mill-race

Leading from Lough Money, a small lake now drained in the Montiagh bogs, in a south west direction for a distance of about 3 furlongs, there stood an ancient mill-race, the sluices of which have been raised about 2 furlongs from the above lough about 70 years back. This mill-race led through a tract of bog and is locally thought to have accommodated the ruins of a Danes' mill discovered at some former period by Patrick McStravoge and others, and which ruins

Parish of Aghagallon

are described on preceding Fair Sheets. The sluices above mentioned were of the best of oak and well made.

Discoveries in Lough Money

John Montgomery, now residing on the remains of the above lough, in labouring about his place in 1834, got about 5 feet beneath the surface of the above remains an ancient wooden vessel constructed out of a solid tree, but quite decayed when found. It was nearly the shape of a churn about 6 feet long, 1 foot in diameter in one end but narrower in the other. Alongside of it lay 2 wooden hand spikes, supposed to have been used in carrying about the above vessels.

In the same place also lay part of a wooden vessel supposed to have been an ancient meddar, but likewise quite decayed when found.

In the same remains of the lough was also found a morticed oak frame nearly the shape of a doorcase. All these articles being decayed when lifted, they have been subsequently broken down for fuel.

About 5 feet beneath the surface of the above remains was also found an ancient bread griddle 2 feet in diameter, tolerably thick and without handles. It is at present occupied as a fire hearth in the aforesaid John Montgomery's dwelling house, and occasionally serves for baking bread. Informants John Montgomery, Henry Welsh and others.

Lough Money in the Montiagh Bogs

Lough Money was formerly the scene of much pleasure in the neighbourhood in which it was situated, both as to fishing and shooting at wildfowl, the latter of which inhabited it to a large extent. It was likewise accommodated with boats for the above purposes. It was likewise ornamented with 2 ancient artificial islands erected on oak frames and sheltered with a handsome planting of ancient and modern willows. Their ruins are now visible but inaccessible by the surrounding morass. This sheet of water, which occupied about 65 English acres, was drained off at the instance of Lord Hertford in 1811, engineer the late Denis Kennedy of Cashel. Informants Neal McStravogue, Anthony Kearney and others. 22nd February 1838.

Forts in Ballymacilrany

In Ballymacilrany, and holding of Henry Shillington, there stands the remains of 2 forts now under tillage.

In the last-mentioned townland, and holding of John Lutton, there stood a fort now quite altered and the site occupied as a fruit and vegetable garden. In demolishing this fort there was a flint arrowhead and stone hatchets found beneath its surface. Informants John Lutton and others, 3rd February 1838.

In Ballymacilrany, and holding of Thomas Thompson, there stands the ruin of a fort now under tillage.

Forts in Ballykeel

In Ballykeel, and holding of Owen Gribbin, there stands the ruins of a fort now occupied as a vegetable garden.

In the same townland, and holding of Widow Magill, there stands the site of a fort now occupied by a fruit garden.

In the above townland, and holding of Charles O'Brien, there also stands the site of a fort which is at present under tillage.

Forts

In Drumaleet, and holding of Stephen Gilbert, stood a fort which is now destroyed. Informants Neal McStravoge, John Bullock and others.

In Derryclone townland there stood 3 forts, which are now destroyed and the sides under tillage.

In Aghadrumglasny, and holding of William O'Hara, there stood a fort which is at present destroyed and the site under tillage. Informants Hugh Lavery, William Glover and others. 13th February 1838.

In the Montiaghs, and holding of James Lavery, there stood a fort, the site of which is now occupied by dwelling houses etc. One of the old bushes still remains. Informants John Mooney, William Glover and others. 14th February 1838.

Manuscripts

This parish formerly possessed within its precincts many valuable and interesting manuscripts, some of which were written up in the English and some in the Irish characters, some procured from remote districts and some the production of local, but late, individuals. Of these old writings many of the parishioners were very fond and careful to preserve, and the bulk of the people most anxious to hear them read; more particularly the prophecies of St Columkille, the latter of which had been pretty numerous in the parish. However, in latter years many of the persons, owners of these old writings, have died and their little libraries subsequently neglected, lent, lost and given unto ruin. Others lent the works to friends in other districts but have never been restored.

On the whole, there is not one of these old books at present acknowledged or to be found within the parish, though it was at no distant period a mart for prophecy books and ancient writings, and its inhabitants very partial to reading and interpretation and fancied construction of those writings, particularly those relating to past and fancied coming events. The latter feelings prevail to a wide extent even to the present period. Informants Neal and Patrick McStravoge, James O'Neill and others.

History and Social Economy

Ancient Families

The Laverys, McStravoges and McCaveneys are locally said to be the most numerous names in the above parish and to have been residents of the townlands of Derrymore, Tiscallen, Ballycairn and the Montiaghs since the 13th century. The McStravoges were in general men of large size, valour and strength. The late Roger McStravoge of Tiscallen was often known to lift 7 cwt between his arms. Informants Neal McStravoge, Owen McCann and others.

Catholic Colony in the Montiaghs

The following townlands, locally denominated the Montiaghs, to wit Montiaghs, Derrymore, Derryclone and Derryhirk, is locally said to be a Catholic colony or settlement. Time immemorial, or particularly since the 1641 war and the continuance of the Penal Code, and even up to a late period, it had been inhabited exclusively by Roman Catholics, so even at the present time there is not more than 12 Protestant families resident in the above 4 townlands. These too have settled here subsequent to the rebellion of 1798. The cause locally assigned for this exclusive settlement in the Montiaghs is that subsequent to the above period or 1641 war the partial withholding of land from the Catholic community was carried on to such an extent, in the surrounding districts of Antrim, Down and Armagh, that many families were banished from their former fertile inhabitations and were consequently obliged to take up their abode in the Montiaghs, a backward, barren, retired portion of the neighbourhood, and then to a great extent occupied by native wood, water and bog. There these exiles resided to a great extent in huts and hovels, and in tolerable safety, the situation being considered a regular fortress bounded on the north west and west by Lough Neagh and Lough Beg and on the east and south by bog and other sheets of water.

Shortly after the settlement of the Catholic exiles in the Montiaghs, they rented tracts of the ground from the original inhabitants, on which they commenced to build mud-wall and stone and lime houses and reclaim patches of remains of bog and native wood, and render their little habitations more comfortable in other respects. Many of them at length became tenants to the Marquis of Hertford, proprietor of the soil. They have also from time to time, in a more or less degree, adopted the plans of foreign settlers in their neighbourhoods, as regards building and planting of forest trees and fruit gardens.

Battle of the Montiaghs

However, in the distracted state of party feelings during the last Irish rebellion an unprincipled portion of their Dissenting neighbours in the surrounding districts of Down and Armagh threatened <treatened> their total defeat and extirpation from the Montiaghs, which, from the fortified situation of the place by bog and water, rendered the project very difficult to effect. However, about the end of harvest 1795 or 1796 a body of men, then denominated the Rackers, and about 200 in number, collected in different parts of Armagh and Down with cars, horses and ammunitions for the purpose of plundering and defeating the inhabitants of the Montiaghs. The latter, who were sometime previous apprised of the Rackers' design, had temporary batteries prepared at different entrances into the Montiaghs and had out occasional sentinels, as daily dreading an attack from their enemy.

However, the Rackers before mentioned made their first effort to enter the Montiaghs at the Cranagh bridge, situated in Tiscallen near the west end of the parish and one of the entrances into the Montiaghs. On the approach of the aforesaid body of Rackers to the Cranagh bridge, which was about 2 o'clock in the evening of day in the year and season of the year before mentioned, the defending party in the Montiaghs had themselves arrayed in arms behind a moss bank near the above bridge and in the verge of the bog. In this moss bank, which stood several feet in the height, they had portholes made to fire through at their besieging enemy.

However, the Rackers, on mounting the bridge, found themselves unexpectedly and instantly repulsed by a volley from behind the moss bank, which volley is supposed to have killed one and

Parish of Aghagallon

wounded several others. Here an exchange of some shots took place, but the result was that the Rackers took to flight and have never since attempted open attack on the Montiaghs.

The spirited conduct of the Montiagh inhabitants, in repulsing and urging to flight the lawless Rackers, on the occasion of the Montiagh battle before alluded to, thereby securing their own lives and properties, at once enlisted on their behalf the high approbation and subsequent patronage and protection of the Marquis of Hertford, lord of the soil, and the local magistrates and gentry. For while they manfully secured their own settlement, they secured the property of the Marquis of Hertford also against a most barbarous and open attempt by a lawless body of strangers on his property, as well as the lives and properties of his tenantry resident on that portion of his estate. Next day after the above battle the inhabitants of the Montiaghs were amply supplied with additional arms and ammunition from the Marquis of Hertford's agent, the late Reverend Dr Trail, and William Smith Esquire, and an immediate application made to government, by the above noblemen and others, for a military force to be stationed in the Montiaghs for protection of its inhabitants. This application was responded to, with orders to station a militia company in the above place. And, in accordance with these orders, the force remained in the Montiaghs till quiet prevailed. 16th February 1838.

The Rackers

The Rackers were first known by the name of Break-of-Day Men. They were composed of persons of the low grade who took out arms to persecute their neighbouring Roman Catholics, under the hidden mask of loyalty, while at the same time they were permitted to have or use those arms for lawful purposes and on lawful occasions only. Instead of loyalty or lawful purposes, they formed themselves into a combined party whose whole pursuit was murder, robbery and plunder of the above sect and their chattels, and at length attacked every class and sect indiscriminately, racking, robbing and destroying themselves and their places. Under the latter circumstances they were denominated the Rackers, a party unknown to the law and prosecuted as such when detected. However, every religious denomination on the Montiaghs, and the parish and surrounding neighbourhood, have lived on the best of good feelings towards each other for many years back.

SOCIAL ECONOMY

Emigration in 1836 and 1837

The following is a list of the persons who have emigrated from the above parish to America during the years 1836 and 1837. It will show the name, age and religion of each person, the ports to which emigrated and the townlands from whence gone, as enumerated from 6th January to 10th February 1838.

1836 [all Roman Catholics]: Patrick Gribbin, 30, Elenor Gribbin, 29, Patt Gribbin, 4, from Derrynaseer to New York.

Patt McStravoge, 24, from Derrymore to Quebec.

Margaret Doone, 25, from Derrymore to Quebec.

James Kelly, 48, Mary Kelly, 46, from Derrymore to Quebec.

1837 [all Roman Catholics except where stated]: Arthur Nugent, 25, from Ballykeel to New York.

Jean McDonnald, 24, from Ballykeel to New York.

James Carvill, 24, Eliza Carvill, 26, James Carvill, 4, Eliza Carvill, 2, from Drumaleet to New York.

Eliza Faloon, 55, Established Church, William Faloon, 23, Established Church, Susana Faloon, 20, Established Church, from Derrypark to New York.

Informants Patrick Cory, John Lutton and many others. Finished 10th February 1838.

Migration

The following is the number of persons that annually migrate to the Scotch harvest from the above parish, enumerated from 6th January to 10th February 1838.

From Ballymacilrany 2, from Tiscallen 1, from Ballycairn 2, from Montiaghs 2, from Derryclone 1, total 8.

It is locally said that want of employ within the parish during the summer or harvest seasons does not oblige the above or any number of persons to migrate to harvest to foreign countries; that they go merely for pleasure and experience's sake, as all of the working class resident in the parish is not sufficient to meet the demand for labourers in cutting and otherwise preparing turf in the Montiagh bogs, together with attending harvest and other processes of farming business. Besides that, very many of the above class are weavers, which trade is extensively carried on in the parish. Information obtained from Patrick Lavery, Henry

Lutton, William Campbell and many others. Finished 10th February 1838.

Size of Farms

Holdings in the parish vary from 1 to 130 English acres, but very few farms of the latter size. There are also some tenements as low as half an acre, but the majority of the holdings is from 10 to 13 acres.

Farmhouses

Of first-class farmhouses, there [are] from 50 to 60 in the parish; of these, about one half are 2-storey high and about one-fourth slated. This class [of] houses are chiefly comfortable, with good sash windows in front, yards and office houses, large and well enclosed, as is also the fruit and vegetable gardens attached to them. In many of the yards are good pumps and in others draw-wells. The interior[s] of the houses are well furnished and in many cases afford handsome clocks. They have in general a taste for cleanliness and have their dwellings well sheltered with forest trees.

The second-class farmhouses are in many respects very comfortable, lit with good sash windows, good yards, offices, fruit and vegetable gardens attached, well enclosed and in many instances well sheltered with forest trees. The majority of the houses are well furnished and afford good clocks. In many of the yards are also draw-wells. This class [of] farmhouses are not so generally whitened with lime as those of the same class in Magheragall.

The third-class farmhouses in this parish and other parishes before described are very numerous, particularly in that portion of the parish locally denominated the Montiaghs and which constitute about a third of the parish. A large portion of the above class houses are mud wall, sod and stone, or of sods altogether, and lit by small glass windows. Some of them are tolerably comfortable in some respects but the exterior exhibiting altogether the materials of which they are built. Besides that, many of them are low and limited in size. Yards too are small and in many instances filthy. On the whole they denote indolence, poverty or want of taste on the part of those who inhabit them.

Cottier Houses

The cottier houses are to a great extent low and limited in size, and denote in many respects, outside and inside, inferior taste or low circumstances. However, much of the inferior state of the latter classes of houses are attributed to the neglect of the persons who inhabit them.

Jurisdiction of Manor Courts

In this parish there is no resident magistrates, peace or revenue police, or other officers. The parish being situated in the manor of Killultagh, consequently all local disputes about the recovery and settlement of money, debts etc. are decided at Lisburn manor court, held on every third Wednesday in the court house of that town, for the above manor; seneschal William Gregg Esquire.

Petty Sessions

All local disputes arising within the parish, and usually decided by a bench of magistrates at petty sessions, are tried and decided at Crumlin petty sessions, held every 2 weeks.

Medical Aid

The poor of this parish get advice and medicine at the infirmary of the county of Antrim, situated at Lisburn, as there is no dispensary or medical man resident in the parish.

Illicit Practices

There is no smuggling or illicit distillation carried on within the parish.

Societies and Money Clubs

There is no reading, temperance or other societies in the parish.

There is no savings banks or money clubs of any description in the parish. 19th February 1838.

Lodges

There is no Orange, Mason or Ribbon Lodges at present. If there were any of the latter at any period in the parish, the local inhabitants are silent on it. However, it is not supposed that any dare be.

Combinations

There is no combinations among tradespeople or labourers in the parish, as regards wages.

Clergy and Places of Public Worship

The Reverend James Denvir P.P. is the only clergyman resident in the parish. The Roman Catholic chapel of Aghagallon is the only house of public worship in the parish; the Catholic community worship at the latter place. The Prot-

Parish of Aghagallon 21

estants worship at Aghalee church and the Presbyterians and Methodists at Moira meeting houses.

Burial Grounds

Maghernagah and Aghagallon old graveyards are the only burial grounds in the parish.

Natural Features

The parish is well accommodated as regards fuel, spring and river waters.

Methodist Meetings

The Methodists have class meetings weekly at different farmhouses throughout the parish. Mr Henry Shillington of Ballymacilrany, a farmer, is the principal class leader.

Public Houses

Temperance is very slightly advocated by any class in the parish. There is above 20 public houses or spirit shops within the precincts of the parish, a number very unusually met with in any parish having neither fair, market town nor village situated within its bounds. Such must be a demonstrative proof of the non-existence of anything tantamount to temperance being as yet cherished in the parish or neighbourhood. The number of publicans here far exceeded the above a few years back. However, there is here a wide inducement for spirit sellers not commonly met with in other parishes or backward places, that is, the vast concourse of people, employers and labourers collected from different districts at the Montiagh bogs during the turf-cutting season, as well as the drawing of same, also those engaged in fishing along the banks of Lough Neagh, as well as at other marketable commodities procured about the bogs; all who are, in more or less degree, supporters of spirit sellers. The majority of the farmers, tradespeople and labourers residing in the parish are likewise favourable to the drinking system. Informants Henry Campbell, Patrick McStravoge, William Ferris and many others.

Longevity

Elizabeth McRory of Derrymore is now in the 97th year of her age and possessed of her faculties to a moderate extent. Her memory is good, her sight tolerable and her features fresh and clean. She still retains several of her teeth and is able to walk in and about her house by the aid of 2 walking sticks, and is at present employed at spinning yarn, 11 hanks to the lb, and now supports herself by spinning and other industry on a small tenement held under Lord Hertford. She experienced little sickness through life except by rheumatic pains and, though married, never bore issue. Her husband, the late Bernard McRory, died about 10 weeks ago at the advanced age of 101 years, and to the latter moments sound in mind and memory but dark of sight for the last 15 years of his life. He was bred in Glenavy and she in Aghagallon. Both their ancestors were residents of these parishes previous to and since the 1641 war.

The late Hugh Heany of Tiscallen, a farmer, died about 40 years ago at the extraordinary age of 108 years and retained his entire faculties to a late period of his life, and died without a struggle. His face and features were so full and fresh to the last moment that, after his departure, he was shaved <sheaved> with as much facility as a boy, nor did he ever drop one of his teeth. Informants Arthur and William McQuillan and others. 23rd February 1838.

John Bullock of Drumaleet, a farmer, is now in the 85th year of his age, fully active and to a moderate extent possessed of his natural faculties. Information obtained from John Bullock, James O'Neill and others.

Extraordinary Childbearing

The late Mrs Ann Gilbert of Drumaleet gave birth to 24 separate children, the offspring of 3 husbands. Her first marriage took place between the 15th and 17th years of her age and [she] was often called into her house from jackstone play among other children after her first birth, and by much flattery got to give her child suck. She died about 30 years back at an advanced age.

Large Family

The townland of Drumaleet gave birth to the following extraordinary family of 17 sons and one daughter, the children of one and the same parents, Patt Brady and Cathrine Brady alias Lavery, his wife, both of whom were of the cottier class. The family lived together till the youngest arrived at maturity. 7 or more of the boys have subsequently joined the army and the remainder scattered into different townlands and parishes in the surrounding neighbourhood. The above Patrick Brady, father to the family, on going to visit his native place in the province of Connaught about 30 years back, was murdered on his way. The aforesaid Cathrine Brady, his wife, married again some years subsequent to the murder of her husband. She was a native of the above parish.

Remarkable Person

This parish gave birth to a deformed male in the person of David McCaveney, bred and still residing in the townland of Drumaleet and now about 40 years of age. The stature, natural talent and deformed or defective order of his hands, feet, legs and arms, together with his extraordinary unprecedented dexterity in pursuing farming business and other performances, render his person well worthy of being sketched, his abilities further developed and the defective order of his aforesaid members accurately shown and described. As ocular demonstration will satisfy the above, I have omitted further and unnecessary remarks on his person or history for the present, till visited by a person competent to take off his sketch.

Character of the People

The inhabitants of this parish are said to be tolerable industrious in their respective callings. Many of them are also said to be pretty regular visitors to the petty sessions for the decision of the assaults, offences, recovery of wages and other disputes arising from within the parish; also to the quarter sessions and the manor courts for the recovery of small debts and the decision of disputes of that nature occurring within the parish also. There are some instances of fowl stealing and other petty thefts in the parish but practised chiefly by modern settlers and travelling beggars, the latter class of which are numerous and constant visitors here on account of the supply of fuel.

The inhabitants of this parish are said to be more attentive to their religious duties than those of the neighbouring parishes of Aghalee and Magheramesk. In Aghagallon, day and Sunday schools and other institutions for the intellectual and moral education of the growing generation are very limited.

Clothing of the People

The wearing apparel of the parishioners is tolerably decent, particularly the first and second-class farmers who generally purchase shop goods of foreign and local manufacture. All classes manufacture the chief part of their linen and stockings but the working portion of the community purchase much of their wearing apparel of every description at the old clothes stalls in Lisburn, Lurgan and other market towns. Brogues and knee breeches are the only remnants of ancient costume now prevailing in the parish. High-heeled shoes was very commonly worn by the females of the parish: Mrs Ann Turtle of Tiscallen retained this portion of the old fashion to her latter days. She died about 40 years back. Since that period the wearing of high-heeled shoes has been relinquished, as also the wearing of shoe and knee buckles, which generally prevailed in the parish at a former period. 27th February 1838.

Amusements

Horse-racing, cock-fighting, gambling, dancing and other amusements prevailed in this parish at a former period but have been altogether abolished by the clergy within the last few years.

Irish Language

The Irish language too prevailed to a great extent throughout the period about 40 years back, particularly in the Montiaghs. A few settlers from other districts still speak Irish fluently but none of the natives of the parish.

Old Stories

Legendary tales and stories also prevailed to a wide extent among the last generation, but very little of either to be had amongst the present. Yet they are very partial to prophecies and old sayings, and the interpretation of them.

Diet

Diet in the parish consists in beef, bacon, fowl, eggs, salt and fresh fish and vegetables, potatoes, wheaten bread, oatmeal bread and porridge, and milk and butter. All classes are very partial to tea drinking, particularly the wealthy farmers and tradespeople. In consequence of its vicinity to Lough Neagh and other sheets of water, fresh fish of various kinds are more abundantly used in this parish than in other parishes before described.

Tradition: Frogs

Local tradition says that since the days of St Patrick frogs do not inhabit or multiply in the waters of Lough Neagh. This tradition seems to be corroborated by recent experience, as several of the inhabitants along the lough shores have cast in frogs procured from neighbouring marshes but immediately returned to the shore. The inhabitants consider the frogs would not live any time in the lough and believe it a peculiar feature not identified with other sheets of water.

Parish of Aghagallon

Early Marriages

Early marriages frequently occurred in the parish at a former period, which may be justly judged from the few instances already given of an unusual number of births in families residing in the parish. However, this practice is greatly fallen off in latter years. Information obtained from John Magee, Arthur McQuillan, John Lavery and many others. 28th February 1838.

PRODUCTIVE ECONOMY

Fuel

Turf is the fuel used by all classes in the parish and is procured within its bounds. Such accommodation being situated plentifully within the parish must in great degree contribute to the comfort of the local inhabitants, more particularly to the comfort of the humbler classes, who in other parishes suffer much privation and cold in the absence of sufficient means to procure coal or other winter fuel.

Bogs and Employment

The extensive tracts of bogs, situated at the subdivision of the above parish locally called the Montiaghs, is the principal support of that description of fuel in the surrounding neighbourhood for many miles. The various processes of cutting, drying and drawing fuel in these bogs is also a source of almost constant employ for hundreds of men, women and children from beginning of June to the end of September of each year, at daily wages varying from 6d to 1s 8d per day. Many of the inhabitants in the neighbourhood of the bogs make the principal support for themselves by cutting turf here and driving it to Lisburn, Moira and surrounding neighbourhood. Several also employ themselves at the making and selling of stable brooms made of the heather got about the bogs; also at cutting and peeling and selling in the surrounding neighbourhood the rushes got about the bogs and used by the country people for rushlights; also in making and selling rush mats, commonly used at staircases and over earthen floors. Several are also employed in lifting and selling for house-roofing and fuels the different kinds of timber got in the above bogs.

On the whole, the working of turf and of other saleable articles got in and about these bogs is not only a source of extensive employment and much of their support for a large portion of the working class and small farmers resident in the parish, but also to a large number of the working class residing in the neighbouring parishes of Aghalee, Magheramesk, Magheragall and Ballinderry etc. during the summer months.

Fishing

Several along the banks of Lough Neagh and within the above parish also make a great portion of the support of themselves and families by fishing for, and selling in Lisburn and Moira and other towns and districts, the fresh fish of various kinds found in the above lough.

Weaving

Weaving of linen, cotton and cambric is carried on to a wide extent by the small farmers and cottier class residing in this parish. Cambric weavers particularly are more numerous here than in any of the parishes before described. There are some diaper weavers also here. These trades are in a great measure the support and comfort of those who pursue them, particularly the cottier class. On the whole, few parishes are more prominent with sources of employment and support for the working class than Aghagallon. Informants William Ferris, John Magee and many others. 12th and 13th February 1838.

SOCIAL ECONOMY

Table of Schools

[Table contains the following headings: name, situation and description, when established, income and expenditure, physical, intellectual and moral education, number of pupils subdivided by age, sex and religion, name and religion of master or mistress, date on which visited. No physical education].

Ballycairn private school, situated on a leading road from the village of Aghalee to Lough Neagh; the house is thatched, stands 1-storey high, 16 by 12 feet in the clear and lit by 2 small windows; school requisites limited, established 1834; income from pupils 20 pounds; annual rent paid by the teacher for the schoolhouse 1 pound; intellectual education: the Bible and Testament, *Murray's Reader*, histories and spelling books, all procured by the pupils; moral education: visits from the vicar and the parish priest, all catechisms taught if required; number of pupils: males, 7 under 10 years of age, 12 from 10 to 15, 1 over 15, total 20; females, 6 under 10 years of age, 4 from 10 to 15, total 10; total number of pupils 30, Protestants 4, Roman Catholics 26; master James Turner, a Roman Catholic; 16th January 1838.

White Hall private school, situated in the townland of Tiscallen, on the leading road between Aghalee and Lurgan; the house is thatched, stands 1-storey high, 16 by 11 feet inside and lit by 2 small windows, school requisites in moderate supply, established 1814; income from pupils 20 pounds, annual rent paid by the teacher for the schoolhouse 1 pound 10s; intellectual education: the Bible, Testament, *Murray's Reader*, histories and spelling books, all procured by the pupils; moral education: visits from the parish priest, all catechisms taught if required; number of pupils: males, 20 under 10 years of age, 17 from 10 to 15, 3 over 15, total 40; females, 10 under 10 years of age, 10 from 10 to 15, total 20; total number of pupils 60, Protestants 20, Roman Catholics 40; master John Finnigan, a Roman Catholic; 17th January 1838.

Derrymore school, situated on the banks of Lough Neagh; is held in a slated house built for the purpose; it is 26 feet 3 inches by 16 feet 3 inches, lit by 4 windows, and school requisites in [moderate ?] supply, established 1831; income from pupils 10 pounds; intellectual education: books published by the Kildare Place Society; moral education: visits from the vicar of the parish, Protestant catechism taught; number of pupils: males, 12 under 10 years of age, 6 from 10 to 15, 2 over 15, total 20; females, 8 under 10 years of age, 2 from 10 to 15, total 10; total number of pupils 30, Protestants 18, Roman Catholics 9, other denominations 3; master Daniel McAlister, a Protestant; 18th January 1838.

Derryhirk private school, situated on the leading road from Lurgan to Antrim, by the Montiaghs; house thatched, stands 1-storey, 13 by 12 feet inside and lit by 2 small windows, established 1834; income from pupils 10 pounds; annual rent for the schoolhouse paid by the teacher 1 pound 6s; intellectual education: Testaments, histories and spelling books, all procured by pupils; moral education: visits from the Revd James Denvir <Dinver>, parish priest, Roman Catholic catechism taught; number of pupils: males, 12 under 10 years of age, 12 from 10 to 15, 4 above 15, total 28; females, 10 under 10 years of age, 8 from 10 to 15, total 18; total number of pupils 46, Established Church 1, Roman Catholics 45; master Owen McCann, a Roman Catholic; 20th January 1838.

Aghagallon Sunday Schools

[Table contains the following headings: name, situation, when established, superintendent, number of teachers, numbers of scholars subdivided by religion and sex, hours of attendance, books read, societies with which connected, observations].

Ballycairn Sunday school, held in the day schoolhouse, established 1835, superintendent James Turner; 4 male teachers; number of scholars: 70 Roman Catholics, 40 males, 30 females, total 70, 50 exclusively Sunday school scholars; open from 3 to 6 p.m. in summer; books read: Bibles, Testaments and catechisms; not connected with any society, no prayer or singing.

White Hall Sunday school, held in the day schoolhouse, established 1832, superintendent John Finnigan; 1 male teacher; number of scholars: 8 Protestants, 12 Roman Catholics, 12 males, 8 females, total 20, 18 exclusively Sunday school scholars; open from 6 to 9 a.m. in summer; books read: Bibles, Testament and catechisms; not connected with any society, no prayer or singing.

Aghagallon parish Sunday school, held in the Roman Catholic chapel, established 1820, superintendent Revd James Denvir, parish priest; 7 male teachers; number of scholars: 280 Roman Catholics, 180 males, 100 females, total 280, 100 exclusively Sunday school scholars; open from 3 to 6 p.m.; books read: Testaments, catechisms and spelling books; not connected with any society, closed by prayer. 16th, 17th and 18th January 1838 [signed] Thomas Fagan.

School Statistics

[Table contains the following headings: name of townland where held, name and religion of master or mistress, free or pay school, annual income of master or mistress, description and cost of schoolhouse, number of pupils subdivided by religion, sex and the Protestant and Roman Catholic returns, societies with which connected. All pay schools, none connected with any society].

Gawley, master Thomas Montgomery, Established Church, income 10 pounds; schoolhouse stone and lime, in pretty good repair, cost 15 pounds; number of pupils by the Protestant return: Established Church 6, Presbyterians 1, Roman Catholics 9, males 9, females 7; by the Roman Catholic return: Established Church 6, Presbyterians 1, Roman Catholics 9, males 9, females 7.

Dernasier, master John Finigan, Roman Catholic, income 24 pounds; schoolhouse stone and lime, tolerably good, cost 13 pounds; number of pupils by the Protestant return: Established Church 14, other denominations 3, Roman Catholics 19, males 28, females 8; by the Roman Catholic return: Established Church 14, other denominations 3, Roman Catholics 19, males 28, females 8.

Ballycairne, master Francis McLoughlin, Roman Catholic, income 9 pounds; schoolhouse mud and thatched; number of pupils by the Protestant return: Established Church 11, Roman Catholics 16, males 15, females 12; by the Roman Catholic return: Established Church 11, Roman Catholics 16, males 15, females 12.

Maghernagagh, master David Rowley, Roman Catholic, income 6 pounds 13s 4d; schoolhouse mud, tolerably good; number of pupils by the Protestant return: Roman Catholics 10, males 8, females 2; by the Roman Catholic return: Roman Catholics 10, males 8, females 2.

Derryclone, master Bernard McGown, Roman Catholic, income 2s 2d to 2s 6d per quarter; held only in summer, no particular schoolhouse, teaches in different places; number of pupils by the Protestant return: 17 Roman Catholics, 11 males, 6 females; by the Roman Catholic return: 17 Roman Catholics, 11 males, 6 females.

Parish of Aghalee, County Antrim

Officer's Statistical Report by Lieutenant George Boscawen, August 1832

NATURAL STATE

Name, Situation and Extent

Aghalee is the ancient and present name of this parish. It is situated in the barony of Upper Massereene, county of Antrim and province of Ulster. It is bounded on the north and east by the parishes of Ballinderry and Magheramesk, on the south by the parish of Moira and the west by the parish of Aghagallon. It is of an oblong form, being about 3 miles from the north west to the south east and contains 2,500 acres 3 roods 32 perches British statute measurement.

Ecclesiastical Union

Aghalee is a vicarage in the diocese of Dromore and is episcopally united to the parishes of Aghagallon and Magheramesk. The union of these 3 benefices is very ancient and no record of the time when it occurred exists. The 2 latter parishes are in the diocese of Connor. It is a lay impropriation, the Marquis of Hertford (who is also the proprietor of the estate) having the right of presentation. The patron receives the rectorial tithes. The present incumbent (the Reverend John Corkew) receives the vicarial tithes and has made an agreement with the parishioners for 5 years, at the moderate rate of 8s 2d per acre.

There is a good glebe house in the townland of Killough. The church is at Soldierstown, in the townland of Poobles. It is a plain neat building and is advantageously situated, being nearly in the centre of the union.

NATURAL FEATURES AND PRODUCTIVE ECONOMY

Surface and Soil

A fine valley intersects this parish, commencing at Aghalee and terminating at Hammond's bridge. A portion of it is inundated and serves as a reservoir for the summit level of the Belfast Canal. On either side there is a chain of rich, fertile and gently undulating hills, covered with neat farmhouses and cottages. From Robinson's Fort, though only elevated 254 feet above the level of the sea, there is a fine view of Lough Neagh and the adjacent country.

Nearly all the land is arable. It is for the most part a fine rich clay and, about Soldierstown, where the immediate substratum is limestone, it is capable of producing the finest crops. There is little waste land in the parish and none exclusively laid out for meadow and pasture.

Agriculture and Produce

The usual mode of culture is to break up the grasslands for potatoes, which is considered the best preparation crop. They are set with the plough. Wheat succeeds, and then oats. Red wheat is much esteemed and the species most raised is the Poland; sometimes barley is sown after the potatoes. A fair average produce of wheat and oats would be 18 cwt per acre and of potatoes 250 bushels. The artificial grasses raised are clover and rye grass. The manure is lime, gravel and the produce of the farmyard. The better order of farmers have generally their own lime-kilns and purchase the limestone by the load, at 6d or 8d, containing about 15 cwt; and for the convenience of the tenantry, the lime is burnt at the quarry and sold at 9d or 10d a barrel.

Turbary

It contains no bog but an abundant supply may be obtained at the Montyaghs in Aghagallon parish. It is usual to rent a bank which is paid for according to its quality, or it may be purchased by the stack varying in size. One of 10 yards by 3 and 30 rows might average 1 pound 10s. It is the chief, if not only, fuel of the tenantry.

Enclosures and Gentlemen's Seats

The enclosures generally consist of a ditch and bank raised from its excavation, which are often planted with forest trees.

There are also some thriving plantations at Broommount, the residence of William Gorman Esquire, to the right of the road leading from Aghalee to Moira.

Streams

There are a few inconsiderable streams. One rises at Aghadavy in Ballinderry <Ballanderry> parish and falls into the Broad water at the Hell Hole; another takes its course through the Friar's glen and the village of Aghalee. There is also a small stream which forms the chief part of the boundary between this and Moira parish.

Parish of Aghalee

MODERN TOPOGRAPHY

Village of Aghalee

The only village in the union is Aghalee, which is situated in a valley near the north west extremity of this parish. There are no public buildings, fairs or markets. The population is [?] 130.

Roads

The direct road from Lurgan to Antrim passes through the north west part of this parish and 2 principal roads branch off from it; one leading from Aghalee to Soldierstown and Moira, and the other, on the north side of the canal, called the Old Church Loning. The first mentioned has a difficult ascent through the parish. They are kept in good repair, the material being in it.

Bridge

[Insert addition by T.C. Hannyngton: Hammond bridge, a small narrow bridge with 2 arches built of [?] hard freestone; an old bridge].

NATURAL HISTORY

Geology

The constituent rock is basalt. It is quarried in several places and is used for building and repairing roads. It is compact and fine grained. On the borders of the parish, at Soldierstown quarry, it is incumbent on the white limestone. The limestone here is very hard and will return a ringing sound to the hammer. It contains numerous beds of flints and but few organic remains. There is some appearance of a whin dyke having traversed the limestone, but it is in a state of decomposition. Marl may be found in several places, and very fine sand near the Old Mill bridge in Poobles. The only minerals observed are quartz and sandstones containing mica and felspar.

ANCIENT TOPOGRAPHY

Antiquities

On the road from Lurgan to Antrim, about one-quarter of a mile north east of the village of Aghalee, are the ancient ruins of a church, the western gable being crowned with ivy.

There are no ruins of castles, round towers in this part of the union, and only one fort or mound, called Robinson's Fort, and situated in the townland of Aghalee.

Some time since, the remains of an urn containing human bones are said to have been found near Soldierstown, as also celts, spears of brass and flint arrowheads, some of which are collected.

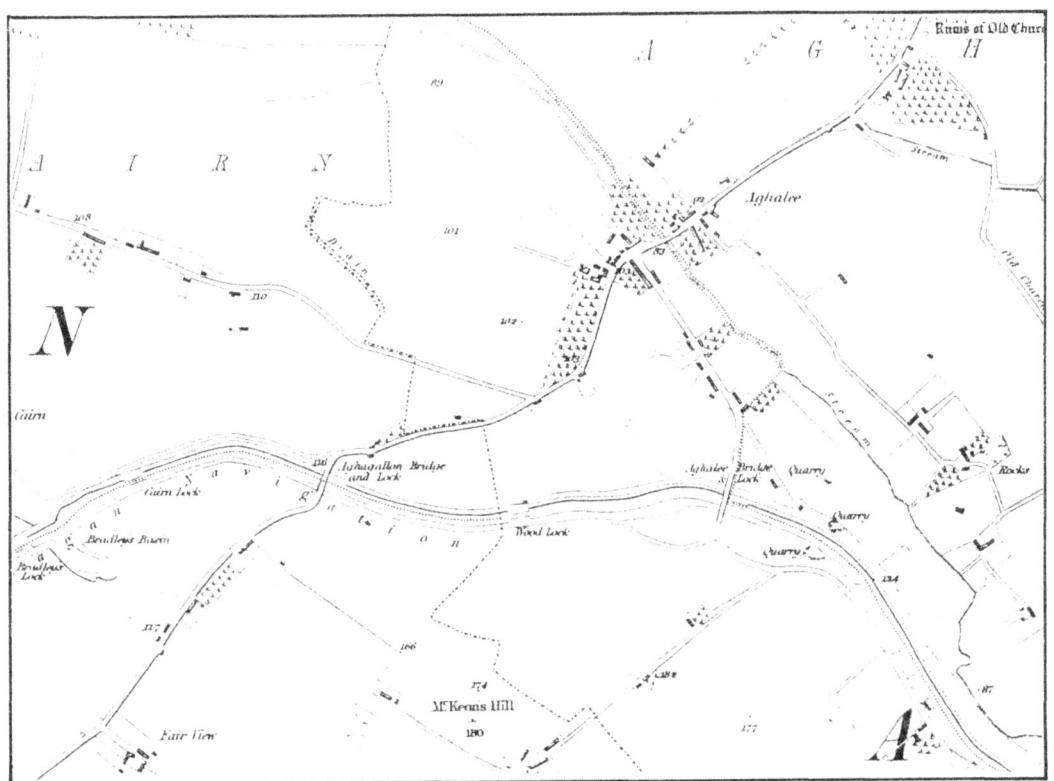

Map of Aghalee from the first 6" O.S. maps, 1830s

Modern Topography

Chapels

None in Aghalee parish: the nearest ones are in Derrynaseer in Aghagallon parish and at Tullyballydonnel in Ballinderry parish.

Social and Productive Economy

Schools

There are 2 permanent schools in the village of Aghalee, one of which has hitherto received a small grant from the Kildare Street Society and the other from the Hibernian Society. There is a school at Soldierstown and another in Ballynaghten. They are not endowed and are supported by the farmers. The rates of tuition vary from 2s 6d to 8s per quarter.

Trade and Manufactures

There are no collective manufactories in this parish. About 78 families are employed in trade and manufacture, a large portion of which are weavers, chiefly of cambrics. In quality it varies from what is called 14 to 20 hundreds, and seven-eighths of a yard wide; the linen is yard wide, and from 14 to 16 hundreds. The nearest markets for the sale of these manufactures and any other produce are at Lisburn and Lurgan.

Population Table

Proprietor the Marquis of Hertford.

Aghalee townland: 773 acres 2 roods 20 perches, families 97, males 201, females 252, total 453.

Aghadrimglasney townland: 37 acres 2 roods 37 perches, families 8, males 12, females 16, total 28.

Ballynaghten townland: 334 acres 29 perches, families 27, males 73, females 71, total 144.

Ballynanaghten townland: 445 acres 2 roods 9 perches, families 37, males 98, females 84, total 182.

Killough townland: 335 acres 1 rood 33 perches, families 61, males 157, females 153, total 310.

Lurgansemanus townland: 120 acres 3 roods 8 perches, families 17, males 38, females 42, total 80.

Poobles townland: 482 acres 3 roods, families 40, males 85, females 129, total 214.

[Totals]: 2,500 acres 16 perches, families 287, males 664, females 747, total 1,411. [Signed] George Boscawen, Lieutenant Royal Engineers, 3rd August 1832.

Fair Sheets by Thomas Fagan, December 1837 and January 1838

Natural Features and Natural State

Native Wood

In Broommount demesne, and along the west side of the canal and that large sheet of water locally called the Broad water, there is about 3 acres of native wood, consisting of a large quantity of hazel, oak and ash, and some underwood. This wood occupied several acres on both sides of the above water at a former period but has been subsequently rooted out and the site reclaimed. That wide extent of ground now occupied by the aforesaid sheet of water was formerly a tract of bog intervening between the 2 woods above stated. After the cutting out of the bog the remains got covered over with water, which serves as a necessary reservoir or feeder to the canal since its foundation. It extends from Soldierstown bridge northwards through a large glen locally called the Friar's glen.

In Ballynaghten, and along the north east side of the canal, there stood about 40 acres of remains of native wood but at present reclaimed to a great extent, yet there are some scattered patches, both in the valley and on the face [of] the adjoining eminence, occupied by oak, alder and ash, and the trees of moderate size. This wood is also in the Friar's glen and formerly extended to the Deerpark at Lough Neagh. Informants Robert Friar, Joseph Walker and others. 9th January 1838.

Natural Features

In this parish there is no mountain nor bog at present. There is no lakes, large rivers or other sheets of water in the parish, save the canal and Broad water connected with it.

Floods

In cases of high floods, the valleys along the east side of the canal are inundated to a wide extent and any crops remaining on the course of the floods injured in a more or less degree, but very little injuries sustained by floods in any other part of the parish. The parish in general is well accommodated with spring and river water.

Improvement and Situation of the Parish

Large tracts of remains of native wood, bogs and rocky ground have been reclaimed within the parish during the last 60 years, and now fertile.

Parish of Aghalee

The chief part of the parish is fertile and well improved in various respects. It is also well situated for agriculture and traffic, as it has the advantage of good communications by land and water to the neighbouring seaports and market towns of Belfast, Lisburn and Lurgan. It is bounded on the north, north west and north east by the parishes of Aghagallon and Ballinderry, and on the south and south west by Moira and Magheramesk. Informants Edward Chapman, Robert Friar, William Ferris, Edward Hull and many others. 12th and 13th January 1838 and preceding days.

MODERN TOPOGRAPHY

Bridge

Soldierstown bridge across the Lagan Navigation near the church of Aghalee has one half-circle arch, turned chiefly with cut freestone, and parapets of rough quarry stone and topped with dressed stone of the latter description. Span of the above arch 24 feet, breadth of the road on the arch 14 foot 6 inches, breadth at one end of the bridge 31 feet and at the other end 28 feet, average height of parapets 4 feet, thickness of parapets 1 foot 6 inches, length of parapets on either side of the road 46 yards. The bridge and parapet are in tolerable good repair. The arch affords a 6 feet wide track to accommodate the lighter horses. This bridge is said to be built by the canal company above 40 years back, engineer the late Mr Owen. Informants Thomas Hannon and others. 25th December 1837.

Aghalee Church

Aghalee church, more commonly called Soldierstown church, is situated about 7 miles west of Lisburn, on a leading road from the latter town to Aghalee and Lough Neagh. It is an oblong edifice 1-storey high and slated, with a handsome tower attached to the west end. It measures 64 and a half feet by 22 feet 3 inches on the inside, walls 3 feet thick and built of stone and lime. The alley is laid with tiles and the pew floors boarded. The interior is lit by 2 Gothic windows on each side and 1 large Gothic window on the east gable, where the communion table stands. There is a gallery on the west end, supported in front on timber columns. The stairs ascending to it are situated in the tower and are made of timber also. The pulpit stands against the north side wall, elevated some feet above the floor. The baptismal fount is of marble and the pedestal on which it stands of cut stone.

The vestry is attached on the north side of the church. It stands 1-storey high and slated, and measures 16 and a half by 7 and a half feet inside. It is lit by 2 oblong windows. In the body of church, to the south side wall, stands a square framed canvas representing the royal arms of His Late Majesty Charles II.

In the north side wall also stands a neat marble monument bearing the following inscription: "Here lyeth the body of Mr John Usher, who departed this life the fourth day of February 1757, in the 63rd year of his age."

The interior of the church is spacious and in plain good order, as is also the pulpit and all other furniture. In the east end stand 2 neat canopied pews, one which belongs to the vicar and the other to Captain Gorman of Broommount. Total pews on the ground floor 26; of these, 16 average 18 foot 4 inches of seats each and will hold 12 persons each pew, total 192; 7 pews averages 9 foot 6 inches of seat each and will hold 6 persons each pew, total 42; 2 pews averages 21 feet of seats each and will hold 14 persons each pew, total 28; 1 pew has 25 feet of seats and will hold total 16; total persons accommodated on the ground 278.

Total pews on the gallery 9; of these, 2 averages 20 feet 6 inches of seats each and will hold 14 persons each pew, total 28; 2 pews averages 14 foot 6 inches of seats each and will hold 10 persons each pew, total 20; 4 pews averages 11 foot 6 inches of seats each and will hold 8 persons each pew, [total] 32; 1 seat has 6 feet of seats and will total 4; total persons accommodated with seats in the church 362, allowing an average of 1 and a half feet to each sitting.

The principal part of the pews and seats on the ground floor are of oak timber and of great age, as is also the reading desk and communion table. Ventilation is afforded by the letting down of the windows. The stairs ascending to the gallery originally stood in the west end of the body of the church, up to 1836. Their removal at the latter period to the tower not only gave place for new pews on the ground floor and 1 new pew on the gallery, but also much improved the west end of the church generally.

The entrance to the church is by a Gothic door on the south side of the tower and secondly by a large oblong door opening from the tower into the body of the church. The entrance to the tower up to 1836 was by a Gothic doorway on the front, which doorway was closed and other improvements made when the present door was opened on the south side at the latter period.

Church Tower

The tower measures 106 feet by 10 feet 4 inches inside, walls built of stone and lime and 3 feet thick, cornices and pinnacles of cut stone. It stands 4-storeys high and lit by 4 Gothic and 1 square windows. The original windows were oblong but very narrow. The bell, about 4 cwt weight, is situated on the top storey and has on its surface the following inscription: "Henry Parkes made mee for a right good sounding bell to be 9, 9." It is still perfect and measures 29 inches in diameter at the mouth and 25 inches in height.

The spire is octagon, 21 feet in height and composed of timber, sheeted over with copper and sanded on the surface. The ballstalk and weathercock about 4 feet high and the tower 42 feet, making on the whole the cock to stand 67 feet above the surface. The tower measures on the outside in the front 16 feet 10 inches and on the side 13 feet.

The exterior of the church, with its handsome spire and large Gothic windows, are all in good order and, from the handsome eminence on which they are situate, surrounded by lofty sycamore and other forest trees, commands a majestic appearance and an ornament to the neighbourhood to which they stand.

It is locally said that this church was built about 1686 and that the original roof was of oak and shingles, which roof remained on up to 1792, at which period the shingles were taken off and a slate roof put on. However, in 1827 it was again unroofed; the old oak with which it was originally roofed sold by auction for the benefit of new repairs. The side walls was then raised 6 feet and an entire new roof put on, together with considerable improvement in other respects, at an expense of 184 pounds. The present spire was also put on at the latter period, at an expense exceeding 100 pounds. Both these sums were levied on the united parishes of Magheramesk, Aghalee and Aghagallon, and paid at 3 instalments, this being the only church in the above union. The date of erection, 1827, is cut in the vane over the present spire; 1713 was cut in the vane which stood over the old spire. The latter spire was composed of timber and covered with shingles similar to the original roof of the church.

The neighbourhood in which the church is situated, and from which it takes its local name of Soldierstown church, derived that term from a troop of horse and 2 companies of foot soldiers having been stationed for some time in a hamlet near the site of the church during the 1641 wars.

Aghalee Graveyard

The churchyard is tolerably large and enclosed partly by a stone and lime wall, and partly by a quickset fence, with a good iron gate at the entrance from the aforesaid road. It is likewise sheltered and ornamented by lofty forest trees.

The following are amongst the Christian names and surnames on tombs and headstones in the graveyard. Male: Andrew, Edward, John, James, Richard, Thomas, William, Henry, Joseph, Josae, Ralph, Jocelyn.

Female: Anne, Ann, Ann Jane, Agniss, Elizabeth, Eliza, Elenor, Jane, Mary, Catherine, Margaret.

Surnames of male and female: Aughee, Allen, Bullock, Charleton, Coshly, Carrol, Clarke, McCully, McConnel, Hammond, Hull, Hall, Hammand, Keenan, George, Lamb, Leich, Logan, Long, Neilson, Spatt, Titterington, Walker, Watson, Richardson, Johnston, Kennedy, [?] Kinley, Ken, Usher, Waters.

Inscriptions at Church

Inscription on a tombstone north of the church: "Here lyeth the body of Richard Owen of Flixton, Lancashire, engineer of the Lagan Navigation, who departed this life 1830."

The oldest stone in the yard is the tomb erected to the Charleton family, 1689. The oldest age on any stone is 79 years. There are some tombs and headstones so defaced by time that the inscription on them cannot be read. There are also several family burials that have neither tombs or headstones to denote their name.

The following inscription is cut on a handsome corniced capstone in the schoolhouse and vestry attached to the north side of the church: "This vestry and schoolhouse was built by the Reverend William Walkington, minister of the parish, in the year 1719, towards the building of which Mr Peter Mason of Moirah gave 8 pounds sterling."

SOCIAL ECONOMY

Congregation and Collection at Church

Divine service is on Sundays during the long days and at 12 o'clock in the morning during winter, but no evening service. Average attendance at Aghalee church on Sundays, in fine weather, 200 and sometimes more, but less in winter.

It is said there is a silver cup or chalice belonging to the church, bearing date 1695.

There is a collection in church on Sundays for the poor of the united parishes of Magheramesk,

Aghalee and Aghagallon, the proceeds of which amount for the present year to about 15 pounds. It is distributed on the first Sunday of each quarter among 46 poor at present on the poor list. The sum given to each applicant is ruled according to the exigency of the case. The above is about an average of the number on the poor list and also of the amount collected towards their support annually for the last 5 years.

Vicar

The Reverend Robert Hill is vicar of the united parishes of Magheramesk, Aghalee and Aghagallon, and gets annual benefice from the above union of parishes, 330 pounds. Information obtained from William Ferris, late churchwarden, James Reid, clerk of the church and also of the church books, John Watson, Thomas Hannon, John McCartney and many others. 27th and 28th December 1837.

MODERN TOPOGRAPHY

Aghalee Glebe

Aghalee Glebe, the seat of the Reverend Robert Hill, is situated about 8 miles north west of Lisburn, contiguous to a leading road from the latter town to the village of Aghalee and also to Lough Neagh. The house is nearly a square building 2-storeys high and slated, with good offices and well enclosed yard in the rear. The garden is neatly laid off and enclosed by a quickset fence. The farm, about 13 and a half English acres, is well enclosed and much improved by partial plantations of different kinds of forest trees. The Marquis of Hertford gave a grant of 1 Irish acre in perpetuity for a site for the house and garden. The other 12 acres is 18s per acre annual rent.

The house was completed 1826, cost of building and other appendages 687 pounds. Of this sum, the Board of First Fruits gave a grant of 400 pounds and also a loan of 250 pounds, the latter sum to be refunded by paying annual interest for it till the interest amounts to the sum lent; the other 37 pounds was given as a gift by the then incumbent, the Reverend Phillip Fletcher.

The house stands on handsome eminence commanding a fine prospect of the surrounding neighbourhood for many miles. It is a very neat commodious house and eligibly situated for a gentleman's residence. Before the erection of this house, the clergy were obliged to procure lodgings as they could. Informants John Watson, the architect, and others. 29th December 1837.

Broommount

Broommount, the seat of William Gorman Esquire, is situated about 7 miles west of Lisburn and 1 mile north of Moira, contiguous to a leading road from the former town to Aghalee and Lough Neagh. The house is a commodious oblong building 2-storeys high and slated, with a wing to the north end. The offices are extensive and the yard is well enclosed. The garden and orchard, about 2 and a half English acres, is well sheltered by forest trees and well enclosed, partly by a stone and lime wall and partly by a quickset fence. This garden contains some glass-roofed hot beds and a small pond, inhabited by trout and tench <tinch> etc. In the rear of the house also stands a neat flower garden. The grounds in front and about the house is ornamented by plantations of forest and ornamental trees. Entrance from the above road to the house by 2 handsome winding avenues.

The demesne or grounds, about 180 English acres, is well enclosed and the seat of extensive and thriving plantations and otherwise much improved, particularly in the neighbourhood of the house. The grounds is also the seat of some acres of native wood.

The seat is bounded on the east and north east by the Lagan Navigation, on the south and south west by a stream or small river dividing the counties of Antrim and Down in the neighbourhood of Moira. The house stands on a handsome eminence contiguous to Aghalee church and in a handsome part of the neighbourhood. The seat has the advantage of the canal and of leading and by-roads on almost all sides which, together with the improved state of the grounds with plantings, render it a convenient and very eligible situation for a gentleman's residence. The chief part of the plantings with other improvements now on the premises were made by the present proprietor within the last 25 years.

Broommount House and an attached farm was for a series of time annexed to Aghalee church as the clergy's residence. A Dean Welsh is said to be the last clergyman who enjoyed it as such. His late widow is said to have sold her right of the place to the Gorman family. However, it is said to be in the latter family above 80 years, and that the present proprietor's late father considerably enlarged the farm, the house and other buildings on the premises. The house is said to have been built by the late Dr Edward Walkington, Bishop of Down and Connor, about 1695 and subsequently improved by the above Dean Welsh, as well as by Mr Gorman. However, the house denotes at present age, both in roof and construction. Informants James Reid, Thomas Hannon, James Hogan and others. 30th December 1837.

Gentleman's Seat

West of, and contiguous to the old church of Aghalee, stands a neat oblong house, now occupied by Mr George Stephenson. It stands 2-storeys high and slated, with good office houses and well enclosed yard attached. The orchard and garden, about 1 acre, is partly enclosed by a stone and lime wall and partly by a quickset fence, and in front of the house a well enclosed courtyard and a handsome iron gate to the entrance. The entire is well sheltered and improved by plantations of different kinds of forest trees. The farm attached to the house, about 72 English acres, is laid off in well enclosed fields, and was the seat of several acres of native wood, all which is now reclaimed except about 4 acres of a mere scrag which is occupied in pasture. The house is situated on a handsome site which, together with its vicinity to the ancient church and neighbouring village of Aghalee, render it an eligible seat for a genteel family.

This house and other improvements on the premises was erected by the Usher family many years back. Captain Edward Lawson Usher was the last of the Usher family who enjoyed the place. He lived here to a late period, but was obliged to dispose of the place under some unpleasant circumstances. It subsequently passed to the present proprietor. Informants William Ferris, Samuel Thompson and others. 4th January 1838.

Gentlemen's Seat and Grain Store

South west of, and contiguous to the old church of Aghalee, also stands a neat oblong house 2-storeys high and slated, now occupied by Mr George Carter, grain merchant. There are good office houses and well enclosed yards attached, also in the rear of the house a fine orchard and garden in which stood a small fish pond. They are enclosed by a quickset fence and the entire premises improved and well sheltered by partial plantations of forest trees. The farm, above 20 English acres, is laid off in well enclosed fields.

On the premises <premis> also stands a handsome grain store 3-storeys high and slated, and a corn kiln 2-storeys high and slated also. The store and kiln was erected about 16 years back by Mr Thomas Elliot of Belfast, merchant.

The place passed to the above Mr Carter in 1827, since which period he deals extensively in the grain trade, by which traffic he not only benefits himself but also affords the farmers of the surrounding neighbourhoods a convenient and speedy sale for their grain, without having to send it to distant markets. He stores on his own premises and prepares for market the grain purchased, and subsequently sends it to Belfast. Also on the above premises there originally stood good farmhouses.

The present house was built by the Usher family many years ago. A Miss Usher was the last of the family who enjoyed the place. The Usher family resided at Aghalee for a series of time and were the proprietors of extensive tracts of land in its neighbourhood, where they erected not only the buildings already discussed but also a flour mill and bleaching establishment in the village, and carried on the manufacture of flour and bleaching business for many years.

Farmhouse

Mr Samuel Thompson has on the north side of, and contiguous to old church of Aghalee, a very neat 2-storey and slated house lately built by his parents. To it is attached good office houses and well enclosed yards, also a handsome orchard and garden enclosed by a quickset fence and well sheltered and improved by plantings etc. He holds 57 English acres of a farm and has also on his premises a good corn kiln for public accommodation.

The aforesaid buildings and other improvements surrounding the old church give the place altogether a beautiful appearance.

MODERN TOPOGRAPHY AND PRODUCTIVE ECONOMY

Village of Aghalee

Aghalee is a small village about 9 miles north west of Lisburn, 3 miles north of Moira and 4 and a half miles east of Lurgan, on the leading road from the latter town to Antrim, in an improved and fertile neighbourhood. It is situated on the 2 townlands of Aghalee and Killough, which are divided by a small river passing through the middle of the village and over which stands a 2-arch bridge to accommodate the above road. The junction of 3 roads towards the west end of the village form it into 3 small streets, one of which lead to Antrim, one to Lurgan and one to Lisburn.

The old church and neighbouring buildings and lofty grain store, and other improvements situated at the east end of the village, contribute

Parish of Aghalee 33

much to the entrance from the east and north east. At the west end also stands a handsome seat and lofty corn store with fine orchard and garden and other improvements in plantings etc., erected by Mr John Heastie, merchant, within the last 25 years, but now occupied by Mr John Turtle, grocer and haberdasher, who is also extensive in the grain trade. The latter concerns contribute much to the entrance at the west end. Contiguous to the village on the south and south west passes the Lagan Navigation, which render great benefits and advantage, not only to persons in trade but to the village generally and surrounding neighbourhood. 4th and 5th January 1838.

Trades and Houses in Aghalee

The following are the trades and callings, and number and height of houses in the village of Aghalee, also the number slated and thatched.

Trades and callings: general grocers and haberdashers 2, spirit and wine sellers 2, grocery and spirit shops 1, grain merchants 2, farmers 8, cottiers 10, dressmakers 2, linen weavers 2, damask weavers 2, surgeons 1, schoolmasters 1, smiths 1, wheelwrights and turners 1, cartmakers 1, tailors 1, shoemakers 1, flaxjobbers 1, pensioners 1, total trades and callings 40.

Houses: houses of 3-storeys 3, houses of 2-storeys 5, houses of 1-storey 30, houses slated 9, houses thatched 29, houses inhabited 35, grain stores 2, schoolhouses 1, houses total 38, not including office houses or small storages.

Commercial

In this village there is neither fairs or markets held. The nearest fair and market town, Lurgan, stands 4 and a half miles west of the village. But in the village there are 2 general stores, William Ferris and John Turtle, who keep in their shops and stores almost every article necessary for country accommodation and also purchase from the local inhabitants, either for ready money or in exchange of goods, all those commodities commonly brought to markets by the country people. Such accommodation in a backward village is very useful for the local inhabitants, as well as beneficial to the persons in trade.

A considerable quantity of grain and other commodities are sent by the canal from Aghalee and surrounding neighbourhood to Belfast etc., and other commodities brought in return by the same conveyance, all which prove useful and accommodating to the above neighbourhood. 5th January 1838.

Flour Mill and Bleach Green

The above village was formerly the seat of a good flour mill and bleaching establishment, both of which were founded and extensively carried on for a series of years by the late Edward Usher of Aghalee, Esquire and his family. However, they declined business about 40 years back, at which period the buildings etc. passed to Mr William Ferris of Belfast, who changed the flour mill and grain stores into a dwelling house and other necessary stores, all which are now occupied in the general grocery and spirit business by his son Mr William Ferris Junior. He also holds the attached farm on which the bleach green was situated, 26 English acres and 24 acres elsewhere. The bleach buildings are gone to ruins.

Bridge

The bridge in the village of Aghalee has 2 half-circle arches, one of which is closed up. Span of the one in use 9 feet, breadth of the road on the bridge 22 feet, average height of parapets 3 feet, thickness of parapets 1 foot 6 inches, length of parapets on either side of the road 40 yards. The bridge arch is in permanent order but the parapets partially dilapidated.

Cattle Pound

Aghalee cattle pound in the village is enclosed by a stone and lime wall 6 feet high, a small iron gate to the entrance and a stream of water passing through one side of it. This is the parish pound but little use made of it for the last 2 years.

Fuel and Supply of Water

The village has the convenience of spring and river water, and turf the chief fuel used by the inhabitants. Informants William Ferris, Thomas Trenor, George Carter and many others.

Canal Bridge

South of and contiguous to the village of Aghalee, and across the canal on the leading road to Lisburn, stands a good 1-arch bridge. Span of the arch 16 feet 6 inches, breadth of the road on the bridge 17 feet 6 inches, breadth at both ends of the bridge 32 feet, average height of parapets 4 feet 3 inches, thickness of parapets 1 foot 8 inches, length of parapets on either side of the road 75 yards. Detached on side of the above arch stands a small arch to accommodate a horse-track, span 3 feet 9 inches. These are half-circle arches, turned chiefly with cut freestone, and the parapets of a blackish quarry stone. The top of the parapets is partially dilapidated and the remainder of the bridge in good order, and the masonry well and handsomely executed.

This bridge was built by the canal company above 40 years back, engineer the late Richard Owens. Information obtained from William Ferris and others. 6th January 1838.

Canal Locks

The following 2 locks are in the above parish. Immediately adjoining the above bridge, on the south side, stands a lock on the canal locally called the Rock lock. It measures 70 and a half feet in length between the floodgates, 16 and a half feet wide and the fall of the water 7 feet 8 inches. A short distance to the west side of the above bridge stands the second lock on the canal, called the Wood lock. It stands opposite the lock-keeper's house and measures 70 and a half feet in length between the floodgates, 16 and a half feet wide and the fall of the water 7 feet 2 inches.

These locks were built of cut stone and were erected above 40 years ago by the canal company, engineer the late Richard Owens. These locks differ in some respects from those in neighbourhood of Lisburn. In the latter locks the sluices are situated in the floodgates and the sills <scills> straight. In the former locks the sluices are situated in the side walls at entering the locks and the sills a half-circle. Informants Arthur Richey, lock-keeper, and others. 8th January 1838.

Canal Stopgates

On the line of the canal intervening between the Lady bridge near Moira and the Rock lock near the village of Aghalee, there stand 3 separate stopgates, the object of which was to keep back the water in cases of breaches occurring in the canal banks, till such breaches were again repaired. These stopgates have been disused many years back.

Canal Quay and Carriage of Goods

At Soldierstown bridge near Aghalee church there is a sort of quay or landing-place on the canal bank where coal, limestone and other commodities brought on the canal to that neighbourhood is landed. About one-fourth of an English mile south of the village of Aghalee, at the top level or Rock lock, there is a second quay or landing-place, where grain and all other commodities sent from the above village and surrounding neighbourhoods to Belfast on the northern direction, or to Newry on the west and southern direction, is put on board the canal lighters; and all commodities brought in return for the village and the neighbourhood is also landed at this quay. This is the last quay on the west end of the canal within the above county where lighters are permitted to load or disload. From the Union Locks to the Rock lock above mentioned there is 10 miles of a level. Carriage per ton from Belfast to Aghalee by the canal, 4s, distance about 24 miles; carriage by land 10s per ton, distance 16 miles. Informant William Ferris and others. 10th January 1838.

Canal

The Lagan Navigation too passes through the parish from south east to north west and affords great accommodation to the local inhabitants, not only in forwarding by it to market grain and other articles at a cheaper rate than by land carriage, but also in getting into the parish, by the same conveyance, coal and other commodities necessary for their accommodation.

Roads

This parish is tolerably well accommodated with public leading and by-roads. The public leading roads are partly made under the new contracts and partly by presentments, and average 21 feet wide clear of banks and fences. The by-roads are all made by presentments and vary from 14 to 19 feet wide clear of banks or fences.

That portion of the road leading from Soldierstown or Aghalee church to Aghagallon, and situated in the above parish, averages 18 feet wide clear of banks or fences and is kept up by presentments. Informants Edward Grey and John McCartney.

Road Contracts

Edward Fletcher and Richard Welch is to keep in repair for 5 years all that portion of the leading road from Antrim to Lurgan situated in the above parish, at 1s per perch per annum. This line of road leads by Lower Ballinderry and village of Aghalee, and averages 21 feet wide clear of banks or fences.

Thomas Patterson and Company is to keep in repair for 5 years all that portion of the leading road from Aghalee to Lisburn by Maghaberry <Magabberry> and situated in the above parish, at [blank] per perch per annum. This line averages 21 feet wide clear of banks or fences.

Parish of Aghalee   35

ANCIENT TOPOGRAPHY

Bronze Hatchet

The brass weapon of which the draft underneath [drawing] is the exact size and shape is at present in the possession of William Ferris, Aghalee.

Urn of Bones

On Broommount demesne there stood a high fort composed of earth and stones. It was totally demolished about 7 years back, at which period there was found beneath its surface an earthern urn containing calcined bones and ashes, but all in a state of decay when discovered and have subsequently crumbled to pieces.

Fort and Causeway

In Ballynanaghten, and holding of Thomas Faloon, there stood a fort of large size. It was destroyed about 20 years back. Nothing of interest was found about it but a quern-stone. Leading from the fort gate towards the south, and a distance of about 140 yards, stood a paved causeway. It has been also destroyed. About 25 yards east of the fort also stood a circular enclosure about 21 feet in diameter and the parapet of stones. It has been likewise destroyed and a quantity of timber cinders found beneath its surface. Informant Joseph Walker and others. 1st January 1838.

Native Wood and Fort

In Ballynanaghten, and holding of John Hall, there stands about 15 English acres of the remains of native wood, but at present reduced to a mere scrag and occupied under pasture.

In the same holding there stood a fort which has been lately destroyed, but nothing of interest found about it.

Ancient Coin in Ballynanaghten

It is locally said that there was a quantity of ancient gold and silver coin found by Henry Mallon in demolishing and removing an old ditch in the above townland at some former period. The coin was deposited in a pot at some depth under the surface of the fence. The amount and description of the coin he concealed from most of his neighbours, but the amount is thought to have been considerable, as appeared from a subsequent and sudden change of circumstances in his family, who were previously in poverty. Informants John O'Neill, Patt Green and others.

Road to Aghalee Ancient Church

That line of road leading from Soldierstown to Aghalee ancient church, and locally called the Old Church Loanen, averages 15 feet wide clear of banks or fences and is kept up by presentments.

William Morrow of the above townland, a farmer, is now in the 87th year of his age and possessed of his faculties to a moderate extent. Informant James McCreanen and others.

Ancient Church of Aghalee

Aghalee ancient church and burial ground is situated on a handsome eminence east of and contiguous to the village of Aghalee, but the church at present reduced to a skeleton. The west gable and 27 feet in length in the clear of both side walls adjoining the above gable is all that now stands. These too are disfigured in a more or less degree, in consequence of many of the well-shaped stones having been picked off the face of the wall and used in other buildings in the neighbourhood. Yet the existing part of the gable and side walls are mantled over with ivy, which gives them a handsome and venerable appearance. As near as can be judged from the present dilapidated state of the walls, their original thickness was 3 feet. They were built of grey stone and run together by grouted lime, similar to other ancient buildings. The masonry was well and handsomely executed, and the side walls from 12 to 15 feet high.

The interior of the church stood 18 and a half feet wide but of its length no accurate account can be given, as the east end is altogether destroyed and the ground occupied by graves. On the west gable stood a door and over it a window, but whether oblong or Gothic could not be at present judged, as the door is dilapidated and the window closed up by ivy.

Directly opposite to each other, on each side wall, stand the ruins of a window. These were oblong and narrow and seemed to afford light to the ground floor. As near as can now be judged, they stood 17 inches by 8 inches on the outside but much wider inside. It would appear from the window on the gable, and some small holes inside in the gable and side walls, that there was a gallery on the church at some period. However, its present ruined state leaves the observer much to conjecture and the tradition of the people, but of the latter there is very little to be found.

Ancient Fount

A few yards on the south side of the church, and placed at the head of a grave, is a grey stone of irregular shape, having in each side an artificial but rude fount for containing water. One of these is oval, 12 by 10 inches and 4 and a half inches in depth; the other approaches to circular, 9 inches in diameter and 2 and a half inches in depth. The stone itself is 22 inches long, 20 inches broad and 12 inches thick. The original berth of this fount stone, whether inside or outside the church, is not at present known.

Ancient Well

About 40 yards west of the church, and on the west side of the road just passing the churchyard, stands a very ancient spring well. It was enclosed by the Usher family with a good stone and lime wall many years ago. 2nd January 1838.

Ancient Graveyard

The graveyard is tolerably large, well occupied by burials but limited in tombs and headstones. It is enclosed by a quickset fence sheltered by a variety of forest trees, and a good iron gate to the entrance. It contains one handsome slate-roofed vault, erected in 1837 to the memory of surgeon James McDonald and Dr Thomas Usher McDonald of Crumlin. James died 1829 and Thomas 1835.

Family Names in Graveyard

The following are among the Christian names and surnames on tombs and headstones in the yard.

Names of male: Bryan, Bernard, Dalway, Edward, Felix, Francis, Mathew, William, Henry, James, Patrick, Ralph, Samuel, Terrence, Thomas.

Names of female: Elizabeth, Elenor, Jane, Matilda, Helena.

The oldest stone legible is 1762. The greatest age on tombs or headstones does not exceed 80 years. The following are the surnames of male and female having tombs or headstones: Johnston, Briens, Bearns, Cousins, Cinnamond, Clark, McDonald, Devlin, Dunigan, Galley, Golley, Holmes, O'Neill, Martin, Lutten, Sharkey. All religious denominations still continue to bury in this old graveyard. Informants Samuel Thompson, Hugh McGrann and others.

Forts

In Killough, and holding of Thomas McConkey, there stood a fort which is at present destroyed and the site under tillage.

In the above townland, and holding of John McKinstry, there stood a fort which is also destroyed and the site under tillage.

In Aghadrumglasny, and holding of John Chapman, there stood a fort which is now destroyed and the site under tillage.

In Lurgansemanus, and holding of William Forsythe, there stood a fort which is also destroyed and the site now occupied under fruit trees.

In Poobles, and holding of William Canning, there stood 2 forts which are now destroyed and the site under tillage.

In Broommount demesne there stood a fort which is likewise destroyed and the site under tillage.

In demolishing the above forts there was nothing of interest discovered.

In Ballynaghten, and holding of Robert Crawford, there stood a fort which is now destroyed.

Forts in Aghalee

In Aghalee, and holding of Richard Gallay, there stood a fort which is now destroyed and the site under tillage.

In the same townland, and holding of Stewart Faloon, there stood a fort which is also destroyed and the site under tillage.

Ancient Quern

Robert McNight of Aghalee found an ancient oval quern-stone beneath the surface in his farm. It stands in his house at present and measures 14 by 10 inches and 5 inches in thickness. It affords holes for handles to turn it with, the same as others before described. Informants Robert McNight and others.

Censer

The censer now in the possession of Mr William Ferris, grocer, village of Aghalee, and of which Mr Boyle has taken a sketch, was found in the parish of Seagoe, county Armagh, several years back. It, together with several small pewter <puter> cups and other pewter vessels resembling a weather-glass, was discovered together a considerable depth beneath the surface. A large leather strap, with brass buckles affixed to it in appropriate places, was attached to the censer, the latter articles having been subsequently in some manner disposed of or lost. Information obtained from Richard Thompson and family, who discovered the above articles, and also from William Ferris, the present possessor of the censer.

Parish of Aghalee 37

Cromlech

In Aghalee, and holding of Samuel Thompson, there formerly stood an oblong enclosure formed by standing columns of stones and covered across by long flat stones by way of a canopy. This cromlech <crumlock> was destroyed many years back. One of standing columns of which it was composed is at present in William Ferris' garden, village of Aghalee. It measures 5 and a half feet long, 2 feet broad and 1 foot thick.

Ancient Gold Coin and Human Skulls

Local tradition says that in demolishing a portion of the walls of Aghalee ancient church about 70 years back, there was a small coffer containing a quantity of ancient gold coin found, deposited in the recess made for the purpose in one of the walls. This treasure is said to be found by some of the Usher family, who were removing the stones to a house they were then building in the neighbourhood of the above old church. But of the amount or description of the aforesaid coin, there is no local account at present.

It is likewise said that in demolishing a portion of the old church subsequent to the above period, that there was 2 or more skulls found deposited in a recess made for the purpose in one of the walls. The above tradition is given by Felix Skelly, Mrs O'Brien, an aged woman, and others, but not generally corroborated.

Druid's Altar

In Aghalee, and holding of John Long, at the base of a rocky eminence, there stood an ancient erection of stone pillars and pavement of stones, supposed to have been a druid's altar. It was demolished above 15 years back but nothing of interest found about it.

Ancient Urns

There were 3 ancient urns found beneath the surface of Aghalee old graveyard; they contained black soil. They were found many years back, but quite decayed. Informants William Ferris, Felix Skelly and others.

SOCIAL AND PRODUCTIVE ECONOMY

Deserted Children

Deserted children on the church books for support, 1837, 2. The support of such is defrayed by the united parishes of Magheramesk, Aghalee and Aghagallon. The number for 1836 did not exceed the above.

Church and Clergy

The church is the only house of public worship in Aghalee parish.

The Reverend Robert Hill, vicar, is the only clergyman resident in the parish.

Private Gentleman

William Gorman of Broommount, Esquire is the only private gentleman resident in the parish. Informants John Magee, William Ferris and others. 10th and 11th January 1838.

Jurisdiction

There is no resident magistrate, or peace or revenue police in the above parish. All local disputes arising within the parish is decided at Crumlin petty sessions. The parish is situated in the manor of Killultagh, consequently all small debts usually recovered or decided at manor courts are decided at Lisburn, held on every third Wednesday for the manor of Killultagh, William Gregg, seneschal.

Medical Aid

There is no dispensary in the parish; the parish poor get advice and medicine at the county of Antrim infirmary, situated at Lisburn.

Societies and Lodges

There is no savings banks, book clubs, reading or temperance societies in the parish.

There is no Orange, Masonic or Ribbon lodges in the parish at present; none of the latter at any period.

Customs

There is no legendary tales or stories, or ancient custom or costume in the parish at present.

Amusements

Bullet-play is partially practised by the youth of the parish, but is the chief amusement now practised.

Party Calamities

Party feuds, burning of people's houses and chapels prevailed to some extent about the village of Aghalee, 1798. Roman Catholics were the chief sufferers. There were 4 persons burned to death and 1 shot in their house. Informants John Rogers, John Magee and many others. 11th January 1838.

Weaving

Linen and cotton and cambric <cambrick> weavers are pretty numerous amongst the small farming and cottier classes in the parish, but very few of the first class farmers carrying on weaving of any description. Fine cambric weavers are more numerous in this than in then neighbouring parishes of Magheragall or Maghermesk.

Character of the People

The parishioners in general are said to be quiet and industrious, and all religious denominations at present on good neighbourhood with each other, but to a great extent lukewarm as regards devotion or religious practice. For on sabbath very many of them employ themselves in prosecuting farming to some extent, farming and housework, or fishing, or some perhaps fruitless pursuits, when those of their neighbouring parishes are engaged in moral and religious duty proper for the day. This neglect of moral practice on Sundays is not confined particularly to any religious class of people, yet they are, in general, civil and communicative, but very defective in the history of their parish. The above relates to Magheramesk also.

Clothing and Fuel

All classes dress respectably, on getting out on Sundays or fair or market days.

Turf is the chief fuel used within the parish. It is procured from the Montiaghs, situated in the neighbouring parish of Aghagallon. Informants Robert Friar, Edward Hull and many others. 12th January 1838.

Migration

The cottier and working class resident in the above parish have all sufficient employment at weaving and farming business throughout the year without being obliged to migrate to foreign countries or remote districts. There is not an instance of any migration from the parish within the last few years.

Emigration

George Crooks Chapman, a Protestant aged 24 years, emigrated to New York 1835, from the townland of Aghadrumglasny. The above is the only person who emigrated from this parish within the last 3 years.

Temperance

Publicans in the parish 5; temperance is but very slighty advocated by any portion of the parishioners.

Roman Catholic Population

The Roman Catholic population of Aghalee worship at Kilwarlin Roman Catholic chapel, situated in the parish of Moira, and pay stipend to the parish priest of the latter parish, who has Aghalee annexed to it in his charge. They occasionally attend divine worship at Aghagallon and Ballinderry.

Presbyterian Population

The Presbyterians of Aghalee attend divine worship at Moira meeting house.

Methodist Congregation

The Aghalee schoolhouse was built by local subscription, cost not at present known. It was designed both for a school and Methodist preaching, both of which it at present accommodates. It is a spacious house. The particular dimensions of this house will be found in school tables relating to the above parish. Methodist preaching is held in this schoolhouse by the Moira preachers once in every fortnight. Divine service commences at 6 in the evening; average attendance 40 to 60 persons. Informants William Graham and others.

Food and Raiment

In consequence of the vicinity of the above parish to Lough Neagh, Lough Beg and other sheets of water, fresh fish of every description is frequently taken and more abundantly used in this than in other parishes before described. Food and raiment is in every other respect the same in this parish as in Magheragall and Magheramesk.

Fuel

Every class of people in the above parish cut and prepare their own turf in the Montiaghs, situated in the neighbouring parish of Aghagallon, and consequently are more comfortable as regards fuel than those of parishes before described, who were obliged to purchase fuel at exorbitant prices from the vendors of turf and coal.

Size of Farms

The holdings in the above parish vary from 3 to 180 English acres. Farms of the latter size are not

Parish of Aghalee

numerous: the majority average from 15 to 40 English acres. There are too several holdings from 1 to 3 English acres. The latter are occupied chiefly by weavers and tradespeople who, by the aid of their industry in weaving etc., live very comfortable on these small holdings.

Farmhouses and Cottiers' Houses

In this parish there are a large number of 2-storey and slated houses which, from their appearance externally, may be reckoned among the first class farmhouses within the above county. The yards, orchards and gardens attached to this class of farmhouses are large, enclosed partly by stone and lime walls and partly by quickset fences, and well sheltered by young and grown plantations of forest trees. Sunk pumps are pretty common in the farmyards and good iron and wooden gates to the different entrances.

The second class farmhouses are also spacious and very comfortable in many respects. The generality of them have well enclosed yards, orchards and gardens attached to them, and principally sheltered by partial plantings. Their office houses too are generally in clean and in neat order, and most of the farmhouses within the parish furnished with good clocks.

The cottier houses, too, in this parish is tolerably comfortable in many respects, but neither these, nor the second class farmhouses, so generally whitewashed with lime outside as those of the same classes in the neighbouring parishes before described.

Population

Population of the united parishes of Maghermesk, Aghalee and Aghagallon.

Summary of the population of the above parish, as enumerated by Mr William Ferris of Aghalee in 1831, and classed into the following religious denominations in 1834: Protestants of the Established Church 1,132, Roman Catholics 208, Presbyterians 54, Moravians 17, total 1,411, male 661, female 750.

Magheramesk parish: Protestants of the Established Church 1,230, Roman Catholics 274, Presbyterians 39, Quakers 157, total 1,700, male 832, female 868.

Aghagallon parish: Protestants of the Established Church 1,283, Roman Catholics 2,304, Presbyterians 40, Quakers 6, total, 3,573, male 1,741, female 1,832. Taken from the above Mr Ferris' book. 15th January 1838.

Table of Schools

[Table contains the following headings: name, situation and description, when established, income and expenditure, physical, intellectual and moral instruction, number of pupils subdivided by age, sex and religion, name and religion of master or mistress, date visited].

Soldierstown parochial school, situated attached to Solderstown church: it is a good slated house, 1-storey high and measures 21 by 16 and a half feet inside; has 3 square windows and 1 entrance door, school furniture all sufficient, established 1719; income: from the rector of the parish 2 pounds, from the pupils 6 pounds; intellectual instruction: *Murray's Reader, Endfield's Speaker*, the Bible, Testament and *Dublin Spelling books*, all procured by the pupils; moral instruction: visits from the rector of the parish, church catechisms taught on Saturdays; number of pupils: males, 13 under 10 years of age, 6 from 10 to 15, total 19; females, 2 under 10 years of age, 3 from 10 to 15, total 5; total number of pupils 24, Established Church 17, Presbyterians 3, Roman Catholics 4; master George O'Mulvenny, a Protestant; visited 21st December 1837.

Coallane national school, situated about one-half mile west of the above church: the house is 1-storey high and thatched and measures 20 by 14 feet inside, and lit by 3 good windows; the school requisites are limited, established under the Education Board 1834; income: from the Education Board 8 pounds, from the pupils 6 pounds; intellectual instruction: books published by the Education Board; moral instruction: visits from the rector of the parish, all catechisms taught on Saturdays if required; number of pupils: males, 10 under 10 years of age, 8 from 10 to 15, 1 over 15, total 19; females, 2 under 10 years of age, 1 from 10 to 15, total 3; total number of pupils 22, Established Church 16, Roman Catholics 6; master James Hare, a Protestant; visited 21st December 1837.

Aghalee classical and English school, situated in the village of Aghalee: the house is a good slated house, 1-storey high, 30 and a half by 17 and a half feet inside, has 1 door and 2 large square windows; the school requisites are all sufficient, established 1824; income from the pupils 28 pounds; intellectual instruction: books published partly by the Kildare Place Society and partly procured by the pupils; moral instruction: visits from the rector of the parish, Scripture, [Authorised?] Version, taught but no catechisms; number of pupils: males, 15 under 10 years of age, 29 from

10 to 15, 1 over 15, total 44; females, 5 under 10 years of age, 7 from 10 to 15, total 12; total number of pupils 56, 50 Established Church, 3 Roman Catholics, 3 other denominations; master William Graham, a Protestant; visited 22nd December 1837, [signed] Thomas Fagan.

Aghalee Sunday Schools

[Table contains the following headings: name, situation, when established, superintendent, number of teachers, number of scholars, books read, hours of attendance, societies with which connected, observations].

Soldierstown Sunday school, held in the day schoolhouse, established 1820, superintendent Edward Lee; 3 male and 2 female teachers, total 5; number of scholars: Protestants 123, Roman Catholics 1, male 58, female 66, total 124, exclusively Sunday school scholars 90. Books read: Bible, Testaments and Sunday school spelling books. Hours of attendance: summer, open from 8 to half past 11 a.m. and from 2 to 5 p.m.; winter, open from 9 to half past 11 a.m. and from 2 to 4 p.m.; connected with Sunday School Society for Ireland for books; no singing or prayers or expenditure for the last year. 23rd December 1837.

School Statistics

[Table contains the following headings: name of townland where held, name and religion of master and mistress, free or pay school, annual income of master or mistress, description and cost of schoolhouse, number of pupils subdivided by religion, sex and the Protestant and Roman Catholic returns, societies with which connected].

1, Peebles, master Daniel McAlister, Established Church; pay school, annual income 17 pounds 10s, schoolhouse stone and lime, good repair; number of pupils by the Protestant return: 16 Established Church; by the Roman Catholic return: 20 Established Church, 11 males, 9 females; parish school, the incumbent gives 2 pounds.

2, Killough, master and mistress John Fishbourne and Jane Fishbourne, Established Church; pay school, annual income 20 pounds, schoolhouse stone and lime, an excellent house, cost 130 pounds; number of pupils by the Protestant return: 30 Established Church, 20 other denominations, 12 Roman Catholics, 42 males, 20 females; by the Roman Catholic return: 32 Established Church, 2 other denominations, 27 Roman Catholics, 40 males, 21 females; connected with the Kildare Place Society and Henry Shillington Esq., the schoolhouse built by subscription of parishioners.

3, Aghalee, master William Graham, Established Church; pay school, annual income 7 pounds 10s, schoolhouse stone and lime, tolerably good, cost 20 pounds; number of pupils by the Protestant return: 28 Established Church, 3 Presbyterians, 1 Roman Catholic, 17 males, 15 females; by the Roman Catholic return: 23 Established Church, 3 Presbyterians, 4 other denominations, 2 Roman Catholics, 19 males, 13 females; associations: none.

4, Aghalee, mistress Miss Mary Meneight, Protestant Dissenter; pay school, income 4s 4d per quarter, schoolhouse stone and lime, tolerably good, cost 15 pounds; number of pupils by the Protestant return: 12 Established Church, 3 Roman Catholics, 15 females; associations: none.

Parish of Ballinderry, County Antrim

Statistical Remarks by James Casey

NATURAL STATE

Situation, Boundaries and Extent

This parish is situated in the barony of Upper Massereene, county of Antrim and province of Ulster. It is bounded on the north by the parish of Glenavy, on the east by the parishes of Derryaghy <Derriaghy> and Magheragall, on the south by the parishes of Magheramesk, Aghalee and Aghagallon, on the west by the parishes of Aghagallon and Glenavy and Lough Beg. The mean distance from north to south is about 4 and a half miles and from east to west 6. It is divided into 26 townlands covering an area of 10,607 acres 2 roods 14 perches statute measurements.

Ecclesiastical: Advowson

It is a lay impropriation in the gift of the Marquis of Hertford, who is the proprietor of the estate. The present incumbent is the Reverend Dean Stannus.

MODERN TOPOGRAPHY

Churches

There are 2 Protestant churches in the parish, though but one is used at present as a place of worship. That built lately (1823), near Largy's Lane Ends in the townland of Ballyscolly, is the one where the service is performed, though the burials still take place in the other in Ballykilly townland.

Meeting House and Chapels

There is a Presbyterian meeting house in the townland of Aghacairnan; is a small neat edifice.

There is also a very neat Moravian chapel and burying ground near Lower Ballinderry.

The Roman Catholics have a small neat chapel in Tullyballydonnell townland, situated near the road from Aghalee to Glen bridge, on the road from Glenavy to Moira.

Schools

The schools in the following townlands are patronised by the Reverend Dean Stannus and they have an endowment from the Kildare Street Society: Lower Ballinderry, Upper Ballinderry and Derrykillultagh. The others are temporary and are situated in the following townlands: Lurganteneill, Ballyscolly and Legaterriff.

NATURAL FEATURES AND PRODUCTIVE ECONOMY

Surface

The higher ground is at the east portion of the parish, which consists of a range of undulating hills. The greatest elevation is [blank] feet. The west portion may be denominated nearly flat, with small eminences convenient to Lower Ballinderry but flat and marshy towards Lough Beg, which constitutes a portion of the parish boundary.

Soil and Agriculture

The soil is generally a strong heavy clay, in many instances extremely difficult to labour. However, if performed in the proper season, it yields abundance of excellent wheat, oats and potatoes. The west portion of the parish is generally a rich sandy soil; gives fine barley. Convenient to Lough Beg there are fine meadows which is generally flooded in winter. The grassland are broken up for potatoes, to which succeed wheat, barley or oats.

Turbary

There is no bog in this parish except a few small patches (which are nearly cut out and reclaimed) near Lough Beg in Ballinderry townland. Turf is the common fuel and is obtained at the Montyagh[s] in Aghagallon parish. The respectable farmers in general have a bank which is paid for according to its quality, and find their own conveyance.

Economical Produce and Price

There is no limestone in the parish but the proprietor of the estate burns lime for the accommodation of all his tenantry, which may be had at 9d a barrel at the kiln or laid down at 1s, including charge for conveyance. The farmers who have kilns prefer buying it by the load at 6d or 8d, containing about 15 cwt, and burning it themselves. The basalt is used for making and repairing roads, for buildings.

MODERN TOPOGRAPHY AND NATURAL FEATURES

Hamlets

There are 2 hamlets in this parish, of small but

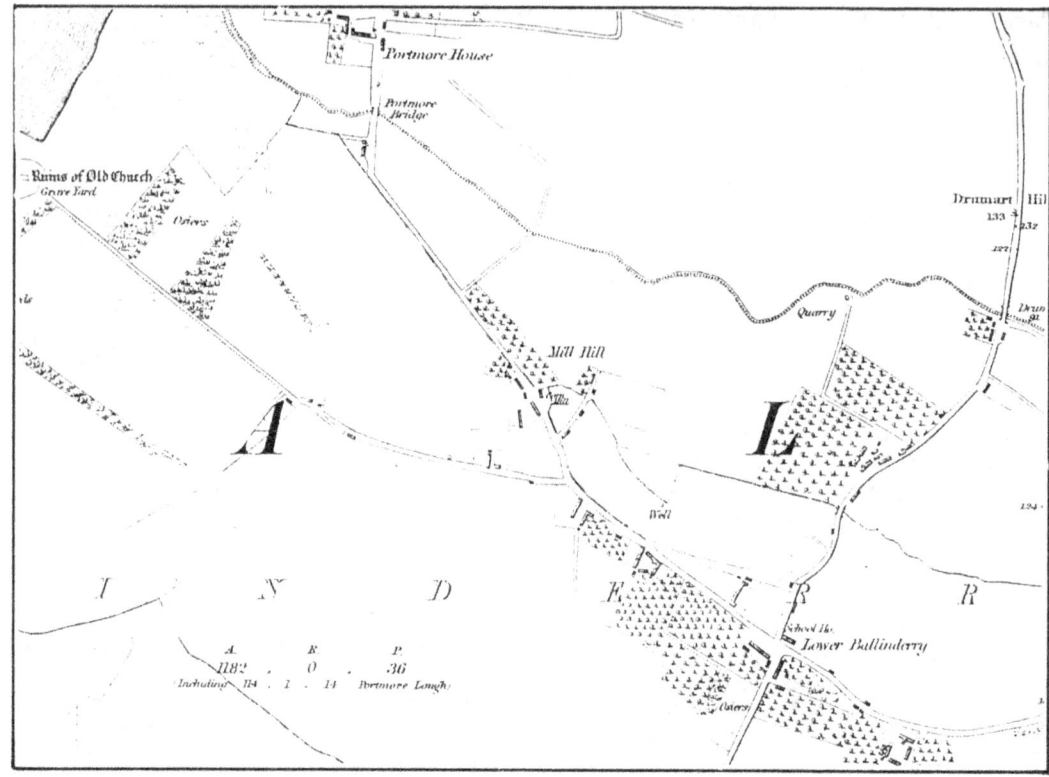

Map of Lower Ballinderry and neighbourhood from the first 6" O.S. maps, 1830s

neat appearance, called Lower Ballinderry and Largy's Lane Ends. The parishioners have a patent for holding a quarterly fair at the latter, but the unhappy party feuds prevented it from rising to any importance and the parish is bereft of both fair and market. The nearest markets are Crumlin, Lisburn and Lurgan.

Scenery

The country present[s] an agreeable surface of undulating ground, watered with frequent small streams. The scenery of the parish is particularly pleasing, exhibiting rich and highly cultivated grounds, with hedgerows in different parts of the parish of ash, fir, alder.

Streams

There are different streams in the parish, but of little magnitude. The principal one is that which joins this parish at Forket bridge between this parish and Magheragall, and continues along the parish boundary for a short distance, where it takes its course through the parish, passing Lane Ends and Lower Ballinderry, and discharges in Lough Beg near Portmore House.

There are various other small streams intersecting the parish at different places, but of very little importance.

Roads

The principal roads are those passing from Antrim to Lurgan, from Glenavy to Lisburn, and from Glenavy to Moira. It is otherwise well intersected with by-roads.

Manufactories

The principal manufactures are linen and cambric, but they are generally carried on promiscuously with agriculture. Since the introduction of yarn spun elsewhere by machinery, spinning is of so little value that it is the occupation of only a few women. The highest wages to be earned by spinning is 3d a day.

ANCIENT TOPOGRAPHY

Antiquities

In Ballinderry and Templecormack townlands are the remains of 2 churches of great antiquity. The former, situated on the border of Lough Beg, is said to have been much resorted to at different periods for the performance of some religious

Parish of Ballinderry

rites. These meetings were called Laa Loo and were held on the 4th August, and were only discontinued in consequence of the factious broils preceding the rebellion of '98. The other called Cormac's Temple, with its burying ground. A curious silver cup was found a few years ago near these ruins, supposed to be a chalice.

There is no other very remarkable antiquities to be seen in this parish, with the exception of some ancient forts which remain in a good state of preservation.

In the townland of Portmore, as tradition says, stood a castle of the O'Neill's, on the ruins of which some of the Conway family built another with magnificent stables, capable of holding 2 troops of cavalry, but there are scarcely any remains of them now.

NATURAL HISTORY

Fossil Wood

Convenient to Lough Beg are to be seen immense quantities of wood coals (so called by the inhabitants) which some of the poorer sorts use as fuel. Whilst burning [it] emits a very disagreeable smell. The waters of Lough Beg and the land contiguous to it have conjointly the curious property of converting wood into stone. Oak, fir, etc. are found at a great depth, many of them in a petrified state.

Minerals

There are several gravelly eminences (called by the inhabitants "drumlins") which, when opened to any considerable depth for the purpose of getting sand or gravel, bones of horses and various animals have been often found. Urns containing human bones are also frequently found in the top of these eminences. [Signed] James Casey, civil assistant.

Draft Memoir, with Additions by George Scott and Another

NATURAL FEATURES

Hills

[Insert note: Mr Hemans, Mr Scott].

The ground in this parish rises gradually from Lough Neagh nearly in the direction of eastwards, till it attains the height of 568 feet above the level of the sea. The hill called Crew is the most striking feature in the parish and may, from its prominent situation, be seen for a long distance. This hill falls in a southerly direction about 250 feet to a small brook, on the opposite side of which runs a chain of hills to the height of 325 feet and slopes gradually to Lough Neagh.

Lakes

Portmore or Lough Beg is situated in the western extremity of this parish, within a half a mile of Lough Neagh. It is as nearly as possible a perfect circle about a mile in diameter. The shores are soft and flat, producing a quantity of coarse grass. There is a small island in the lough called Sally Island, most probably from a few osiers growing on it. [Insert marginal note: See account of Portmore House for the island]. There is a drain called the Main Drain leading into Lough Neagh, by which small boats pass. There are eels, perch and trout found in the lough.

Rivers

There are no rivers in this parish. There are a few tributary streams, the most considerable of which is the brook running from Upper Ballinderry to Lower Ballinderry and thence discharges itself into Portmore lough. It rises in Magheraghall parish.

Bogs

There is a bog of some extent in this parish, situated in the townland of Lower Ballinderry, the average depth about 7 feet. There are some stumps of timber found in this bog, some oak and some birch. Many little undulating hills exist in the bog, composed of sand and gravel. They are called islands by the inhabitants, as for instance George's Island, Rabbit Island. They are not artificial as in some cases. The height of the bog is about 58 feet above the level of the sea.

Coast

The coast along the shore of Lough Neagh is flat and abounds with small pebbles. It is soft close to the shore.

MODERN AND ANCIENT TOPOGRAPHY

Public Buildings

Portmore House, situated in the townland of Portmore, parish of Ballinderry: it is now a ruin, within 300 yards of Portmore lough, therefore the situation of the house was pleasing. As this house was the residence of the eminent rector Jeremy Taylor, some account of him may be interesting.

He was chaplain to Charles I in 1690 and, in recompense for his attachment to the house of Stewart, he was promoted to the sees of Down and Connor, to which was annexed the administration of the bishopric of Dromore. Previous to this he had been honoured with a seat in the Privy Council of Ireland, and the University of Dublin conferred on him the office of their vice-chancellor. He died in August 1667 at Lisburn.

This prelate is said to have written some of his deepest works in a sort of summer house on the small island on Lough Beg. A situation like this, secured almost from the possibility of interruption, was very much in unison with the meditations of this worthy man, whose spiritual works have given celebrity to his name. In the parish of Ballinderry, where this island is situated, his name is held in admiration to this day. The principal work which he finished at Portmore was the *Ductor Dubitantium* or *Rule of conscience*.

Old Church

There is an old church in the parish of Ballinderry, situated in the townland of Ballykilly close to the road leading from Upper to Lower Ballinderry. From its present appearance I conclude it is many years since erected. The dimensions of the church are 66 feet by 27. There are 25 pews in the house and 4 in the gallery. The former would contain 250 persons and the latter 24. The burial service is only performed here and there seems to exist a dispute amongst the parishioners whether the church should be thrown down or repaired. It is impossible to ascertain either the cost of erecting this church or the date of its erection.

Moravian Chapel

There is a Moravian chapel in the townland of Lower Ballinderry and parish of Ballinderry. It is a simple oblong square. There are no pews and it contains 400 persons. It cannot be ascertained when this building was erected or what it cost.

Post Office

There is a post office in the village of Lower Ballinderry, which receives Dublin letters at half past 7 o'clock a.m. and receives northern letters at half past 5 in the evening.

SOCIAL ECONOMY

Schools by G. Scott

[Table contains the following headings: name of townland, number of pupils subdivided by religion and sex, remarks on how supported, when established].

Derrykilultagh, 36 Protestants, 3 Catholics, 25 male, 18 female, 43 total; supported by the parents of the children, established 1830.

Ballyscrolly, 59 Protestants, 10 Catholics, 54 male, 15 female, 69 total; under the Association for Discountenancing Vice; the master receives 8 pounds from the association and is partly supported by the parents of the children, established [?] 1835.

MODERN TOPOGRAPHY BY G. SCOTT

Ballinderry Church

Ballinderry church is situated close to the village of Upper Ballinderry, in the townland of Ballyscrolly. It is rather a handsome building 70 feet by 36, erected in the year 1824 at the expense of 2,200 pounds, 1,000 of which was given as a donation by the Marquis of Hertford and the remaining 1,200 was collected from the parishioners. There are 57 seats in the hall, would contain 296 persons; and 38 seats in gallery, would contain 144 persons; total number 440 persons.

[Insert query: There is no graveyard attached to this church, the parish burial ground being at the old church].

Presbyterian Meeting House

Ballinderry Presbyterian meeting house is a small slated house very much out of repair. There are collections made at various periods to defray the expense of repair but, as the congregation is very small, the collections made are not near sufficient. It is 60 feet by 24. There are 35 seats, would contain 215 persons. This meeting house was formerly a thatched cabin and the alteration cost between 60 and 70 pounds. The cost of this building since erection has been 200 pounds and it would cost 50 pounds more to put it in moderate repair.

Roman Catholic Chapel

Ballinderry chapel, a very small slated house, 38 feet by 18, without seats: there are 2 small windows. It is upwards of 100 years built and the congregation pay the expense of the repairs.

MODERN TOPOGRAPHY

Corn Mill

Situated at Lower Ballinderry: it is well supplied

Parish of Ballinderry

with water. The wheel is 13 feet diameter, breadth 2 feet 6 inches, an overshot wheel with a fall of 12 feet.

Villages of Upper and Lower Ballinderry

There are no towns in this parish. The villages of Upper and Lower Ballinderry are only worthy of notice. At the former village there are 2 public houses, a smithy and a few neat-looking cottages. The new church and a neat cottage built by one of the innkeepers give a very pleasant appearance to the place. One of the innkeepers, or indeed both, sell groceries. The road from Glenavy to Moira runs through the village.

Lower Ballinderry is pleasantly situated at crossroads similar to the upper village. It consists of a public house and grocery shop, post office and smithy. There is also a corn store built for a speculator, but failed. It is therefore not used. The road from Crumlin to Lurgan passes through the village.

Gentlemen's Seats

There are no resident gentlemen in the parish. The Marquis of Hertford is the lord of the manor, who resides constantly in England. Dean Stannus of Lisburn is his agent.

Communications

The road from Crumlin to Moira passes through this parish for a distance of nearly 4 miles, breadth about 22 feet. It is in very bad repair. There is a new road in progress but not yet complete. It is making at the expense of the county and the present road repaired (or rather nominally so) by the same means. The new road runs to the eastward of the present one.

The road from Crumlin to Lurgan passes through this parish for the distance of 3 and a half miles, its average breadth 22 feet, in moderate repair, which is done by the county.

The cross and by-roads are numerous (commonly named "lonins" by the inhabitants). They are in some cases most injudiciously laid out and in very bad order. What repairs are made on them are at the expense of the respective townlands in which situated.

General Appearance and Scenery

There is nothing striking or bold in the scenery of this parish. At the same time it presents many very pleasing rural landscapes. From some points there are fine and extensive views, as for instance from Crew hill. The Mourne Mountains in the county of Down may be seen clearly from many parts of the parish. Of a clear day they may be seen very distinctly.

SOCIAL ECONOMY

Local Government

There are no magistrates resident in the parish. A court leet is held in Lisburn, at the office of the Marquis of Hertford, for the manor of Killultagh, in the month of May but not at any stated time in the month. The court is empowered to try actions under the sum of 20 pounds. Appeals from decrees pronounced here lie to the judges of assizes. Cases of attachment are tried as records. Appraisers are appointed for valuing damages and a cess levied on the townlands for the repairs of their respective by-roads.

Habits of the People

The general style of the cottages are rather improved when compared with the northern part of the county. They are built of stone, whitewashed and generally consist of 2 apartments. The fuel made use of is turf, but generally very sparingly on account of its scarcity. The usual average number in a family consists of 6 persons and they are rather particular as to cleanliness in their dress or arrangement of their houses. Any old customs seem to be out of date. Whiskey drinking is often resorted to as a recreation; even the women sometimes partake of a drop.

PRODUCTIVE ECONOMY

Fairs and Markets

There are neither fairs or markets held in the parish. The produce of their farms is sold either in Lisburn or Belfast. The spinning and weaving produce is for the most part sold to dealers.

Rural Economy

Cultivation is much improved in the parish. The iron plough is generally used instead of the old Irish one. The farms consist on an average of about 30 acres, for which the average rent is about 7s per acre. The fields are well fenced with quickset hedges and consist of from 3 to 4 acres. There are some leases given but the tenant is required to pay a fine of the fourth part of his rent per annum; in lieu thereof he is allowed a lease of 3 lives. The farmers are a respectable class of people but hold their farms as a means of subsistence.

There are no lime quarries in the parish: any lime burnt is brought from Mullaghcarton and sold in town quarries, for which 5d per load is paid. There is no rotation of crops laid down by the landlord as in some cases. It seems at the pleasure of the tenant and, from what I can learn, there is a crop of potatoes every 5 years and white or green crops in the interim.

Fair Sheets by Thomas Fagan, March 1838

MODERN TOPOGRAPHY AND SOCIAL ECONOMY

Parish Schoolhouse

The Ballinderry parish schoolhouse was built by liberal subscriptions from the Marquis of Hertford, Dean Stannus, his agent, and the parishioners; cost about 170 pounds. It is a good house of stone, brick and lime, stands 1-storey high and slated, well finished in every respect for the purpose. The grounds is neatly planted with forest trees laid off in the garden-like manner and a neat wrought-iron gate to the entrance, and is situated contiguous to the new church of Ballinderry.

Killultagh Schoolhouse

The Killultagh schoolhouse, situated on a leading road from Lisburn to Glenavy, is a good slated house built of stone, brick and lime, principally at the expense of the Marquis of Hertford and Dean Stannus, his agent, cost about 120 pounds. It stands 1-storey high and is in every respect well fitted out for the purpose. The grounds are also planted with a variety of forest trees and laid off in the garden-like manner.

Divine Service in Killultagh Schoolhouse

This house accommodates a church service, held there on every second Friday at 5 o'clock in the evening, by the Reverend Savage Hall, vicar of the parish, average attendance from 200 to 300 persons. It also accommodates a Primitive Wesleyan meeting, held there every second Sunday at 5 p.m., average attendance from 80 to 100 persons. Informants James R. Hendren and others. 5th and 6th March 1838.

Temperance Society

Killultagh Temperance Society was established in 1834 and is held quarterly in Killultagh schoolhouse, president the Reverend John Brown of Magheragall. This society is conducted on the same principles of other societies of the above description and consists at present of 120 members, of adults of both sexes and of various religious denominations.

Connected with the Killultagh sunday school is also a juvenile temperance society, consisting at present of 94 members, of both sexes and of different religious denominations. The meetings are held monthly and the rules the same as other societies of a similar nature. It is superintended by James R. Hendren and the meetings held in the day schoolhouse.

Roman Catholic Chapel

Ballinderry Roman Catholic chapel, situated in the west side of the parish, about 4 furlongs east of the village of Aghalee and about 1 mile from the village of Lower Ballinderry: this is an oblong building, 1-storey high and slated, and measuring 38 feet 8 inches by 18 feet 8 inches inside; walls of stone and lime, 1 foot 10 inches thick, and the floor made of sand, lime and clay. It is lit by 4 arch windows, entrance by 1 door, situated on one of [the] gables. The altar, composed of timber and stonework, stands against the other gable. There is neither seats or galleries in the chapel. Attached to one end of the chapel is a small vestry, 1-storey high and slated; measures 9 by 6 and a half feet inside and lit by 1 small window.

The yard is enclosed partly by a stone and lime wall and partly by a quickset fence, and an iron gate to the entrance. It is partially sheltered by forest trees, but has no burials in it. The grounds was originally purchased from a farmer for a term of years, but is at present a free gift from the Marquis of Hertford. The original chapel on this site was a thatched house and was consumed by fire about the rebellion of 1798. The present one was rebuilt and slated above 20 years back, cost about [blank] pounds, subscribed chiefly by the congregation. Divine service in the chapel at 10 o'clock a.m. on every Sunday; average attendance from 200 to 400 persons. Collections are made, the proceeds of which go partly to keep the chapel in repair and partly to relieve distressed poor.

The Reverend James Denvir is the pastor of the Ballinderry Catholic congregation. He holds a portion of Ballinderry annexed <annext> to Aghagallon parish. Information obtained from Patrick Green and others.

Ballymacravin Schoolhouse and Divine Service

The Ballymacravin school, situated about 1 and a

half miles from the village of Lower Ballinderry on the Antrim road, was built by subscription in 1835, cost 80 pounds, of which sum the Marquis of Hertford gave 30 pounds, Dean Stannus 20 pounds of a bequest left by the late John McInstry of the above parish for charitable purposes, and of which Dean Stannus was left the manager; the remainder in smaller sums from the neighbouring farmers. It is a good 1-storey house and slated, built of stone, brick and lime, and when finished inside will be very well adapted for the above purpose.

This schoolhouse accommodates a church service, held there on every second Thursday at 7 o'clock p.m. by the vicar of the above parish, average attendance from 200 to 300 persons.

Legatarriff Schoolhouse and Divine Service

The Legatarriff schoolhouse accommodates a Methodist meeting held there by the Lisburn Methodist preachers on every fourth Thursday at 6 o'clock p.m., average attendance from 100 to 200 persons; also prayer meetings by the same class of people at 8 o'clock p.m. on Sundays. This schoolhouse is a small thatched house, built by subscription for a school above 22 years back, cost about 20 pounds.

Schoolhouse of Lower Ballinderry

The Lower Ballinderry schoolhouse, situated in the village of Lower Ballinderry, was built by subscription in 1827, cost about 273 pounds. The Marquis of Hertford granted the school grounds and liberally subscribed to the erection of the schoolhouse, as did also the Very Reverend Dean Stannus, his agent, and several other gentlemen and farmers in the neighbourhood.

The house is a handsome slated house, 1-storey high in the front and 2-storeys in the rear, and divided into 2 divisions, one for the males and the other for the females, and lit by 7 large oblong windows, 4 in front and 3 in the rear. The lower storey, consisting of 2 rooms and a kitchen, is fitted out for the male and female teachers' lodgings. Attached to the school is also a good garden for the use of the teachers. The grounds is improved by shrubberies and forest trees. The house accommodates a Sunday school in the summer. Information obtained from the teachers also from John Carroll and Harden Byrnes. 8th and 10th March 1838.

Ballinderry Corn Mill

Ballinderry corn mill, situated contiguous to the village of Lower Ballinderry, is leased by Mr Thomas Walkington; Marquis of Hertford, proprietor. The mill is of stone, 2-storeys high and thatched. There are 2 water wheels, one of which drives 2 pairs of stones, one pair of which grind wheat and the other oats. The second wheel drives a third pair of stones for grinding oats also. The large wheel is of wood and iron, and overshot, diameter 15 feet 6 inches, breadth 3 feet 5 inches. The water is conveyed to the top of this wheel by a wooden trough from the reservoir, and has a slanting fall. The small wheel is of wood and iron also, and is undershot, diameter 13 feet 6 inches, breadth 2 feet 3 inches, fall of the water 11 feet 8 inches. The entire machinery is in good order, but the supply of water to the mill is limited in June, July and August.

The quantity of grain annually manufactured into meal here is averaged at about 5,400 sacks, of 4 cwt each sack. The mill and machinery was much improved in 1837 by Mr Walkington, the present owner, who also erected new kilns, 2-storeys high and slated, all at a considerable expense. The mill was founded by the Messrs Dogherty, Bunton, Gorman and Company of Glenavy about 240 [24 ?] years back. Informants John Carroll, John Fleming and James Johnston. 12th March 1838.

Moravian Chapel

The Moravian chapel of Ballinderry is situated on a very handsome site adjoining the village of Lower Ballinderry, with a burial ground attached in the rear. The chapel is a very neat oblong edifice, 1-storey high and slated, and situated nearly north and south. Over the south end stands a neat cupola, a bell and vane, and attached to the north end a very handsome 2-storey and slated house for the minister's dwelling, with other necessary accommodations. The interior of the chapel is spacious and well lit by 3 large arch windows on the west side, entrance by a large arched door on the south gable in front of the adjoining road. It measures 38 and a half by 23 and a half feet inside, walls of stone and lime and 2 feet in thickness.

The pulpit, a modern and neat structure, stands to the north gable elevated some feet above the floor, and suspended from the ceiling a handsome brass chandelier, and a communication from the chapel to the minister's dwelling by a door on the north gable. The floor is of lime and sand. Forms are the only seats as yet erected; total seats in this chapel 33 and each averaging 9 feet 2 inches in length, and will accommodate 6 persons each seat, total 198 persons accommodated with seats in the chapel, allowing 1 and a half feet to each sitting. It is not as yet completed inside, but when finished will be a very neat edifice externally and internally.

The garden and grounds in front of the chapel is tastefully laid off in garden-like manner, ornamented with shrubberies and stocked with fruit trees, enclosed by neat quickset and laurel fences and partially sheltered by lofty forest trees. Entrance from the adjoining road by 2 iron gates, one opening to the chapel and the other to the minister's dwelling. The buildings and place is altogether in neat order and form an ornament to the village in which it is situated.

Divine service in the chapel at 11 o'clock morning and at 6 o'clock evening on Sundays; Reverend John Chambers, minister.

Burial Ground

The burial ground in the rear of the above chapel is enclosed by a quickset fence. The following are amongst the Christian names and surnames on the tombstones in it: Anthony, George, Henry, James, Robert, Vernon, Thomas, William, Anna, Ann, Elizabeth, Eve, Mary, Easter, Margaret, Jean, Sarah.

Surnames: Boyes, Barns, Campbell, Ferriss, Bell, Bates, Fearis, Laughlin, McNees, Hopes, Johnston, Thompson, Maise, Tipping, Spence, Mays, Neilson, Syms, Weathered. The oldest stone is not earlier than 1767. The greatest age on any stone is 96 years. Several of the stones are defaced and cannot be read, and many families bury in it who have no stones.

The tombstones in the Moravian burial ground are all short and nearly square, and situated on the top of the earthern graves near the head, and unsupported by any other stones, save that the head is a little elevated and looking to the east.

Foundation of Moravian Chapel

The Moravian settlement at Lower Ballinderry was founded by the late Reverend John Cenick about 85 years ago. The chapel grounds, about 2 English acres, was then purchased for an unexpired term of years from a farmer, the late Ben Haddick. The grant was subsequently renewed by the Marquis of Hertford at 1 pound 10s annual rent. The original chapel, built here at the above period, was thatched and constructed at the expense of the English and other foreign Moravian congregations.

However, in 1821, it was rebuilt and slated, furnished with a valuable organ, and various improvements made on and about the place, at an expense of about 700 pounds, to which the Marquis of Hertford subscribed 20 pounds. The Very Reverend Dean Stannus, Captain Watson of Brookhill, Major Houghton of Springfield and many other clergymen and gentlemen of the surrounding neighbourhood gave liberal subscriptions, as did also persons of all religious denominations subscribe according to their means. Their own brethren of other congregations also subscribed. A late Mrs Bates, of Gracehill, an English lady, also subscribed to the erection and completing of the chapel and other appendages the liberal sum of 325 pounds. However, it is said to have been a very handsome edifice and to be much admired by all for its style and cleanliness.

There was an academy for the education of young ladies attached to it and conducted on the same principle as those at Gracehill or Gracefield. But in 1835, on Easter Sunday morning, the chapel with all its furniture was consumed by accidental fire. The present chapel was subsequently erected and opened for divine service on the 16th June 1836. Cost of erection can only be obtained by applying at Gracehill, the senior Moravian settlement in this county.

Moravian Congregation and Minister

The Moravian settlement at Lower Ballinderry is rather on the decline in latter years. The congregation at present does not exceed 40 members. The average attendance at divine service is from 30 to 40 persons, including strangers.

The Reverend John Chambers is the present minister and receives average annual income from various sources about 40 pounds; a house and the benefit of 2 good gardens in addition, the ground rent of which is paid by the congregation. Collections are made in the chapel, the proceeds of which go to the poor. Information obtained from the Revd John Chambers, James Johnston and others. 13th March 1838.

Lower Ballinderry

Lower Ballinderry is a small village situated on the leading road from Antrim to Lurgan, 10 miles south west of the former and 6 miles north east of the latter, and about 8 miles north west of Lisburn, and formed at the junction of 4 roads in the neighbourhood of Lough Neagh, and surrounded by a well-improved and fertile neighbourhood. The following are the trades and callings, number and height of houses in the village and suburbs,

Parish of Ballinderry

also the number slated and thatched, inhabited and uninhabited.

Trades and callings: grocers and spirit dealers 2, 2 houses; grocers and farmers 1, 1 house; farmers 5, 5 houses; labourers 5, 5 houses; masons 2, 2 houses; smiths 1, 1 house; clergymen 1, 1 house; schoolmasters 1, 1 house; schoolmistresses 1, 1 house; postmistresses 1, 1 house; trades and callings total 20.

Houses inhabited 20, Moravian chapel 1, schoolhouse 1, grain stores 1, grain kilns 1, forge 1, waste house 1, building 1, houses total 27. Houses of 4-storeys 1, houses of 3-storeys 1, houses of 2-storeys 9, houses of 1-storey 16, total 27. Houses slated 8, houses thatched 19, total 27. 14th March 1838.

In the vicinity of the village stands a good corn mill and kilns and mill-dam, also several first-rate farmhouses and handsome orchards.

The receiving or post office was established here in 1822, Miss Ann Jane McCann, postmistress. The office is held at Mr Harden Byrne's house adjoining the village. Mr Byrne is contractor for the conveyance of the mail by a 1-horse car from Crumlin to Banbridge, distance 18 miles. The mail arrives from Crumlin at Lower Ballinderry daily at 5 to 5.30 p.m., and from Banbridge at 7 to 7.30 a.m. daily also.

The corn stores and kilns in the above village were built 1822 by Mr Harden Byrne at a considerable expense. He dealt extensively in the grain trade for several subsequent years. They are now held by Mr Ralph Russell, who carries on the grain trade to some extent. A part of these stores stands 4-storeys high, part 3-storeys and the kilns 2-storeys, and all slated.

Temperance Society

Lower Ballinderry Temperance Society was established February 1838 by Mr John Thompson of the above place. Meetings of this society are to be held monthly in the Lower Ballinderry schoolhouse at 7 o'clock p.m. It is to be conducted on the same principles as others of the same description and to be superintended by a committee of 12 persons, these to be changed from time to time as circumstances may require. Present committee: Messrs John Thompson, Harden Byrne, John Montgomery, James Creaney, Alexander Ross, Thomas Taylor, Samuel Thompson and Joseph George Wilson etc.

The society consist[s] at present of 90 members of both sexes, of different ages and of various religious denominations. This laudable institution, though but yet in its infancy, is much esteemed and likely to prosper in the neighbourhood. Information obtained from John Thompson and others. 15th March 1838.

Presbyterian Meeting House

The Ballinderry Presbyterian meeting house, situated in the townland of Aghacarnan, on a by-road leading between the Glenavy and Ballinderry roads to Lisburn, and about 1 mile south east of the new church of Ballinderry: this is an oblong edifice, 2-storeys high and slated, and measuring 57 by 21 and a half feet inside, walls of stone and lime and 2 feet in thickness, and floor boarded. It is situated east and west and well lit by 4 Gothic windows in front, 2 Gothic windows and 4 oblong windows in the rear.

Entrance to the lower storey by a large door on the front or south side and to the galleries by a door on each gable, with stone stairs ascending to them on the outside of the house. The pulpit is situated about the middle of the house, against the north side wall, and elevated some feet above the floor. Pews on the ground floor 35: of these, 32 average 9 and a half feet of seats each and will hold 6 persons each pew, total 192; 1 has 19 and a half feet of seats and will hold 13 persons; 1 has 15 and a half feet of seats and will hold 10 persons; 1 has 7 and a half feet of seats and will hold 5 persons; total accommodated with seats on the ground floor 220. The galleries are not yet seated but, if seated, would accommodate about one half of the above numbers, say 110. That would leave the house, if finished, to afford accommodation for 330 persons, allowing 1 and a half feet to each sitting.

The pulpit and pews are in decent order and the house whitewashed with lime outside.

In the yard stands a neat, 1-storey and slated session house. It is partially planted with forest trees and laurels, and enclosed partly by a stone and lime wall and partly by a quickset fence, but no burials in it. Entrance from the aforesaid road by a good iron gate.

The meeting house was overhauled and newly roofed, slated and seated, with other improvements, in 1826 at an expense of about 150 pounds, exclusive of horse and manual labour done by the congregation free of expense. To the aforesaid sum the Marquis of Hertford subscribed 25 pounds. The Very [Reverend] Dean Stannus, Captain Watson of Brookhill and several other gentlemen liberally subscribed, as did also liberal persons of all religious denominations.

Divine service in the meeting house in winter at 12 o'clock noon and in summer at half past 11 mornings on Sundays, average attendance from 100 to 200 persons. Collections are made, the proceeds of which go to repairs on the house. There is also instructions in the Scripture given to an average attendance of about 100 adults in the meeting house for 1 and a half hours before divine service on Sunday mornings, by the minister.

Minister and Income

The Reverend Henry Leebody is minister of the Ballinderry Presbyterian congregation and receives average annual stipend of 25 pounds, royal bounty of 50 pounds, total annual income of 75 pounds.

ANCIENT AND MODERN TOPOGRAPHY

Original Meeting House

The original meeting house was thatched. It was founded above 100 years back by the late Reverend John Heastie, who was also the first Presbyterian minister that preached in the above parish. It was he also gave the site of the house at the above period. The site was subsequently granted by the Marquis of Hertford, free of expense. The meeting house was rebuilt and slated for the first time about 33 years back, but on a more limited scale in length and breadth than the former or the present one. The cost of the first building or rebuilding in 1805 is not at present known. However, they were built by subscriptions from liberal persons of various creeds.

Succession of Ministers

The following were the Presbyterian ministers of Ballinderry since the establishment of a congregation there: first the Reverend John Heastie, who was the founder, second the Reverend [blank] Brown, third the Reverend [blank] Rowen, fourth the Reverend Robert Carlisle, fifth the Reverend William Whitla, sixth the Reverend John Shaw, present the Reverend Henry Leebody. Information obtained from the Revd Henry Leebody, William Adams, Mrs Russell and others.

Old Church of Ballinderry

Ballinderry old church is situated on a handsome site adjoining the road leading from the village of Lower Ballinderry to Lisburn. It is an oblong edifice, 1-storey high and slated, and situated nearly east and west, and measuring 64 and a half by 22 and a half feet inside; walls of stone and lime and 3 feet in thickness, and an entrance door on the west gable. It is lit by 2 windows on the south side, 3 on the north side and 1 large [one] on the east gable over the communion table. These windows are approaching to square, except 2 that are oblong. They are on the old fashion, the casing of wood, strong and clumsy.

There are 2 circular windows on the west gable to light the gallery erected on that end of the church. Entrance to this gallery by a door on the north side of the church, and stone stairs ascending to it on the outside. The gallery is small and supported in front on 2 timber columns. The communion table stands in the east end of the church and over it, on a framed parchment of canvas, the Royal Arms with the letters C and R at the top, and at the foot the words Dieu et Mon Droit.

The pulpit stands against the north side and about the middle of the church. The alley and area around the communion table is laid with freestone and the remainder of the floor partly of lime and sand and partly boarded; total pews on the ground floor 26, each averaging 18 feet of seats, and will accommodate persons each 12; total accommodated on the ground floor 312. There are 4 seats or pews on the gallery, each averaging 14 feet of seats, and will hold 9 persons each, total 36; total accommodated in the church 348.

The pews are of oak-panelled work, but the interior and furniture of the church is falling fast to decay and is now merely preserved for antiquity's sake and the accommodation of funeral services.

On the west gable stands a sort of chimney or belfry and bell. This bell is now split and much injured, but seldom used since the erection of a bell on the new church. This bell was designed for Aghalee church but was brought here by mistake, and continues so to the present period. The Ballinderry bell was put up in Aghalee church and remains there to the present period also, and much a better bell than the one above mentioned. These 2 bells were cast at the one period. By this it would appear that the above churches were built about the one period.

Graveyard at Ballinderry Old Church

The graveyard is enclosed partly by a stone and lime wall and partly by a quickset fence, and partially sheltered by forest trees, with a good iron gate to the entrance. The following are amongst the Christian names and surnames on tombs and headstones in the yard.

Male names: Anthony, Alexander, Adam, Allen, Humphrey, Jonathan, Charles, Edward, Francis, Hugh, John, James, William, Samuel, Ralph, Henry, Thomas.

Parish of Ballinderry

Female names: Agness, Alethea, Ann, Allice, Charity, Dorathea, Elenor, Maria, Joanna, Elizabeth, Margaret.

Epitaph on a headstone: "Here lieth the body of Mr Thomas Johnston of Portmore, who departed this life the 30th July 1800 in the 90th year of his age; he was descended from the Honorable and Reverend Thomas Johnston, third son of the Earl of Annandale in Scotland, who was rector of Drumgooland and vicar of Ballynahinch, county of Down, in the reign of King Charles I."

Surnames on tombs and headstones: Allen, Blizard, Close, Clarke, Eken, Higginson, Johnson, Moore, Weatherhead, Culbert, Cinnamond, Casement, Eden, Gilbert, Johnston, Maze, Patterson, Yar, Ravonscroft, Ross, Peel, Shillington, Tatnal, Thompson, Thomson, Taylor.

The oldest stone legible in the burial ground is 1679 and the greatest age on any tomb or headstone is 92 years. Some of the tombs and headstones are defaced and consequently can not be read.

A chest belonging to the old church is at present in the tower of the new church and on its sides cut in figures 1706, which is said to be the period at which the old church was built; also a silver cup with the following inscription on it: "The cwp of Balanderey chwrch." This cup belonged to the old church and is in good order. Informants John Johnston and others, 16th March 1838.

New Church of Ballinderry

Ballinderry new church, situated north of and contiguous to the leading road from Lower Ballinderry to Lisburn, is an oblong edifice, 1-storey high and slated, and situated nearly east and west. It measures 65 by 33 and a half feet inside, walls of whin quarry stone and lime, and nearly 2 and a half feet in thickness. Entrance through a large Gothic door on the south side of the tower, and from the tower into the body of the church by an oblong door on the west gable. The interior of the church is spacious and well lit by 3 Gothic windows on the north side, 3 Gothic windows on the south side and 1 large Gothic window on the east gable over the communion table; ventilation afforded by lattices <lettises> situated in those windows.

The galleries along the 2 sides and on the west end of the church are plain but very neatly constructed, and supported in front on 10 metal columns. The communion table stands at the east gable, enclosed by timber railing, and in front of it, about the centre of the church and elevated some feet above the floor, stands the pulpit, and contiguous to it in front a marble baptismal fount supported on a timber pedestal. The alley, tower floor and area around the communion table is laid with cut stone and the pew floors boarded. Ascent to the galleries by stone stairs situated in the tower, and light afforded them by the aforesaid windows, the tops of which nearly reach the ceiling.

Pews on the ground floor 37: of these, 32 average 13 and a half feet of seats each and will hold persons each 9, total 288; 2 pews, 22 and a half feet of seat each and will hold persons total 30; 2 pews, 19 and a half feet of seats each and will hold persons total 26; 1 pew, 28 feet of seats, and will hold persons total 19; total persons accommodated with seats on the ground floor 363. On the galleries there are 36 pews: of these, 28 average 5 feet 10 inches of seats each and will hold persons each 4, total 112; 6 pews average 6 feet 3 [inches] of seats each and will hold persons each 4, total 24; 2 pews average 11 feet of seats each and will hold persons total 14; choir's seat, 28 feet of seats and will hold persons total 18; total persons accommodated with seats in the church 531, allowing an average of 1 and a half feet to each sitting.

The interior of the church, the pulpit, galleries, pews and all fixtures are permanently constructed and in decent order. The vestry is attached to the east end of the church; stands 1-storey high and roofed with lead, entrance to it by 2 doors from the church and a third door on the outside. It is 20 feet 3 inches by 10 and a half feet inside, lit by 2 windows, and afford a coal store for the use of the vestry.

Attached to the west end of the church stands a handsome tower and beautiful spire of cut stone, topped with a handsome brass ball and stalk, all which are said to stand 128 feet in height. The tower stands 3-storeys high, built of whinstone and lime, walls 5 feet 3 inches in thickness, corners, pinnacles, door casings and other ornaments of cut stone. It is lit by 5 Gothic and 2 square windows, and measures 17 feet 10 inches by 17 and a half feet on the outside. The bell, which is said to weigh 6 and a half cwt and have a superior tone, is situated on the third storey. It is 8 feet 8 inches in circumference, 2 feet 9 and a half inches in diameter and 2 feet 2 inches in height. It was made at the Lagan foundry by Coates and Young, and is said to have cost 60 pounds.

Exterior and Grounds of New Church

The corners, cornices, pinnacles and other ornaments of the church is of whitish cut stone. These pinnacles and other ornaments along the church roof, together with the cut stone in the spire and tower, is said to be partly of foreign stone and partly procured from Tyrone. The quarry stone used in the church and tower were quarried contiguous to the church. It is altogether internally and externally, with its handsome and lofty spire attached to the west end, one of the handsomest country edifices perhaps in the north of Ireland; and situated on a very handsome site containing about 2 English acres, enclosed partly by a stone and lime wall and partly by a quickset fence, and a neat wrought-iron gate to the entrance. The grounds is beautifully laid off and ornamented with shrubberies of forest and ornamental trees and gravel walks.

There is no burials at the new church. The following inscription is cut on a handsome corniced stone in front of the church tower: "Erected AD 1824, by a donation from the Marquis of Hertford of 1,000 pounds and 1,200 pounds presented by the parish, Reverend James Stannus, vicar, Turtle Bunting and Thomas Russell, churchwardens."

Mr Boyd, architect, Belfast, was contractor for the erection of the above church. The old church was disused, except for funeral services, after the completion of the new church in 1824 or subsequent. Information obtained from John English, John Johnston and others. 20th and 21st March 1838.

Old Church: Templecormac

Ruins of Templecormac old church and burial ground, situated about 1 mile east of Ballinderry new church, is tolerably large, enclosed by a quickset fence, partially sheltered by forest trees, and a small iron gate to the entrance. Nothing of this old church now remains but the foundation walls, which are at present grown over with earth and grass. It was situated nearly east and west and, as near as can be now judged, it stood 44 by 20 feet inside; walls of rough stones and grouted lime, similar to other ancient buildings, and 2 feet 10 inches in thickness.

The interior of the building is partly occupied by graves. The graveyard, too, is to a great extent occupied by burials, but very limited in headstones. Different religious denominations still continue to bury in it but Roman Catholics are the most numerous. The Irish cry accompanied funerals of the latter class of people coming to this graveyard up to about the year 1800.

The ground for interment was much larger formerly than at present. The following are amongst the names and surnames on the headstones in the yard: Archibald, Alexander, James, Thomas, Elizabeth, Grizel, Margaret, Jane. Surnames: Larmor, Maze, Smyth, Scott. At the heads of graves are several rude stones without any inscription.

The church is said to have been demolished by Oliver Cromwell. A large portion of the walls remained up to about 1790, as did also part of the clergy's dwelling and office houses that stood contiguous to the church, on the site now occupied by Robert McAleavey's dwelling.

Contiguous to the church also stood 2 ancient springs, one [of] which is at present closed up. These wells are said to have been formerly visited by people for the cure of disordered eyes.

Templecormac is said to have been an extensive seat of learning at a former period; that there was a temple for the education of students; and that the establishment was superintended by 3 friars, which was the number of clergy always resident there. One of the friars are said to have divine service at the ruins of the old church about 60 years back. There was a tract of ground attached to the temple for the use of the clergy and students. It was called the Church Fields, and is now occupied by Robert McAleavey and James Gibson, farmers.

Templecormac was formerly called Cormac's Temple, and is said to have been founded by a Cormac Akilly, to whose name it was subsequently dedicated, and afterwards gave name to the townland in which it was situated, and is to the present day called Templecormac. Information obtained from James Dunnigan, William Brennagh, his wife, and others, 21 March 1838.

Tullyrusk Ancient Church

The ruins of Tullyrusk ancient church and burial ground is situated on a handsome eminence in the townland of Tullyrusk and contiguous to a leading road from Castle Robbin to Antrim. Of this ancient church, which was situated nearly east and west, nothing at present remains but the ground or foundation walls, which are grown over with earth and grass. As near as can be judged from the present dilapidated state of the walls, the church stood 61 by 19 feet in the inside, walls of rough whinstone and grouted lime, and 3 feet in thickness. The interior is now occupied by graves. The graveyard is enclosed by a quickset fence and an iron gate to the entrance, which stands on the south side, and several stone stairs ascending the gate.

The following are amongst the names and surnames on headstones in the graveyard: Andrew, Bernard, Bryan, Daniel, Eneias, Felix, Patrick, John, James, Robert, Roger, Thomas, William, Ann, Eleanor, Elizabeth, Letitia, Molly, Mary, Margaret, Hannah.

Surnames: Boyes, Close, McGee, McLernon, McLornan, Tolan, Matchet, Medowel, Hammill, Hovron, Potts, Kennedy, Weatherup, Waters.

1724 is the earliest date legible on any headstone and 88 years the greatest age. At the heads of graves are several rude headstones without any inscription on them, and the majority of graves without any headstones whatever. Few bury here at present but Roman Catholics. The Irish cry accompanied the funerals of the latter class of people to this graveyard up to 1817.

A large portion of the church walls remained up to 1800, when they were taken down to build a schoolhouse in its neighbourhood. The altar, which is said to be of stonework, was discovered in sinking graves in the interior at some former period. It stood at the east gable.

The church is said to have been destroyed by Cromwell, but of its founder or to what saint's name it was dedicated there is no local account, save that it was founded under the direction of St Patrick. It is said to have been a chapel of ease attached to Shankill, Belfast, and also that the 4 townlands of Tullyrusk, to wit Tullyrusk, Budore, Dundrod and Knockcairn, constituted a small parish for its support.

Ancient Castle

A short distance to the north of the old church stood an ancient castle said to have been founded and occupied by the Norton family. A portion of the ground walls are said to still remain, but grown over with earth. At the castle also stood a fort, a great part of which still remain, but in a disfigured state. To the south of the old church stood a hamlet or small town called Leathemstown, said to have been nearly 6 furlongs in length. The fire hearths and part of the ground walls of above 100 houses have been raised on the site of this town, which is at present under tillage. There was also raised on the site the ruins of 2 corn kilns and a mill-race.

Tradition also says that there was a great battle fought at Knockcairn at some former period, between the Norton family of Tullyrusk Castle and Dunn of Dundrod Castle, both of whom were allied by marriage connection. However, further inquiry in the neighbourhood of Tullyrusk might glean more tradition regarding this battle. Information obtained from John McLernon, Jane Cory and others. 22nd March 1838.

Camlin Ancient Church

The ruins of Camlin or Crumlin old church, situated east of and contiguous to the town of Crumlin, and on the banks of Crumlin river, is situated nearly east and west and measures 72 by 21 feet 10 inches inside. The walls are of extraordinary strength and thickness, built of whin and greystone bound together by grouted lime similar to other ancient buildings, and varying from 5 to 5 and half feet in thickness. The east gable, together with the west gable to the square and the larger portion of both side walls, still stand, but greatly disfigured by dilapidation and the extracting of well-faced stones from [the] surface of the walls, yet they are to a great extent mantled over with ivy which gives them a venerable appearance. A large piece of the west end of the north side wall is altogether destroyed, as well as a portion of the same end of the south side wall.

On the east gable, at a height of several feet above the surface, stands the ruins of a Gothic window 5 and a half feet high, 3 feet wide inside and 2 feet wide outside. Inside, in the south corner of the latter gable, stands the ruins of a safe 2 and a half feet broad, 2 feet 3 inches deep and 4 feet high, but as the walls are dilapidated, its original or accurate height cannot be judged. On the south side wall, 21 and a half feet from the east gable, stands the ruins of an arch window 3 feet 10 inches wide by 3 feet 8 inches high inside.

In both side walls, and nearly opposite to each other, stands 4 arches in each wall. These arches are now partly dilapidated. It is difficult to judge their original size but they seem to have stood 7 and a half feet wide at the base, 2 feet 10 inches deep and from 5 to 6 feet high; of their use there could be no information gleaned. The columns between the arches, which are of masonry, stood 2 and a half feet thick.

Within 15 feet of the west gable, and on the north side wall, stands the ruins of a door, as may be seen by a portion of one side of it still remaining and having to the east side of it, through the wall, a bolt-hole 7 inches wide by 8 inches high and 5 feet in length. If there were any other doors or windows on the church than those described, they cannot be at present traced. However, the interior of the building was curiously constructed and the entire masonry well executed.

Graves

There are several graves inside and outside of the church, but no tombs or headstones, save part of one headstone erected 1765, as follows and in rude cut letters: "Here lieth the body of John Armstrong, who departed this life August 13th 1765, aged 35 years." In the graveyard, at the heads of graves, are several large rough stones without any inscription on them.

The graveyard is enclosed by a quickset fence and partially sheltered by forest trees. Of the founder of the old church or to whom it was dedicated, there could be no local information obtained, but it is said to have been destroyed about the 1641 war, as was also a number of the clergy who belonged to it. Information obtained from Robert Durham, an aged man, and his wife. 23rd March 1838.

Ballinderry or Laa Lau Ancient Church

The ruins of Ballinderry ancient church and burial ground is situated on a small but handsome island in the east side of Lough Beg, contiguous to Portmore and the village of Lower Ballinderry. Of the old church, nothing at present remains but the 2 gables. It was situated nearly east and west and measured 62 and a half by 24 and a half inside. Walls of whin and grey and a few freestones, 3 feet 3 inches in thickness, and bound together by grouted mortar similar to other ancient buildings, and the masonry well executed. The gables are to a great extent covered with ivy, which gives them a handsome and venerable appearance. On the east gable, and 4 feet above the present surface, stands the ruins of an oblong window 6 feet 3 inches high by 2 and a half feet broad on the outside, but much larger inside. On the west gable also, and 2 feet above the present surface, stands the ruins of 2 oblong windows 2 feet 9 inches high by 8 and a half inches wide each on the outside, but larger inside. The tops and sides of these windows are much disfigured. The body of the church is now occupied by graves to a great extent.

Graveyard of Ancient Church

The graveyard is large, enclosed by a quickset fence and tolerably occupied by graves. It contains several tombs and a large number of headstones bearing the family names who bury there. At the heads of many other graves are large stones taken from the church walls. 9 yards to the south west of the west end of the church stands a fount stone of the hard grey kind. This fount stone is of irregular shape, but measures 3 feet 2 inches in length, 2 feet 2 inches in breadth and 1 foot 3 inches in thickness. The fount approaches to circular shape, 1 foot 1 inch in diameter and 7 inches in depth, and a sunk passage on one side of it for letting out the overflow of water occasioned by the rain.

24 yards south west of the above stone stands a second fount stone, which seems to have had 2 founts in it but one of them is now nearly destroyed. This stone is the same quality as the one before described and measures 2 feet 10 inches long, by 1 foot 6 inches broad and 11 inches thick. The existing fount in it is oval shaped, 12 by 10 inches and 5 and a half inches deep, with a passage for the water to flow out as above described. The broken fount seems to have stood 7 inches in diameter and 8 inches in depth.

These stones are locally called St Patrick's Knee Stones, and said that the holes was left in them by St Patrick while in the attitude of prayer. They were frequently visited by hundreds for the cure of warts, which the application of the water contained in the stones is said to have effectually cured on various occasions, and other diseases also.

The graveyard stands a considerable height above the shore, or meadow ground enclosing it. The principal entrance is on the east side by 2 ancient piers of masonry and several stone stairs ascending them. A short distance from them stands 2 circular piers of masonry also, but seem of modern date and stand at the entrance of the meadow above mentioned.

The graveyard, though only about 2 furlongs from dry land, is accessible by boats only during the winter months and floods, but in summer can be got into by 2 bridle roads leading to it, one of which approach the gate situated on the east side, and described [above]. The other passage stands to the south west side, a considerable distance from the latter.

Names in Graveyard

The following are amongst the names and surnames on tombs and headstones in the graveyard. Male names: Allen, Arthur, Charles, Domnick, Bernard, Hugh, William, James, John, Farrell, Robert, Patrick, Thomas, Anthony, Richard, Roger, Con, Henry, Enes.

Female names: Ann, Elizabeth, Cicely, Sarah, Susanna, Cathrine, Frances, Mary, Rose.

Surnames: McAravay, McDonnell, McDonald, McCorry, Magill, Magee, Crossey, Ravenscroft, Breedin, Brankin, Cormic, O'Brian, Lavery,

Parish of Ballinderry

Johnston, Clark, Gregory, Daragh, Hanan, Smith, Finn, Horbison, Gerneby, Closse, McKaven, McKavney, Lamb, Hant, Davey, O'Doran, O'Dowd, Monoghan, McGuckin.

There are several tombs and headstones defaced and cannot be read. The majority of families bury without tombs or headstones, save rude and unlettered ones. The oldest headstone legible is 1707, and 85 years the greatest age on any.

Inscriptions on Headstones

Epitaph on a headstone near the south corner of the west end of the old church:
"DSBR 1732,
A husband kind,
A father dear;
A faithful friend,
Lieth here;
My days is spent,
My glass is run;
Children dear,
Prepare to come.
Cormick O'Dowd, aged 82 years."

Inscription on a clergyman's headstone inside the church: "Sacred to memory of the Reverend Bernard O'Doran, late vicar of Killead, who departed this life on the 16th of October 1815. This stone is erected as a small tribute of affection by his son, James O'Doran, also to Susannah, wife of the above, aged 81 years. Obit, 2nd February 1837." This is a very handsome cut stone, situated to the west gable of the church, inside. The above clergyman was in early life a Roman Catholic priest.

Tradition of St Lau

The church is said to have been founded by St Lau, a Justinian B&C, and to have been destroyed by Cromwell, at the period of his destruction of many others. Ballinderry ancient church, better known by Laa Lau church, is dedicated to St Lau, who is said to be the founder of it, and in memory of whom, for time immemorial, the 4th August was held in great veneration, as patron day or day of indulgence of the above old church. At that period of the year thousands of persons congregated here, from local and remote districts, and performed stations outside of the graveyard on the shores along the edge of the water, as well as about the church.

Along the shore or edge of the water stands a great number of large stones, at arranged distances, and at each of which a portion of the ceremony was performed. These stones or stages are still visible when the floods fall in summer. However, about 40 years back, the multitude of all shades and grades assembling at the above old church became so great that drinking, quarrelling <quarling>, cock-fighting and sundry other vices, as well as party feuds, practised on the occasion, destroyed the original design and endangered the peace and well-being of the surrounding neighbourhood, to such extent that the late Reverend William Dawson, the then parish priest of Ballinderry, found it necessary for the peace and safety of the neighbourhood to abolish the stations at the old church altogether 40 years ago. But before drinking, gaming, and quarrelling destroyed the original design of the Laa Lau stations the meetings on the occasion were large and moral as intended, and regularly conducted by the clergy of the Roman Catholic religion.

On account of the beauty and antiquity of the place, situated in a large and elegant sheet of water, and the graveyard, partially studded with thorn and board-tree bushes, as well as the large assemblage of pilgrims collected on the occasion of the Laa Lau stations, the scene annually was most desirable and admired in the neighbourhood in which the old church is situated. Information obtained from James Johnston, John Magee, Patrick Green and many others. 28th and 29th March 1838.

Portmore

Portmore, once the seat of an ancient castle and of some of the most extensive and elegant stabling, offices and sundry other improvements known to have been within the kingdom, or perhaps many others at the period in which they were extant, is delightfully situated near the east end of Lough Beg, on an eminence commanding a fine prospect of Lough Neagh, Lough Beg, Ram's Island, the Old Church Island, as well as the surrounding scenery for many miles. Nothing now remains to denote this once healthy and splendid seat but the wall surrounding the bowling green, a few pear and other fruit trees, and some dilapidated patches of the castle and stabling walls that are partly roofed-in for cottier and office houses, and in other cases serving as fences.

However, their present broken and disordered state renders it quite difficult to give any accurate outline of either the castle or stabling, save that the walls may vary from 2 to 3 feet thick, a few feet of the lower part built of stone and the remainder of brick of a hard and superior quality, and the cornicing of cut freestone. However, the ruins of the castle, as shown by a caretaker in the place, measure 81 by 27 feet in the clear; walls, partly of stone and partly of brick, measures from 2 and a half to 3 feet thick and in some parts 5 feet high. The interior is now dug up for crop. The floor is said to be paved with black stones of moderate size and beneath the pavement, arched with brickwork and leading in different directions. The bowling green, now occupied as a fruit and vegetable garden, is walled in with a high stone and lime wall, but dilapidated in several parts; stands 80 by 70 yards inside and possess several of the old pear trees, both inside and outside the wall.

History of Ancient Castle

Tradition says little on the founder of the old castle, or its age. However, it is locally said that the stabling, towers, castles and other improvements in the place were made by Earl Conway, or Sir George Seymour, about 1664; and that the stabling etc. were 140 feet long, 35 feet broad and 40 feet high; that there were accommodations for 2 troops of horse and rooms for the men; that the cisterns were marble and the water conveyed by pipes to the horses' heads or mangers from Lough Beg, situated contiguous to the ruins above mentioned. These splendid buildings are said to have been pulled down by orders of Lord Hertford above 90 years back. The entire timberwork, which was of the best of oak, as well as the cut freestone and other valuable materials were sold out to different purchasers by private sale, by the late William Johnston, then employed by Lord Hertford's orders.

Sally Island, Songs and Wildlife

Contiguous to Portmore, and situated in Lough Beg, stands a small island now covered with water, except a few willows from which it takes its name of Sally Island and on which stands the ruins of some ancient building, but cannot be at present inspected. However, it is said that the late Dr Jeremy Taylor, formerly Bishop of Down and Dromore, and who resided at Portmore for many years during the reign of Cromwell, wrote much of his valuable writings on the Sally Island, apart from bustle and annoyance. Informants Mr James Johnston, Mr John Carroll, Thomas Bell and many others.

There were some elegant songs locally made about the beauties of Portmore, and which could be obtained in the neighbourhood.

Portmore deerpark, containing about 2,000 acres, stood a short distance from the castle; contained a large store of deer, jays, pheasants, hares, rabbits and other game, as well as large oaks and other timber, also canals and quays for pleasure boats. [Signed] Thomas Fagan, 29th and 30th March 1838.

School Statistics by Thomas Fagan and Another, March 1838

SOCIAL ECONOMY

Table of Schools

[Table contains the following headings: name of townland where held, name and religion of master or mistress, free or pay school, annual income, description and cost of schoolhouse, number of pupils subdivided by religion, sex and the Protestant and Catholic returns, societies with which connected].

Ballinderry, master William English, Established Church; schoolhouse a new house about to be built, for which Lord Hertford has given an acre of land and the Lord Lieutenant's Fund granted 56 pounds; number of pupils by the Protestant return: 17 Established Church, 1 Roman Catholic, 10 males, 8 females; the parish school, to be connected with the Association for Discountenancing Vice, Lord Hertford patron; the incumbent is to contribute towards the payment of the master's salary.

Derry Kiltullagh, master Patrick McVeagh, Established Church; pay school, annual income 10 pounds 10s; schoolhouse a small thatched cabin in sufficient repair; number of pupils by the Protestant return: 24 Established Church, 6 Presbyterians, 1 Roman Catholic, 20 males, 11 females; by the Roman Catholic return: 28 Established Church, 6 Presbyterians, 1 Roman Catholic, 20 males, 15 females; Lord Hertford gave 10 pounds towards the house.

Legaterriff, master William Entwistle, Established Church; pay school, annual income 12 pounds; schoolhouse stone and lime, good repair; number of pupils by the Protestant return: 21 Established Church, 3 Presbyterians, 2 Roman Catholics, 14 males, 12 females; by the Roman Catholic return: 20 Established Church, 3 Presbyterians, 3 Roman Catholics, 12 males, 14 females; schoolhouse built by subscription.

Aughacarnon, master James Kirnahan, Established Church; pay school, annual income 7 pounds 10s; schoolhouse stone and lime, in good repair, cost 25 pounds; number of pupils by the Protestant return: 23 Established Church, 1 Roman Catholic, 12 males, 12 females; by the Roman Catholic return: 23 Established Church, 1 Roman Catholic, 12 males, 12 females; associations none.

Ballyscolly, master John Kane, Roman Catholic; pay school, annual income 30 pounds; schoolhouse a part of a dwelling house; number of pupils by the Protestant return: 39 Established Church, 3 Presbyterians, 3 Roman Catholics, 35 males, 10 females; by the Roman Catholic return: 39 Established Church, 3 Presbyterians, 3 Roman Catholics, 35 males, 10 females; [patrons] William Sefton and Alexander Paterson.

Lurgill, master John Gally, Established Church; pay school, annual income 35 pounds; schoolhouse a room in a private house; number of pupils by the Protestant return: 29 Established Church, 5 Presbyterians, 3 Roman Catholics, 22 males, 15 females; by the Roman Catholic return: 29 Established Church, 5 Presbyterians, 3 Roman Catholics, 22 males, 15 females; associations none.

Magiestown, master Robert Barber, Roman Catholic; pay school, annual income 16 pounds; schoolhouse a room in a p[rivate] house; number of pupils by the Protestant return: 20 Established Church, 10 Roman Catholics, 18 males, 12 females; by the Roman Catholic return: 20 Established Church, 10 Roman Catholics, 18 males, 12 females; associations none.

Lower Ballinderry Moravian school, mistress Mrs Willey, Protestant, Church of the United Brethren; pay school, annual income 160 guineas a year; schoolhouse in the Brethren's house, spacious room; number of pupils by the Protestant return: 5 Established Church, 1 Presbyterian, 3 Protestants of other denominations, 4 Roman Catholics, 4 males, 9 females; by the Roman Catholic return: 5 Established Church, 1 Presbyterian, 3 Protestants of other denominations, 4 Roman Catholics, 4 males, 9 females; associations none.

Portmore, mistress Jane Thompson, Established Church; pay school, annual income 6 pounds; schoolhouse the mistress's own kitchen; number of pupils by the Protestant return: 13 Established Church, 3 Roman Catholics, 10 males, 6 females; by the Roman Catholic return: 13 Established Church, 3 Roman Catholics, 10 males, 6 females; associations none.

Legateriff, master Clements Fitzgerald, Established Church; pay school, annual income 8 pounds; schoolhouse held in a barn; number of pupils by the Protestant return: 16 Established Church, 3 Presbyterians, 1 Roman Catholic, 12 males, 8 females; by the Roman Catholic return: 16 Established Church, 3 Presbyterians, 1 Roman Catholic, 12 males, 8 females; associations none.

Derry Kiltullagh, master John O'Neill, Roman Catholic; pay school, annual income 2 pounds 10s; schoolhouse held in his own kitchen; number of pupils by the Protestant return: 3 Established Church, 5 Presbyterians, 3 Roman Catholics, 6 males, 5 females; by the Roman Catholic return: 1 Established Church, 9 Presbyterians, 1 Roman Catholic, 7 males, 4 females; associations none.

Ballinderry, mistress Anne Bushe, Moravian; free school, Kildare Place Society gave a gratuity last year; the school only held on Wednesday; schoolhouse held in the Brethren's chapel; number of pupils by the Protestant return: 7 Established Church, 6 Protestants of other denominations, 17 Roman Catholics, 30 females; by the Roman Catholic return: 7 Established Church, 6 Protestants of other denominations, 17 Roman Catholics, 30 females; connected with Kildare Place Society, superintended by Mr and Mrs Willey.

School Statistics

[Table contains the following headings: name, situation and description, when established, income and expenditure, physical, intellectual and moral instruction, number of pupils subdivided by age, sex and religion, name and religion of master or mistress, date on which visited].

Ballinderry parish school contiguous to Ballinderry church, stone, slated, stands 1-storey high, 35 and a half by 23 and a half feet, well lighted by 6 square windows, school furniture and requisites all in good order, established 1825; income: 2 pounds from the Revd Savage Hall, 15 pounds from pupils, also the benefit of about 3 roods of arable ground; intellectual instruction: books published by the London Hibernian Society; moral instruction: visited by the vicar and the church catechism taught; number of pupils: males, 26 under 10 years of age, 5 from 10 to 15, 31 total males; females, 13 under 10 years of age, 2 from 10 to 15, 15 total females; total number of pupils 46, 43 Established Church, 3 other denominations; master Samuel Thomson, a Protestant, visited 1st March 1838.

Lower Ballinderry female school, situated in the village of Lower Ballinderry, in a good house built 1827 for the use of a male and female school; the schoolroom is 17 by 15 feet inside and well lit by 3 large oblong windows, school requisites in good repair and lodgings afforded the teacher, established 1833; income from pupils 12 pounds; intellectual instruction: the Bible, Testaments, *Dublin Reading and spelling books* read and procured by the pupils; fancy and plain needlework and knitting is also taught the females; moral instruction: visits from the vicar of the parish and the church catechism taught; number of pupils: males, 6 under 10 years of age, 2 from 10 to 15, 1 above 15, 9 total males; females, 3 under 10 years of age, 4 from 10 to 15, 8 above 15, 15 total females; total number of pupils 24, 20 Established Church, 4 Roman Catholics; mistress Elizabeth Sedgwick, a Protestant, visited 2nd March 1838.

Moygarriff private school, situated on a by-road between the Lurgan road and the Dublin road by Ballinderry, and held in a room 1-storey high and thatched, 16 by 15 feet inside and lit by 2 small windows, established 1837; income from pupils 20 pounds; annual rent paid by the teacher 1 pound; intellectual instruction: books read the Bible, Testaments, *Dublin Reading and spelling books*, all procured by the pupils; moral instruction: visits from the parish priest, all catechisms taught if required; number of pupils: males, 27 under 10 years of age, 8 from 10 to 15, 35 total males; females, 12 under 10 years of age, 3 from 10 to 15, 15 total females; total number of pupils 50, 36 Established Church, 2 Presbyterians, 12 Roman Catholics; master Thomas Turner, a Roman Catholic, visited 3rd March 1838.

Killultagh school, situated on a leading road from Lisburn to Glenavy and held in a good slated house built for the purpose in 1830; it stands 1-storey high and measures 31 and a half by 17 and a half feet inside and lit by 6 oblong windows, all furniture and school requisites in good order, established 1831; income from pupils 15 pounds; intellectual instruction: books read are Testaments, *Dublin Reading and spelling books*; moral instruction: visits from the vicar of the parish and all catechisms taught if required; number of pupils: males, 14 under 10 years of age, 11 from 10 to 15, 25 total males; females, 23 under 10 years of age, 6 from 10 to 15, 29 total females; total number of pupils 54, 27 Established Church, 5 Presbyterians, 15 Roman Catholics, 7 other denominations; master James R. Hendren, a Protestant, visited 6th March 1838.

Lower Ballinderry male school, situated in the village of Lower Ballinderry; the schoolroom is 24 by 17 feet inside and lit by 4 oblong windows, furniture and other school requisites in good order, the house slated and 1-storey high, established 1828, latterly in 1838; income not yet known; the house affords lodging for the teacher, he has also a good garden; intellectual instruction: books published partly by the Kildare Place Society and partly by the London Hibernian Society; moral instruction: visits from the vicar of the parish and the church catechism taught; number of pupils: 6 under 10 years of age, 2 from 10 to 15, 8 total, all males, Established Church; master Joseph G. Wilson, a Protestant, visited 8th March 1838.

Ballymacravin school, situated about 1 and a half miles from the village of Lower Ballinderry, on the leading road to Antrim and held in a good slated house built for the purpose, 1835; it stands 1-storey high and measures 28 and a half feet by 16 feet 9 inches inside, lit by 3 oblong windows in front and 2 oblong windows in the rear, entrance by 1 door, school furniture in good order, established 1837; income from pupils 24 pounds; intellectual instruction: books published by the London Hibernian Society; moral instruction: visits from the vicar of the parish, church and Presbyterian catechism taught; number of pupils: males, 19 under 10 years of age, 11 from 10 to 15, 30 total males; females, 10 under 10 years of age, 3 from 10 to 15, 13 total females; total number of pupils 43, 39 Established Church, 4 Roman Catholics; master John Mulvena, a Presbyterian, visited 10th March 1838.

Legatirriff school, situated on a by-road leading between Killultagh and Lough Neagh, and a thatched house built for the purpose, 1817, by local subscription, cost about 20 pounds; it stands 1-storey high and measures 20 by 14 and a half feet inside, lit by 5 good glass windows, furniture and other school requisites all sufficient, established 1817; income from pupils 10 pounds; intellectual instruction: books published by the London Hibernian Society; moral instruction: visits from the vicar of the parish and the church catechism taught; number of pupils: males, 24 under 10 years of age, 20 from 10 to 15, 1 above 15, 45 total males; females, 10 under 10 years of age, 5 from 10 to 15, 15 total females; total number of pupils 60, 50 Established Church, 5 Presbyterians, 5 Roman Catholics; master William Entwistle, a Protestant, visited 9th March 1838.

Lurgill female school, held in a farmhouse about 1 mile from the village of Lower Ballinderry; the schoolroom is 15 by 12 and a half feet inside and lit by 3 good windows, school requisites in moderate order, established 1837; income from pupils 20 pounds; intellectual instruction: books read the Bible, Testaments and *Dublin Reading and spelling books*, fancy and plain needlework are also taught; moral instruction: visits from the church clergy and the church catechism taught; number of pupils: 9 under 10 years of age, 9 from

Parish of Ballinderry

10 to 15, 6 above 15, 24 total pupils, all female, 22 Established Church, 2 Roman Catholics; mistress Mrs Elizabeth Hope, a Protestant, visited 9th March 1838.

Sunday Schools by Thomas Fagan

[Table contains the following headings: name, situation, when established, superintendent, number of teachers, number of scholars subdivided by religion and sex, books read, hours of attendance, societies with which connected, observations].

Ballinderry parish Sunday school, held in the day schoolhouse, established 1825; superintendent Revd Savage Hall, vicar of the parish; 4 male and 8 female teachers, total 12; number of scholars: 84 Protestants, 6 Roman Catholics, 40 males, 50 females, total 90, 70 exclusively Sunday school scholars; books read: Bible, Testaments and Sunday school spelling books; hours of attendance: open from 3 to 5 p.m. and catechism from 10 to 11.30 a.m; societies with which connected: Sunday School Society for Ireland for books; observations: opened and closed by singing and prayer.

Killultagh Sunday school, held in the day schoolhouse, established 1823; superintendent James R. Hendren; 14 male and 10 female teachers, total 24; number of scholars: 120 Protestants, 55 Presbyterians, 6 Roman Catholics, 97 males, 84 females, total 181, 110 exclusively Sunday school scholars; books read: Bible, Testaments and Sunday school spelling books; hours of attendance: open from 7 to 10 a.m. and 3 to 5 p.m; societies with which connected: Sunday School Society for Ireland for books; observations: opened and closed by singing and prayer.

Legateriff Sunday school, held in the day schoolhouse, established 1823; superintendent Revd Savage Hall, vicar of the parish; 5 male and 5 female teachers, total 10; number of scholars: 90 Protestants, 4 Presbyterians, 6 Roman Catholics, 40 males, 60 females, total 100, 80 exclusively Sunday school scholars; books read: Bible, Testaments and Sunday school spelling books; hours of attendance: open from 3 to 4.30 p.m. summer, none in winter; societies with which connected: Sunday School Society for Ireland for books; observations: opened by prayer, closed by singing and prayer.

These Sunday schools done between 2nd and 10th March 1838, [signed] Thomas Fagan.

Parish of Camlin, County Antrim

Officer's Statistical Report by Lieutenant
R.J. Stotherd, May 1833

NATURAL STATE

Name and Situation

This parish appears to have been known by the name of Camlin from an early period. It was anciently situated in the territory of Killultagh, in the south or Upper Claneboy and county of Down, and now belongs to the manor of Killultagh, barony of Upper Massereene and county of Antrim.

Boundaries, Divisions and Extent

It is bounded on the north by the Crumlin river and parish of Killead, on the east by the parish of Tullyrusk <Tullyrousk>, south by the Glenavy river and parish of Glenavy, and west by Lough Neagh.

It is divided into 10 townlands, namely Aghnadaragh, Ballycessy, Ballydonaghy, Ballygortgarve, Ballymacrevan, Ballyshanaghy, Ballytromery, Ballyvollen, Lanygarve and Gobrana. There appears to be a townland named Ballycamlin in all the published documents of this parish, but it is not specified in the boundary surveyor's sketch map, nor were the boundaries pointed out by the mearsman.

It is of an oblong form, its greatest extent from east to west being about 5 miles, from north to south 2 and a half and contains 5,709 acres 20.4 perches.

NATURAL FEATURES AND PRODUCTIVE ECONOMY

Surface

It forms a part of that extensive level tract of country which extends through the south of the barony of Antrim and the west of Massereene, along the shores of Lough Neagh, until it meets the county of Down. Its surface is even, the highest point being at Donald's Mound, 382 feet above the level of the sea, from which point to about 1 mile westward it is of a tabular form, from which the descent is gradual and regular to the high water mark of the lough at 50 feet above the level of the sea. From Donald's Mound eastward it is very even, with a gradual slope north to the Crumlin and south to the Glenavy rivers.

Soil

The general character of the soil is clay, mixed in some parts with gravel and near the Glenavy river and lough shore with sand, forming on the whole a very productive surface soil. Towards the mouth of the Crumlin river, in the townland of Ballymacrevan particularly, the depositions from the higher grounds have formed, when mixed with the substratum of clay, a soil which amply repays the cultivator's labour <labor>.

Produce

Wheat, barley, oats and potatoes are the principal productions. The heavy clay lands are fallowed, but the potato fallow appears to be preferred as a preparative for grain. Turnips are sometimes grown by the wealthier farmers but in other respects the mode of culture and succession of crops does not differ from that followed in the adjacent parishes.

SOCIAL ECONOMY

Advowson, Tithes and Right of Presentation

The parish of Camlin is included in a union with Glenavy and Tullyrusk. It is not known in what year this union took place, but it is certain that there was no union in the year 1633. It has been referred to the time of the dissolution of the abbeys in the reign of Henry VIII or to that of Queen Elizabeth, in consequence of the small number of Protestants in some parishes at that period. It is a vicarage in the diocese of Connor, the reputed patron being the Marquis of Hertford, to whom the rectorial tithes belong. Camlin is called a grange in the registry of Connor and the church is designated the chapel of Camlin, both in the registry and the regal visitation book.

Proprietor

The Marquis of Hertford is proprietor and lord of the manor. The only perpetuities derived from him are the 4 townlands Ballymacrevan, Ballytromery, Ballygortgarve and Ballyshanaghy, leased to Sir Hercules Langford Baronet by Lord Conway, about the year 1670. They are now the property of the Honourable Colonel Pakenham of Langford Lodge, under whom several individuals hold farms in perpetuity.

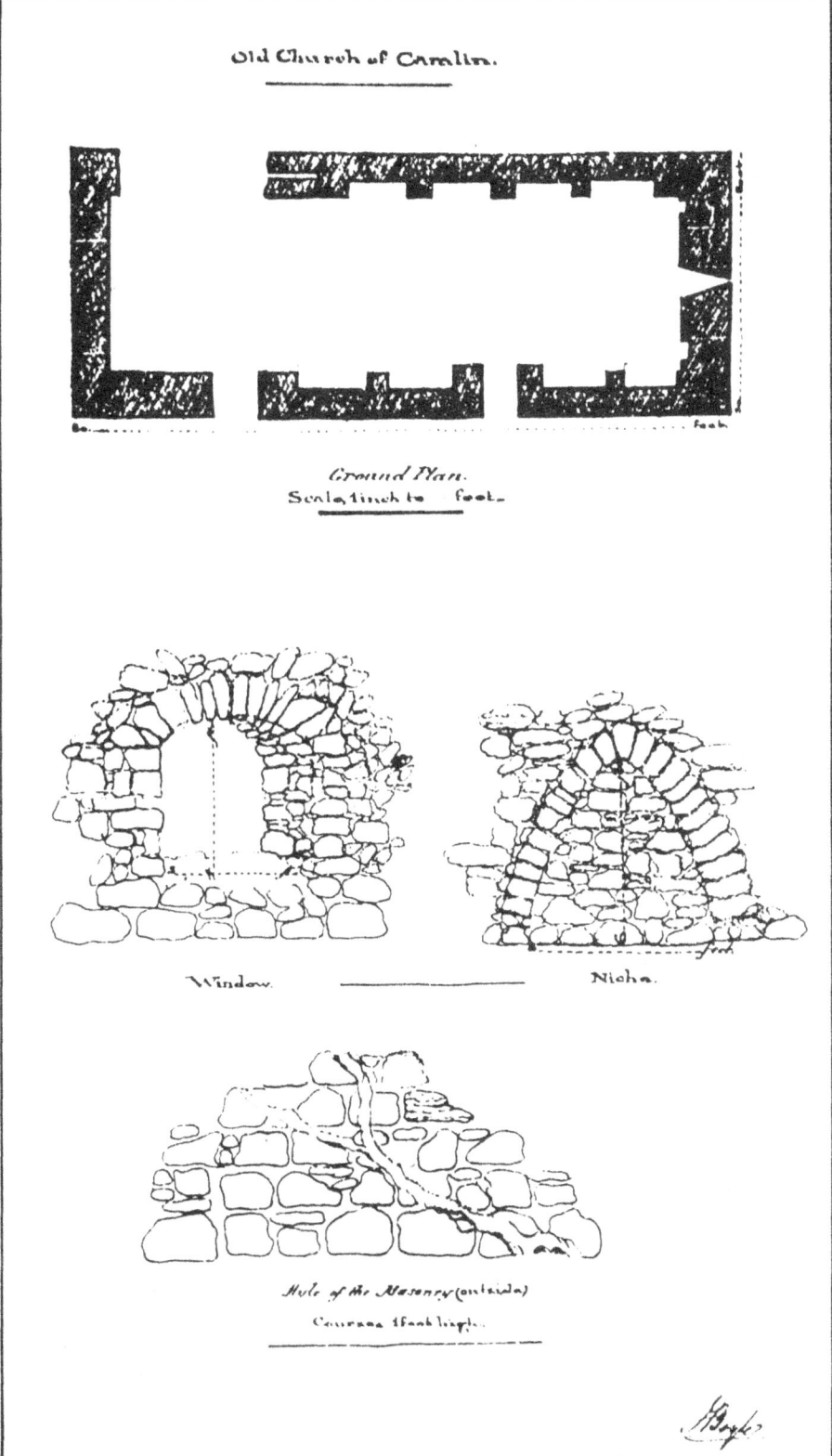

Old church of Camlin

Leases

The farms are generally leased for 21 years and 1 life, or for 3 lives, the actual rent being fined down to two-thirds or three-quarters by paying a certain sum on the lease being taken. This seems an advantageous mode of letting land: it ensures a substantial tenant and enables the landlord to let his lands at a much lower rent than he otherwise would be able to do.

MODERN TOPOGRAPHY

Roads

The parish is well intersected by good roads to Antrim, Belfast, Lisburn and Moira to Dublin. The materials are scarce, being field stones broken with the hammer, or gravel and trap rocks from the beds of the rivers Crumlin and Glenavy. A good road on the lough shore appears desirable, being easy of construction and the material at hand. The principal roads are made and repaired at the expense of the county, the by-roads by the court leet of the manor.

NATURAL FEATURES

Rivers

The Crumlin and Glenavy rivers, which bound the parish, are of little importance but as mill-streams. They abound in trout, eels, bream, pike and perch.

Woods and Plantations

[Insert marginal note: See *Statistical account of Glenavy, Camlin and Tullyrusk* by the Reverend Edward Cupples]. There is no doubt but that at an early period the whole of this country was covered with wood. Boate, in his *Natural history of Ireland*, says that "there were great forests in his time in the county of Antrim, especially in Killultagh." From the time of James I to within the last 70 years considerable vestiges of them still remained, and 1,400 acres in the neighbouring parish of Glenavy, covered with forest trees on the banks of Lough Neagh, were held as a park by the Lords Conway.

This park was stored with deer, pheasants, hares and a variety of game. About 50 years since, a considerable portion of it was leased to tenants and cleared of wood. The remainder, under the name of the Hogg or Little Deer Park, continued to be appropriated to the same purpose till about 32 years since, when it was also given up to cultivation and leased to tenants.

In the parish of Camlin the only plantation of grown wood of any magnitude is at Cherry Valley, in the townland of Ballymacrevan [insert addition: on the shore of Lough Neagh]. There is also a good deal of young planting in hedgerows in the same townland and on the lough shore, also at Thistleborough in the townland of Ballyshanaghy, at Gobrana and on the banks of the 2 rivers, Crumlin and Glenavy.

Lough Neagh

For particulars relative to Lough Neagh, its pebbles and petrifaction, see *Statistical account* by the Reverend Edward Cupples, and *Statistical survey of the county Antrim* by Reverend John Dubourdieu.

Rocks

Trap is the only rock found in the parish. It is not quarried for any useful purpose, being in the bed of the 2 rivers and difficult of access.

MODERN TOPOGRAPHY

Town of Crumlin

Crumlin is a neat, regular-built and improving little town. About 70 years since it consisted of only 2 houses, a public house and a smith's forge. It is a post town and has a monthly market, held on the first Monday in every month.

Schools

In the town of Crumlin is a good classical boarding school kept by the Reverend Mr Alexander, the Presbyterian minister.

Adjacent to the town is a parish school, supported principally by the Honourable Colonel Pakenham of Langford Lodge, and the Kildare Street Society. The former gives 50 pounds per annum, the society 18 pounds, namely 10 pounds to the male and 8 pounds to the female school. On the 1st December 1832 there were 61 males and 62 females, between 30 and 40 of whom are Roman Catholics <Catholicks>. The parents of the children also pay, according to their means, from 1s to 3s per quarter. The schoolhouse is a very neat building.

There are also 3 small schoolhouses in the parish: 1 in Aghnadaragh, on the roadside; 1 in the townland of Ballycessy, on the Camlin side of the Glenavy river; and 1 at Donald's Mound, in the townland of Ballydonaghy.

Gentlemen's Seats

Cherry Valley, the residence of John Armstrong

Parish of Camlin

Esquire, Thistleborough, that of Stafford Whittle Esquire, are the principal houses in the parish. There are several other very respectable places within its limits, including Gobrana and the rectory. The farmhouses in general are very comfortable and of a superior class to those met with in the north.

Churches

The church of Camlin is a venerable ruin overgrown with ivy, situated about half a mile north east of the town of Crumlin, on the banks of the river. The duty is now performed at the parish church of Glenavy. In the town is also a meeting house for Protestant Dissenters, of which the Reverend Mr Alexander is minister.

Markets

The principal markets for the sale of grain are Belfast, Lisburn, Lurgan and Antrim.

NATURAL FEATURES

Waterfalls

On the Glenavy river there is a very pretty waterfall of about 40 feet, over trap rocks, to which the surrounding trees add beauty and variety. There is also a waterfall on the Crumlin river under Glendarragh but it is much more broken, and it is necessary, to see either in perfection, to await a flood.

MEMOIR WRITING

Memoir Writing

Memo: For more ample details, see *Statistical account of the union*, by the Reverend Edward Cupples. See also a list of townlands, with their derivations, at the end of the same work. [Signed] R.J. Stotherd, Lieutenant Royal Engineers, 17th May 1833.

Memoir by James Boyle, [1837 ?]

NATURAL FEATURES

Hills

This parish includes the extremity of one of the features extending westward from Divis mountain, terminating at the shore of Lough Neagh, and being included between the 2 streams forming the northern and southern boundaries of the parish. This feature also forms a portion of the vast tract of flat country extending along the eastern shore of Lough Neagh, from the southern side of the barony of Upper Antrim to the southern side of the county where it meets that of Down.

This parish presents little variety in its surface. Its highest point, Donald's Mound, 382 feet above the sea, is near its eastern side. For a mile westward from this the country is flat but then begins to fall gently towards the lake, presenting, except near the shore where there is a trifling bank, one almost unbroken and unvaried slope. There is a gentle and trifling slope northward and southward, terminating in the banks along the Crumlin and Glenavy rivers, those along the former being for some distance lofty and almost precipitous.

The principal points are Scotstown, 382 feet, Donald's Mound, 382 feet, Oaks, 335 feet and Gobrana, 308 feet above the level of the sea.

Lakes

The western side of this parish forms the eastern side of that part of the coast of Lough Neagh called Sandy bay, the northern side of the bay, which is somewhat of a horseshoe form, being formed by the southern coast of Killead and its southern side being formed by the coast of Glenavy parish. There are 708 acres 1 rood 4 perches of the surface of Lough Neagh included within the limits of this parish and 1 and a quarter miles of its coast are formed by its western side.

Its shore is low and shingly and along them are several small quays constructed of stones piled without mortar, forming a breakwater and a small basin capable at one time of admitting vessels drawing 6 feet water. These have for many years fallen into disuse and are now ruinous and partly filled with sand. The extreme depth of the lake in this parish is more than 20 feet. It is shallow along the shore. It rises in winter, generally to a height of 5 and a half or 6 feet above its summer level, but does not encroach on any cultivated ground in this parish.

The waters of Lough Neagh possess a strong petrifying power, enormous lumps of partially and perfectly petrified wood being found along its shores, and in the ground at a considerable distance from them where they are low. The descriptions of wood thus found are either oak, ash or holly. The last is celebrated for making the best stones. The pebbles along it are beautiful and many of them valuable, some of chalcedony, beautifully varied, others white or opaque, and inferior to the diamond only in hardness.

The scenery along the shore of this parish is of the most cheerful and interesting description, the views from it being wide and beautiful and terminated by lofty ranges of mountains. When viewed from a distance, the shores of this parish have a very beautiful effect: their broad and gentle slopes, in the highest state of cultivation, studded with numerous snug residences and clusters of trees and traversed by bushy hedgerows which, almost covering each other, give it all the appearance of a thickly wooded country.

Crumlin River

There are 2 inconsiderable streams, the Crumlin and Glenavy rivers, which form the northern and southern boundaries of this parish.

The Crumlin river takes its rise in the western side of Divis mountain in the more easterly parish of Shankill, at an elevation of about 1,058 feet above the sea and 1,010 above Lough Neagh. From this it pursues a westerly course for 1 mile and, descending to a level of 323 feet above the sea, enters on the northern boundary of this parish, along which it flows in a circuitous and westerly direction for 4 miles (separating it from the more northern parish of Killead) and discharges itself into Lough Neagh at the north west corner of the parish. It also forms the northern boundary of the barony of Upper and the southern of Lower Massereene.

Towards the east of the parish its bed is soft and clayey and its banks low, but in the neighbourhood of Crumlin it flows through a deep and narrow ravine, the banks rising abruptly on either side to an elevation of upwards of 100 feet above its bed, which is of trap rock, broken and irregular, and during heavy rains producing a succession of waterfalls. Its banks decline in height towards its mouth and its bed becomes gravelly. Its average breadth is 28 feet and its depth very variable, being affected by the seasons, the irregularity of its course and a high carry built across it about half a mile east of Crumlin for the purpose of turning water to the mills. Its average fall is 1 foot in 65 feet but its inclination is very variable, except for the last mile and [a] half of its course. It is subject to very sudden floods which, from the dry nature of the neighbouring country, very quickly subside and commit no injury. Its situation for machinery is valuable but it does not afford a sufficient supply of water power for more than 7 months in the year, owing to the causes before mentioned. It is applicable to drainage and irrigation.

In the neighbourhood of Crumlin the scenery along it is romantic, its steep and lofty banks being thickly wooded and forming a deep and narrow dell, and the course of the river below being interrupted and varied by a succession of little waterfalls. This glen is well known by the name of Glendarragh and is much frequented in summer by parties of pleasure from the neighbourhood.

Glenavy River

The Glenavy river is a small stream which takes its rise in the south western side of Divis mountain in the parish of Derryaghy, and at an elevation of about 950 feet above the sea. From this it pursues an irregular and north western course between the parishes of Tullyrusk and Glenavy, and, descending to a level of 302 feet above the sea, enters on the southern boundary of this parish, along which it flows westerly for 4 and a half miles, separating it from that of Glenavy; and, after flowing through the village of that name, it discharges itself into Lough Neagh at Sandy bay, after a total course of 9 and a half miles.

Its average breadth is 18 feet and its depth varies from 1 to 6 feet. Its banks are in many parts composed of clayey cliffs, on which it is encroaching. In some places they are high and steep, and in general sufficient to confine it in its frequent but harmless floods which rise and subside very rapidly. Its bed is chiefly composed of small gravel but in the townland of Ballyvollen, 1 mile from its mouth, its course is interrupted by a ledge of trap rocks, which produce a very fine waterfall of about 40 feet, the beauty of which is greatly enhanced by the steepness of its banks which are here wooded. Its average fall is 1 foot in 78 feet. It is very usefully situated for the purposes of machinery and is applicable to irrigation and drainage.

Springs

Pumps are very numerous in this parish as spring water is otherwise very scarce. Water is usually found at depths of from 11 to 25 feet, being deeper towards the lake, except immediately at the shore. From the flatness of its surface, the parish is but badly supplied with water from rivulets or streams, particularly along its western side.

Bogs and Woods

There is no bog in this parish.

There is every indication of this parish having at one time been well wooded, and the tradition of the country is that it at one time was covered with oaks. The quantities of petrified wood found, some of very large dimensions, and the young oak saplings growing in the old hedgerows tend to

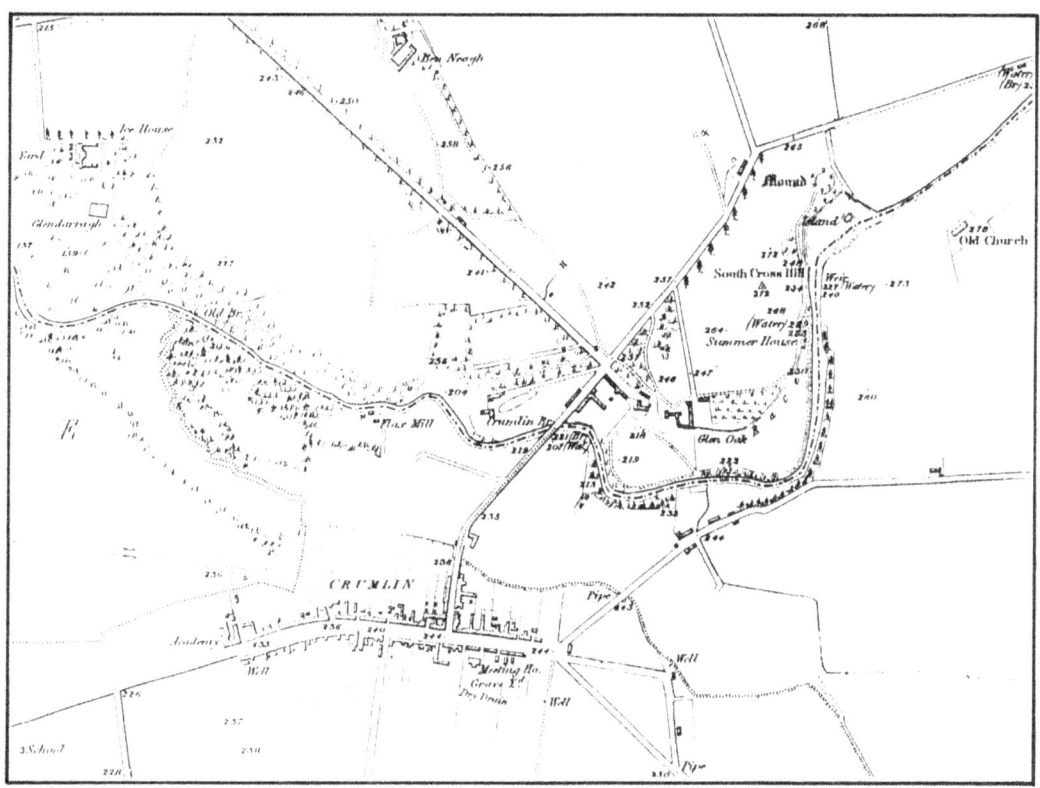

Map of Crumlin from the first 6" O.S. maps, 1830s

corroborate this. Holly and cherry also seem indigenous to the soil. The sallow, though not natural, grows here to a great size. At Cherry Valley are a few old oaks, evidently the remains of the natural woods. It is within memory of some old people since there [were] more evident vestiges of natural wood, and Boate, in his *Natural history of Ireland*, says, "There were in his time great forests in the county Antrim, particularly in Kilultagh" (the manor in which this parish is included).

Climate

The air is pure and dry, though, from its flat surface and exposure to Lough Neagh and the prevailing south west wind, it is not very mild. The high and thick hedgerows afford considerable shelter to the country. The seasons are about 1 week later than in Glenavy. Harvest generally commences in Ballinderry, next in Glenavy and then in this parish.

MODERN TOPOGRAPHY

Towns: Crumlin

The little market and post town of Crumlin is pleasantly situated on the left bank of the Crumlin water and on the main road from Antrim to Dublin, 2 and a half miles east of Lough Neagh, 113 miles north of Dublin, 14 miles west of Belfast and 7 miles south of Antrim. It is situated at the northern side of the parish of Camlin, in the barony of Lower Massereene, manor of Killultagh, diocese of Connor and north east circuit of assize. It consists of a main street 54 feet wide, extending for a third of a mile from east to west. From the northern side of this a lesser street extends for a short distance along the road to Antrim. In the town itself there is nothing interesting, nor does it tend to ornament or improve the landscape. Its situation is very cheerful and healthy, being situated on the summit of a bank which slopes gently from east to west, and in the middle of a rich and highly cultivated country, varied and ornamented by clusters of planting around the comfortable houses of the farmers.

The origin of Crumlin is of modern date and has been caused by the erection of the very extensive, well-known flour and corn mills of the Messrs MacAulay in 1765, at which period Crumlin consisted solely of a public house and a smith's forge. The mills alluded to are situated on the opposite bank of the Crumlin water, and in the parish of Killead, but they are said to have been the nucleus which caused the origin of the town. It must have sprung up very rapidly, as it has not increased during the last 20 years.

Crumlin, as has been before stated, consists of a main and a lesser street, containing 138 houses, 11 of which are on the Killead side of the river. Of these, 41 are 2-storeys and 97 1-storey high, all built of stone and lime, roughcast and neatly whitened. Nearly all the 1-storey cottages are thatched. The others are slated. The streets are of a good width and kept pretty clean and the houses, though nearly all of an inferior description, have, from a liberal use of lime, a cheerful and cleanly appearance.

The people are almost all of the humbler class. The 2-storey houses are occupied by persons in business as dealers and the cottages chiefly by a few mechanics and those employed at the mills, which afford employment to a great many labourers and carriers; and, except the labourers, mostly all hold some land in addition to their other business. The people are very quiet and industrious, and generally comfortable in their stations.

Public Buildings

The public buildings in Crumlin consist of a Presbyterian meeting house, a court house and a bridge.

The meeting house is situated on the south side of the town. The former house, near which it stands, was erected in 1723. It presents a plain but substantial appearance. It measures 58 feet long and 24 feet wide. It contains a gallery and would accommodate 800 persons. The expense of erecting it will amount to 1,000 pounds, to be defrayed by subscription.

The court house is situated near the centre of the town. It is a neat, little 2-storey building, erected in January 1832 at an expense of 190 pounds, defrayed by the county. The understorey is suitably fitted up as a court house for holding petty sessions. The upper storey is fitted up as [a] police barracks and contains accommodation for 4 men.

The bridge over the Crumlin river is a plain old structure, consisting of 5 circular-segment arches and measuring 114 feet long and 23 feet wide. It is a skew bridge. It was erected by the county about the year 1780, previous to which time there was only a wooden footway of planks, with a handrail, across the river at this point.

There is an inn in Crumlin at which post cars and horses may be had for hire. Petty sessions are held in the court house in Crumlin on every alternate Tuesday. There are usually at least 2 magistrates in attendance.

PRODUCTIVE AND SOCIAL ECONOMY

Markets and Commodities

A market is held in Crumlin on the first Monday in each month. A considerable number of pigs, cows and some sheep, pedlar's goods, yarn and crockery ware are the commodities principally exposed for sale. No tolls or customs are levied at these markets. These markets are improving. A horse fair was attempted to be established in this town but without success. It was held for 3 successive months but then given up.

Belfast is the mart from which the dealers procure their commodities and to which the people take their farm and other produce for sale. It is 14 miles distant and the carriage of goods cost 5d per cwt. [Insert footnote: The carmen who draw for the flour mills receive only 3d per cwt but they are almost constantly employed]. It is from thence that timber, coals, iron and slates are procured.

Crumlin is well supplied with shops of different descriptions and also with milk, butter and fruit. Fish is brought in abundance from Lough Neagh. There is but little butcher's meat consumed here. Building stones are easily procured and lime, which is brought from Shankill, 9 miles distant, costs when laid down 1s 1d per barrel. Ground around the town lets for grazing at from 3 pounds to 3 pounds 10s per acre. The town is well supplied with water from a public pump at the end of the town.

Dispensary and School

A dispensary, supported partly by local subscription and partly by the county grand jury, was established here in 1832 and has been useful in its effects.

There is an academy for both boarders and day scholars kept here by the Reverend Nathaniel Alexander, the Presbyterian clergyman, who established it here in 1801. It is a respectable school and formerly bore a high character and was well supported.

General Remarks

Crumlin is not increasing nor has not lately increased in size, no new house having for a long time been built in it. The people are thriving and industrious, peaceable and well conducted.

Modern Topography

Gentlemen's Seats

Cherry Valley, the residence of Charles Armstrong Esquire, J.P., agent to the Honorable Colonel Pakenham, is a modern and gentleman-like 2-storey house, pleasantly situated in the townland of Ballymacrevan near the shore of Lough Neagh, and 1 and one-eighth miles west of Crumlin. It commands a tolerable [crossed out: beautiful] view of Lough Neagh and its distant shores. There is a good deal of planting and some old oaks (apparently natural timber) about the house.

Thistleborough, the residence of Stafford Whittle Esquire, is a good 2-storey house, prettily situated a little to the south of Cherry Valley and in the townland of Ardoragarragh near the shore of Lough Neagh, and 1 and a half miles west of Crumlin. There is some thriving planting about the house.

The Glebe, the residence of [blank] Charters Esquire, is agreeably situated on a gentle eminence at the south of the parish and near the village of Glenavy. The house is modern, 2-storey and commodious and was [built ?] by [blank].

Mills

The machinery of the parish consists of 1 corn and 2 flax mills. The corn mill is situated in the townland of Ballygortgarve, on the Crumlin water. It is propelled by a breast water wheel 16 feet in diameter and 3 feet 6 inches broad; fall of water is 3 feet. There is sufficient water for only 7 months in the year.

The flax mill in the same townland is propelled by a breast water wheel 14 feet in diameter and 3 feet 6 inches broad, with a fall of water of 5 feet. The supply of water is sufficient during but 5 months in the year.

The flax mill in the townland of Ballytromery is propelled by a breast water wheel 12 feet in diameter and 1 foot 6 inches broad. The supply of water is sufficient during only 7 months in the year.

Communications

This parish is amply provided with the means of intercourse with the neighbouring towns and districts. Generally speaking, the roads are well laid out and kept in good repair. The materials used in their repair are broken stone, procured either from field stones or from the trap rocks in the beds of the rivers, or from the quarries of that rock. The main roads and most of the by-roads are kept in repair by the county and some of the by-roads by the manor.

The main roads are the road from Antrim to Banbridge through Crumlin and Glenavy, which intersects the centre of the parish. There are 2 and a third miles of it in this parish. Its average breadth is 23 feet. It is level and well laid out, and in pretty good repair.

The road from Antrim to Lurgan through Crum[lin] traverses the parish for 2 and a half miles, parallel to and a little to the west of the former; its average breadth is 23 feet. Except at its northern end it is quite straight and level. It is in tolerable repair.

The road from Glenavy to Belfast passes through the eastern side of the parish for 3 and a quarter miles. It is a pretty well laid out and good road, average 21 feet broad.

There are 2 roads leading from the Crumlin and Glenavy road to the lake. That along the northern side of the parish is good, well laid and, except at its eastern end, level. The second, along the south west side of the parish, is not in good order and there is 1 very steep hill on it.

There is a good level road passing for 2 and three-quarter miles along the north side of the parish, between the town of Crumlin and the village of Dundrod. The average breadth of these roads is 20 feet.

Bridges

There are 8 bridges in this parish, 5 of which are over the Crumlin and 3 over the Glenavy rivers. The principal of these are that at Crumlin, which is a skew bridge, consisting of 5 circular-segment arches and measuring 23 feet wide and 114 feet long; and the bridge in the village of Glenavy, consisting of 3 semicircular arches and measuring 24 feet wide and 80 feet long. These are, like the others, plain old structures, suitable in every respect but not worthy of further notice.

Scenery

In all the districts of this parish its appearance and scenery are pleasing, possessing all the beauty with which a rich and highly cultivated country, interspersed with neat farmhouses peeping out from among clusters of shady trees, its smooth slopes traversed with bushy hedges, the lanes and roads mostly sheltered by rows of trees, which, with its numerous orchards, give it from a distance the appearance of a thickly wooded country, more resembling a rich English than an Irish district.

Social Economy

Inhabitants

The inhabitants of this parish are chiefly, indeed almost all, the descendants of the settlers who came over in the reign of Elizabeth under the families of Langford, Seymour (Lords Conway) and Rawdon, but chiefly under the Seymour or Conways, the ancestors of the present Marquis of Hertford, the largest landed proprietor in the county. The people are partly of English and partly of Scottish extraction, the latter being principally found along the northern side of the parish, which may be termed as the link of connection between the 2 races, those to the south being almost exclusively English and those to the north of the county of Scottish descent. Among the names commonly met with in this parish are those of Ferris, Campbell, Bell, Palmer, Whitla, Whittle, Finton and McGrady (the last 2 are Roman Catholics).

Early Improvements

The colonisation of the county by a peaceful and industrious people may be regarded as one of the principal, if not the earliest, cause of its improvement. It is said that previous to this period this parish was one vast forest, and this, from several circumstances (such as the prevalence of natural underwood), is not improbable. The other succeeding causes were the establishment and toleration of religion and the diffusion of knowledge, the opening of roads and the establishment of markets in the neighbourhood. The erection of the very extensive flour and corn mills in the vicinity of Crumlin in 1765 gave encouragement for the growth of grain, and the Corn Law of 1788, which, when grain fell below a certain price in this country, granted a bounty on it if exported here, tended to confirm it in being an exclusively agricultural district, little else than wheat, oats and potatoes being raised in it. The prices to which grain rose during the wars succeeding this period still further encouraged the cultivation of the ground and there is at present but little, if any, waste ground in it.

Progress of Improvement

The soil is naturally stiff and not so fertile as the aspect of the country would lead the traveller to suppose, but the industry of the people and the expense they have been at in bringing lime from a considerable distance for it has made up the deficiency, and there are few parishes which present a more interesting appearance of fertility, industry and substance, it being by no means inferior to the generality of English rural districts.

The leases are generally for 3 lives and 31 years, few being perpetuities, and the lands are reasonably let. A considerable number of the working class are employed about the extensive mills of the Messrs Macaulay and the remainder are not more numerous than is necessary for the cultivation of the ground. The facility of procuring instruction at the schools in the parish, some of which are of a most excellent description, and the exertion, influence and example of the Honourable Colonel Pakenham, who possesses a portion of this parish, and his being almost constantly resident in the adjoining one of Killead, have been the means of much improvement in the people.

It should have been stated that the people along the western side of the parish are much the most independent, have the largest farms and the best houses but here they would seem to be almost exclusively English in their extraction, from their taste for gardens and orchards, there being scarce a house that has not an orchard attached, and these are in general very profitable. A good orchard of an acre, producing an average crop, will on an average let for 13 pounds for the season. Persons called "apple men" take the orchard and draw off the apples to Belfast, where they sell them to persons who export them to England and Scotland, and formerly this country was remarkable for the quantity of fruit exported from it.

Obstructions to Improvement

Some say the tenures or leases granted by the Marquis of Hertford (3 lives) is so uncertain as to discourage improvement. This is not the case, as the tenants have every confidence in their renewal, and such, unless where the arrears are not paid up, is always the case.

The Presbyterian minister is an old man and there is only 1 Protestant curate (the rector being non-resident) for the union, comprising an extent of 27 and a half square miles. [Crossed out: This is too much for 1 person and in the more remote districts the Protestants are much neglected].

Local Government

There is 1 magistrate (local), Charles Armstrong of Cherry Valley, Esquire, whose residence is conveniently situated 1 and a third miles west of Crumlin. He possesses the confidence and respect of the people. Petty sessions are held in Crumlin on every second Tuesday. 2 magistrates (the

Parish of Camlin

Honorable Colonel Pakenham and Mr Armstrong) form the bench. The causes tried are of a very trivial description, being merely a few petty assaults and disputes about wages and trespass.

This parish is included in the manor of Lisburn, the courts being held in the town of that name. The manor courts are held once in 3 weeks and courts leet twice a year. Sums not exceeding 20 pounds are recoverable by civil bill process and sums of 100 pounds are recoverable by attachment. Outrage is almost unknown here, as is also illicit distillation.

Insurance

There are some insurances of property but few, if any, life insurances. The Messrs Macaulay have their mills in this parish insured at the Shamrock Insurance office for about 3,000 pounds, and those in the adjoining parish for about 19,000 pounds. Though these mills have been established since 1765, no loss has ever been sustained at them by fire.

Dispensary

A dispensary was established here in 1832 and has been very beneficial in affording immediate relief in cases of emergency, accidents, and also the facility of procuring vaccination, but in a parish where the people are comparatively free from disease, its effects have not been so perceptible. There is occasionally, in winter, a little fever along the lake and among the poorer class but there is no complaint to which they are particularly subject. No statement of the numbers of cases or of each case is preserved. For further particulars, see Table of Benevolence.

Schools

From their description and the manner in which some of the schools in this parish, particularly that in the townland of Ballytromery, are conducted, they are calculated to do a great deal of good in this parish. The people are desirous of having their children instructed in reading, writing and arithmetic, and a few of them are learning mensuration, book-keeping and geography, but a great drawback to their being permanently educated is the early age at which they are generally taken from school. The girls are now getting into the business of flowering muslin and, as they can earn a little at this at the age of 13, they are by that time taken from school and employed at it at home.

There is a taste for education among the people and there is at present, in the townland of Ballytromery, a book club consisting of 100 volumes of historical and useful works, which was got up in 1833. There are 16 subscribers who pay 7s 6d entrance and 6d per month. It may be worthy of remark that the children in most of the schools in this parish appear unusually neat and cleanly in their persons.

Poor

The active poor in this parish are but few. The collections at the places of worship on Sundays and the voluntary charity of the people is adequate to their support. The circumstance of an aged parent being deserted by his children is unknown, and objects of compassion are never disregarded.

Religion

This parish is episcopally united to those of Glenavy and Tullyrusk, and constitute a vicarage, of which the Reverend Edward Cupples, the vicar-general of the diocese, whose resides at Lisburn, is the vicar. The name of this parish is but little known by the people, the union being generally, indeed almost only, known by that of Glenavy. The vicarial tithes amount to 380 pounds per annum and the lay tithes (payable to the Marquis of Hertford) to 101 pounds, being altogether about 8d per acre. The vicar keeps only 1 curate, who resides in this parish and to whom he pays a salary of 75 pounds per annum. A second curate is much required as the union includes an area of 27 and a half square miles [crossed out: and in some districts the people are pretty neglected].

There is but one Presbyterian congregation in the parish and it is in connection with the Remonstrant Synod. The minister, the Reverend Nathaniel Alexander, receives 100 pounds regium donum and 30 pounds stipend.

In the Roman Catholic Church, this parish is united to that of Killead, the priest of which is supported by his flock in the usual variety of ways.

By the revised census of 1834 there are in this parish 1,124 Episcopalians, 631 Roman Catholics, 590 Presbyterians and Protestant Dissenters.

Habits of the People

There is but little difference between the habits of the people in this parish and those in the adjoining one of Killead. Like it, it is exclusively an agricultural district, no flax being sown except what is required to give occupation to the females in spinning. The people are, however, less wealthy than those in Killead, the farms being generally from 30 to 40 acres. There are a few of from 80 to 120 [acres], but there are few leases in perpetuity and there is a greater equality as to circumstances. All hold more or less land, except those employed at the extensive mills of the Messrs Macaulay and the agricultural labourers who are scarcely numerous enough to cultivate the ground. All classes therefore are employed and all may be said to be comfortable in their stations.

The system of subletting does not exist here, and instead of dividing his farm among his children, the farmer almost always leaves it to one, chargeable with a certain sum for each of the rest, and this circumstance tends also to promote emigration.

Houses

Their houses, though generally sufficiently roomy, comfortable and cleanly, are not so much so as those in Killead, there being few 2-storey houses. Lime being less used in roughcasting or whitening, and there not being the same attention to neatness, they do not bear the same appearance of substance or wealth but, like them, they are almost hidden in clusters of shady trees and these, with the bushy hedgerows of sallow and hawthorn, give the parish all the appearance of a thickly wooded country. But, excepting Killead, they are scarcely inferior in most respects to any other district in the county.

Food

The better farmers consume a good deal of bacon and hung beef, fish from Lough Neagh, baker's bread, meal and potatoes, the lower class but little animal food, potatoes being their chief food. Fish from Lough Neagh, such as perch, pullen and trout, are abundant and cheap in summer, and are quite within the reach of the people. Less meal and more baker's bread is now consumed than formerly. Milk is not abundant, owing to the quantity of grain sown and the little pasture in the parish. Tea, from its reduced price, is now pretty generally used. The want of fuel is a great privation which the lower class suffer, as, from its being 7 miles distant, a horse can draw but one load in a day.

Dress

They dress very well and comfortably, and this, particularly as respects the females, is to be wondered at, as formerly when yarn was more profitable the women generally clothed themselves from the profits of their spinning. Now it yields little or nothing and they work more generally in the fields, particularly during the harvest. Of late they have got into the habit of flowering muslin, which gives them employment and is a little more profitable. Calicos, however, have fallen in price and their apparel (second-hand) is now sold in the markets and fairs at a very low rate. The latter is mostly exported from England to this country. The females all wear bonnets and shawls and most of them gloves. Breeches are but little worn except by the old men. A dark blue coat, blue drab or corduroy trousers <trowsers>, a beaver hat and coloured waistcoat is the usual dress of the men. An umbrella is an indispensable appendage to the equipment of both sexes. Watches are numerous and a clock is to be found in almost every house.

Marriage and Longevity

They are rather long-lived than otherwise and marry rather earlier than usual. 5 is the usual number in a family.

Amusements

Their amusements consist of dancing, attending the summer fairs, a little cock-fighting and on Easter Monday all classes join in the play of "thread-the-needle", which consists in a number of persons of all ages and sexes taking hands and forming a line, the person at the head runs under the hands of a couple further down the line, then again under another, and so on, the entire line holding together and following, and this they keep up along the road from Crumlin to Glendarvagh. Formerly they used to call at Mr Macaulay's of Glenoak and at Glendarragh, where they used to receive some money but this practice has been given up.

Cock-fighting and "pitch-and-toss" are kept up during the morning of Easter Monday. A play termed the "battle of Aughrim" used sometimes to be performed by the Orangemen in a barn or public house and the receipts devoted to some charitable purpose, but this has been given up latterly. This play is in print and represents some of the incidents attendant on King William's visit to Ireland. But their taste for amusement has rather declined of late years, partly from money being less plenty and partly from their habits having become more settled and steady. They are fond of music, and drums, fifes and violins are their favourite instruments. [Crossed out: There a great many Orangemen in the parish and there used to be some party riots in the fairs in Glenavy, but these have latterly been given up].

Parish of Camlin

Character

All classes are charitable and humane, honest, peaceable, industrious and obliging but they are not a sober race, being much prone to whiskey drinking. Neither are they a very moral race, as marriage is rather a subsequent proceeding and there are too many loose characters in the neighbourhood.

Emigration and Migration

Emigration has not decreased in the same proportion in this as in most of [the] parishes. There certainly is not the same spirit for it as previous to the last 3 or 4 years but still, from 15 to 20 annually emigrate to Canada and few ever return. The prevalence of emigration from this parish is probably owing to the circumstance of a farmer's generally leaving his farm to his eldest son, who is charged with a certain portion to each of the other children. The other sons, having got a little capital, usually emigrate; or perhaps the son to whom the farm is left, finding the encumbrances on it too heavy, gives it over to the next, receiving a portion of money instead, and then emigrates.

Perhaps an individual or two may annually go to the Scottish harvests, but there is rather a scarcity of hands here during the harvest and labourers sometimes come here from the opposite shores of Tyrone and Derry.

There are not any remarkable events upon record.

Crumlin: Table of Trades and Occupations

Apothecary and surgeon 1, baker 1, butcher 1, clergyman 1, copper and tinsmith 1, constabulary 4, carpenters 2, grocery and spirit shops 3, grocery and hardware shop 1, houses of entertainment 3, innkeeper and leather cutter 1, milliners 2, mantua makers 3, nailer 1, painter and glazier 1, tailors 6, physician and surgeon 1, reed maker 1, spirit sellers 9, saddlers 2, shoemakers 7, smith 1, watchmaker 1, weaver 1, and cooper 1, [total] 56.

ANCIENT TOPOGRAPHY

Drawings

Interior of the old church of Camlin showing gravestones.

Old church of Camlin, ground plan, main dimensions 80 by 30 feet, scale 1 inch to [blank] feet.

Window, 4 feet high; niche 9 feet high by 8 feet broad.

Style of the masonry (outside), courses 1 foot high.

Draft ground plan of old church with dimensions.

Draft drawings of old church, showing detail of window with dimensions, windows 6 feet high, 13 feet from the top, gable 24 feet high; gable in which window situated; another view of church.

Glendarragh, view of old mill and stream, 24th August 1837.

Rough drawings of 5 circular objects, with list of dimensions.

Draft ground plans and section drawings of 19 forts: 5 in Ballydonaghy, 5 in Ballyshanaghill, 7 in Ballyvollen, 1 in Ballymacrevan, 1 in Aghnadarragh.

Draft ground plans and section drawings of 10 forts, 2 described as near Crumlin.

Draft Memoir by T.C. Hannyngton, G. Scott and Another

NATURAL FEATURES

Coast

Along the shores of this parish the remains of several old quays still exist. They are formed of large stones built without mortar and consist of a breakwater and small basin. They would admit a vessel of 6 feet draft of water. Formerly vessels traded regularly to these harbours, bringing corn and turf from the Tyrone and Derry side of the lough, and merchants were always in attendance. These quays cost about 300 pounds in building. They are now only used by fishing boats and are falling to decay and rapidly filling up with sand. Along the shores beautiful pebbles are found and sometimes in the fields at a considerable distance from the shores when they happen to be very flat. [Insert marginal note: Give specimens of petrified wood]. Very fine specimens of petrified wood are also found, some of enormous dimensions. One at Langford Lodge, a log of petrified oak, is 6 feet long and 4 feet in diameter. The knots and grain of the oak are still visible. They are by no means rare and are often found partially petrified, with portions of stone and wood mixed.

Lakes

Lough Neagh forms the western boundary of this parish. The shores within its limits are flat with stony beaches.

Bogs

There is no bog in this parish. Consequently the people are badly off for fuel. They draw it from the parish of Aghagallon but, as a horse cannot make more than 2 journeys in a day, they find it expensive.

Woods

At Cherry Valley, the residence of Charles Armstrong Esquire, there are a few old oaks, evidently the remains of the old natural woods which at one time covered this country. Although there are no extensive tracts of wood in this parish still, from a distance, it has the appearance of a well-wooded district, in consequence of the numerous hedgerows which, from a distance, so cover each other as to give the appearance of wood.

MODERN TOPOGRAPHY AND SOCIAL AND PRODUCTIVE ECONOMY

Crumlin

This town consists of 2 streets which are kept in good order. They are not lighted at night but have broad footpaths, which are mostly kept clean. The houses are regular, mostly slated and are 2-storeys high. There is a court house and dispensary, an inn, where accommodation may be had, and post cars. The town is well supplied with shops. There is a good pump near the end of the town for public use. It has a market the first Monday in every month, where cows, pigs, sheep are offered for sale, as well as all kinds of haberdashery. Meat is also brought in for sale. There was a horse fair held in this town for 3 successive months, but would not succeed.

Many attend the markets for pleasure. The women arrive in town on market days early in order to sell their yarn, which is generally bought by merchants and taken to Belfast.

Post

[Insert marginal note: The hour when the post leaves Crumlin should be stated]. There are 2 post deliveries in the day. The post car leaves Crumlin at 8 o'clock in the morning, meets the Belfast and Derry mail in Antrim at ten minutes past nine in the morning, remains there until quarter past three afternoon and arrives in Crumlin at quarter past four afternoon, with Derry and Belfast's letters.

The Crumlin and Banbridge car leaves Crumlin at half past four evening, meets the Dublin mail in Banbridge at twenty minutes past three morning and arrives in Crumlin at quarter past eight a.m.

The usual force of police stationed in the town are 6.

Crumlin: Trades and Occupations

Surgeon and apothecary 1, innkeeper and leather warehouse 1, grocers 2, grocers and spirit shops 3, grocer and hardware shop 1, spirit shops 9, milliners 2, tailors 6, shoemakers 7, watchmaker 1, saddlers 2, baker 1, butcher 1, reed maker 1, painters and glaziers 2, nailer and smith 1, tin man 1, houses of entertainment for the poorer classes 2.

Insurance and Employment

There are some houses insured from fire by the [blank] insurance office in Belfast. [Insert marginal query: What office?]. The insurance can easily be effected in Belfast, a distance of 10 Irish miles.

The labourers find constant employment at the surrounding mills.

Public Buildings

Crumlin bridge was erected between 1770 and 1785, previous to which there were planks and handrails; the expenses paid by the county. It is a plain bridge with 3 arches raised but little. The cost cannot be ascertained.

The church that is resorted to at present is Killead, there being no church in this parish, and Glenavy church is also partly attended by the [Episcopalians or inhabitants ?] of the parish of Camlin.

The Presbyterian meeting house [was] erected in the year 1723, the expenses defrayed by general subscription. There are 46 seats in the aisle, would contain 288 persons; and 23 seats in gallery, would contain 196 persons; total number 484 persons; dimensions 58 feet by 24; supported by donations and collections. It is a very plain building much out of repair: the seats in gallery are all falling to pieces.

Table of Schools

[Table contains the following headings: name of townland where held, number of pupils subdivided by religion and sex, how supported, when established].

Ballydonaghy, 12 Protestants, 12 Presbyterians, 9 Catholics, 20 males, 13 females, total 33; under the Kildare Street Society, the master supported solely by the scholars; established 1819.

Parish of Camlin

Ballycessy, 32 Protestants, 4 Presbyterians, 16 Catholics, 40 males, 15 females, total 55, 3 Quakers; supported by the scholars; established 1813.

Arragh [Aghnadarragh ?], 41 Protestants, 3 Presbyterians, 1 Catholic, 28 males, 16 females, total 44; supported by the scholars; established 1815.

Ballytromery, 46 Protestants, 39 Presbyterians, 50 Catholics, 62 males, 55 females, total 115; this school is chiefly supported by the Honourable H.R. [insert footnote: Hercules Robert] Pakenham, who contributes 50 pounds per annum, and partly by the parents of the children; established 1825.

Ballytromery, 14 males, total 14; private academy of Mr [blank] Alexander; established 1800.

Social Economy: vide the adjoining parish Memoir (Killead).

Court House

The petty sessions are held here on Monday every second week. The number of outrages committed in this town are very few and have much decreased within these last few years. There is seldom or never any disturbance takes place here, with the exception of some fights which terminate market and court days. The number of magistrates generally in attendance on court days are 3 or 4: the Honourable Hercules Robert Pakenham, Charles Armstrong Esquire, James McCauley Esquire. The residences of the 2 latter are within a very convenient distance.

Dispensary

The health of the people has much improved since the establishment of this dispensary, Dr McDonnald physician, which was in the year 1832. [Table]: average number of patients 360, cured 360; typhus and inflammatory fever with dyspepsia and chronic complaints; supported by private subscription and grand jury presentments.

Mills

Flax mill belonging to James Greer: diameter of wheel 12 feet, breadth of buckets 1 and a half feet, fall of water 3 feet, breast wheel, water sufficient 7 months in the year.

Corn mill belonging to Robert McCauley Esquire: diameter of wheel 16 feet, breadth of buckets 3 and a half, fall of water 3 feet, breast wheel, sufficient water 7 months in the year.

Flax mill belonging to Robert McCauley Esquire: diameter of wheel 14 feet, breadth of wheel 2 and a half feet, fall of water 5 feet, water sufficient 5 months in the year.

General Appearance and Scenery

There is nothing striking in this parish. It is well cultivated and full of comfortable farmhouses. It is a good wheat country and is well sheltered, with hedgerows of fir and poplar and thick thorn hedges. Towards the [shores or south ?] it becomes rich in wood, and from the lake looks very much like a well-cultivated English district. The houses are all of stone or brick, whitewashed. The farmers are rich and keep good houses. [Signed] T.C. Hannyngton.

Fair Sheets by J. Bleakly, [1838 ?]

MEMOIR WRITING

Memoir Writing

Forwarded to Lieutenant Bennett, Royal Engineers, 22nd August 1840, [signed] James Boyle.

SOCIAL ECONOMY

Crumlin Petty Sessions

Report of the Crumlin petty sessions from the 1st January 1828 till the 1st January 1829. Number of summons issued 200: number of cases of assault 96, of theft 16, of housebreaking 3, rescue 4, riot 2, trespass 1, illegally cutting timber 2, miscellaneous 4.

Report from 1st January 1829 till 1st January 1830. Number of summons issued 336: cases of assault 91, rescue 4, breaking of game laws 1, housebreaking 1, riot 4, theft 4, miscellaneous 2.

Report from 1st January 1830 till 1st January 1831. Number of summons issued 330: cases of theft 15, assault 87, rescue 5, drunkenness 1, murder 1, miscellaneous 5.

Report of the Crumlin petty sessions from 1st January 1831 till 1st January 1832. Number of summons issued 158: cases of theft 30, assault 62, trespass 1, rescue 2, miscellaneous 6.

Report from 1st January 1832 till 1st January 1833. Number of summons issued 300: cases of theft 22, assault 100, rescue 5, breaking of game laws 1, rape 1, miscellaneous 4.

Report from 1st January 1833 till 1st January 1834. Number of summons issued 350: cases of assault 100, theft 18, riot 2, rescue 4, housebreaking 1, trespass 1, miscellaneous 4.

Report from 1st January 1834 till 1st January

1835. Summons issued 361: theft 11, assault 122, rescue 3, number of cases of robbery from the person 4, robbery of property 1, riot 3, trespass 6, housebreaking 4, miscellaneous 9.

Report from 1st January 1835 till 1st January 1836. Number of summons issued 399: assault 133, trespass 20, theft 20, disputes as to wages 6, breaches of excise laws 2, rescue 6, riot 4, drunkenness 4, housebreaking 4, miscellaneous 10.

Report from 1st January 1836 till 1st January 1837. Number of summons issued 366: cases of larceny 47, assault 79, trespass 37, drunkenness 30, rescue 9, breaches of excise laws 2, miscellaneous 6.

Report from 1st January 1837 till 1st January 1838. Number of summons issued 616: cases of larceny 47, number of cases of common assault 78, trespass 38, drunkenness 29, rescue 9, breaking of excise laws 2.

Petty session days on every second Wednesday. The petty session house or court house in Crumlin measures 43 by 20 feet in the clear. The police barracks is the upper storey of the court house and is of the same dimensions. Information obtained from Mr William English, petty sessions clerk, and Sergeant Philips of the constabulary.

Crumlin Dispensary Reports 1833-36

Report of the Crumlin dispensary from 1st March 1833 till 15th March 1834. Thomas McDonald Esquire, M.D. was medical attendant. The following are the diseases with the number of cases, with the number of dispensations of medicine and number of gratuitous visits in each year.

Dispensations of medicine 1,731, gratuitous visits 143.

Asthma 81, anasarca 5, amenorrhoea 12, ascites 14, abscess in the breast 2, burns 3, cardialgia 10, chronic cough 3, cephalgia 5, cholera morbus 1, cramp in stomach 4, constipation 5, chronic hepatitis 3, dyspepsia 213, diarrhoea 13, dysmenorrhoea 10, dysuria 3, erysipelas 1, febris 110, gonorrhoea 2, haemoptysis 8, haematemesis 5, haemorrhoids 14, herpetic eruptions 4, hysterites 5, hydrocele 2, herpes 6, injury of the loin 1, influenza 80, leucorrhoea 7, lepra 5, lumbago 13, lump in breast 5, menorrhagia 10, ophthalmia 19, otites 2, pulmonary affection 14, pleuritis 20, paralysis 10, paronychia 2, palpitatio 6, pyrosis 20, phlegmatic <plematic> erysipelas 3, rheumatism 117, scabies 6, secondary syphilis 10, staphylonia 1, scrofula 103, urticaria 10, ulcer in leg 50, ulcer in throat 50, vermes 57. The number of applicants corresponds with the number of dispensations of medicine.

Report of the Crumlin dispensary from 15th March 1834 till 15th March 1835. Number of dispensations of medicine 3,178, which is also the number of applicants, number of gratuitous visits 127.

Asthma 60, ascites 30, amenorrhoea 8, aphtha 1, burn 6, cephalgia 3, cynanche tonsilla 4, catarrh 2, cough 6, dysuria 35, dyspepsia 200, dysenteria 2, diarrhoea 30, dysmenorrhoea 6, erysipelas 3, epilepsy 1, epidemic fever 3, febris 10, gonorrhoea 3, glut 3, hepatitis 10, herpes 7, haemoptysis 5, herpetic eruption 3, influenza 50, insanity 1, inflammation 2, icturus 3, lumbago 10, leucorrhoea 6, lepra 2, mesenterica 2, opthalmia 12, otites 2, pulmonary affections 12, pyrosis 7, paronychia 3, pleuritis 12, palpitation 10, phle[g]mon 2, psora 10, porrigo 1, purpura 1, rheumatism 226, ringworm 1, scrofula 40, scabies 8, staphylonia 1, schirrus pictora 2, scarlatina 3, ulcer in leg 20, ulcer in throat 20, ulcer in nose 2, ulcer in vulva 5, ulcer in ears 2, ulcer in foot 3, ulcer in tongue 3, urticaria 8, vermes 37.

Report of Crumlin dispensary from 17th March 1835 till 17th March 1836. Dispensations of medicine during that year 2,106, gratuitous visits 93; number of applicants is the same as the number of dispensations of medicine.

Asthma 30, anasarca 4, amenorrhoea 20, ascites 10, anthrax 1, aphtha 2, abscess 2, cough 9, catarrh 6, cynanche tonsilla 4, dyspepsia 220, dysmenorrhoea 5, diarrhoea 20, erysipelas 4, epilepsy 2, epitaxis 2, febris 25, gonorrhoea 4, glut 2, herpes 4, haemorrhoids 9, insanity 4, icturus 1, lepra 3, leucorrhoea 6, lumbago 6, opthalmia 12, otites 3, psora 12, phthisis 5, phlegmon 2, paralysis 6, pyrosis 6, palpitation 5, pleuritis 10, phoraphymosis 1, rheumatism 300, rubeola 6, scarlatina 6, scrofula 100, ulcer in leg 20, ulcer in tongue 3, ulcer in vulva 3, urticaria 6, vermes 40.

School Statistics by James Boyle and Another

SOCIAL ECONOMY

Table of Schools

[Table contains the following headings: name, situation and description, when established, income and expenditure, physical, intellectual and moral education, number of pupils subdivided by age, sex and religion, name and religion of master or mistress].

Crumlin academy, a boarding and day school; in a suitable and cheerfully situated 2-storey house adjacent to the village of Crumlin, having a good playground, ballcourt; income from pupils 366 pounds; expenditure: 1 assistant resides, board and lodgings, an annual salary of 40 pounds; intellectual education: the classics, containing the works usually read in the entrance course, mathematics, algebra, history, geography and the works necessary for an English and mercantile education; moral education: Authorised Version of Scriptures and prayers every morning, and the boys are catechised in a compendious catechism on Saturdays; total number of pupils 14, all male; master the Reverend Nathaniel Alexander, principal, [blank] Montgomery, assistant, Presbyterians.

In an extremely neat and spacious and airy house, cheerfully situated in the townland of Ballytromery, containing 2 large schoolrooms with apartments for the male and female teachers, built at an expense of 400 pounds defrayed jointly by the Honourable Colonel Pakenham, the Kildare Society and a grant from the said society's fund; established 1825; income: the male and female teachers (who are married) receive jointly, besides a free house, garden and an acre of ground, from Colonel Pakenham 40 pounds, 40 pounds from pupils; intellectual education: the females learn needlework, all learn spelling, reading, writing, arithmetic; geography, history, mensuration, book-keeping are taught; moral education: the school is always opened with prayer, Authorised Version of Scriptures daily; Sunday school, occasionally visits from a Protestant curate; number of pupils: males, 21 under 10 years of age, 18 from 10 to 15, 6 over 15, a total of 45; females, 20 under 10 years of age, 15 from 10 to 15, 5 over 15, a total of 40; total number of pupils 85, 28 Protestants, 29 Presbyterians, 28 Roman Catholics; master and mistress John and Elizabeth Wilson, Protestants.

In an excellent schoolhouse built at a cost of 80 pounds, defrayed partly by the Kildare Society, local subscription and 20 pounds from Lord Hertford, situated in the townland of Ballysessy; established 1820; income from pupils 25 pounds; intellectual education: reading, writing, arithmetic, books of the Kildare Society, *Murray's Grammar*, *Jackson's Book-keeping*, mensuration, algebra; moral education: Sunday school, occasional visits from the Protestant curate, Authorised Version of Scriptures daily, catechisms afternoons; number of pupils: males, 16 under 10 years of age, 12 from 10 to 15, 1 over 15, a total of 29; females, 15 under 10 years of age, 6 from 10 to 15, a total of 21; total number of pupils 50, 26 Protestants, 2 Presbyterians, 22 Roman Catholics; master Michael Carr, Roman Catholic.

In a neat and excellent house built for the purpose by local subscription and situated in the townland of Ballydonaghy; established 1805; income: 22 pounds from public donation, 22 pounds from pupils; intellectual education: reading, writing, English grammar, books of the Kildare Society, *Thomson's Arithmetic*, *Jackson's Bookkeeping*, mensuration, algebra; moral education: Sunday school, occasional visits from the Protestant curate, Authorised Version of Scriptures daily, catechisms afternoons; number of pupils: males, 11 under 10 years of age, 15 from 10 to 15, a total of 26; females, 8 under 10 years of age, 6 from 10 to 15, a total of 14; total number of pupils 40, 18 Protestants, 17 Presbyterians, 5 Roman Catholics; master John Smyth, Presbyterian.

In a very neat and suitable house built for the purpose by local subscription and situated in the townland of Aughnadarragh; established more than 30 years; income: from the rector of the parish annually 22 pounds, 16 pounds from pupils; intellectual education: *Dublin Spelling and reading book*, *Murray's Grammar*, writing, *Thomson's Arithmetic*, any books brought by the children; moral education: visited by the Protestant curate, Church of England catechism, Authorised Version of Scriptures daily; number of pupils: males, 7 under 10 years of age, 9 from 10 to 15, a total of 16; females, 8 under 10 years of age, 6 from 10 to 15, a total of 14; total number of pupils 30, 23 Protestants, 6 Presbyterians, 1 Roman Catholic; master Benjamin Chasse, Protestant.

Education

[Table contains the following headings: name of townland where held, name and religion of master or mistress, free or pay school, annual income of master or mistress, description and cost of schoolhouse, number of pupils subdivided by religion, sex and the Protestant and Roman Catholic returns, societies with which connected. All are fee paying].

Aghnadaragh, master Henry McHenry, Established Church; annual income 28 pounds; schoolhouse stone and lime, built by vestry and subscription, cost 20 pounds; number of pupils by the Protestant return: 23 Established Church, 18 males, 5 females; by the Roman Catholic return: 23 Established Church, 18 males, 5 females; the incumbent gives 2 pounds and superintends the parish school.

Ballygortgarve, master Arthur Rea, Dissenter;

annual income 26 pounds; schoolhouse stone and lime and thatched, cost 15 pounds; number of pupils by the Protestant return: 6 Established Church, 15 Presbyterians, 5 Roman Catholics, 18 males, 8 females; by the Roman Catholic return: 6 Established Church, 15 Presbyterians, 5 Roman Catholics, 18 males, 8 females; associations none.

Lanygarvy, master Michael Mulholland, Roman Catholic; annual income 18 to 20 pounds; schoolhouse a private house; number of pupils by the Protestant return: 10 Established Church, 2 Presbyterians, 12 Roman Catholics, 15 males, 9 females; by the Roman Catholic return: 10 Established Church, 2 Presbyterians, 12 Roman Catholics, 15 males, 9 females; associations none.

Camlin, master Reverend Nathanial Alexander, Presbyterian; annual income 6 guineas per annum and 1 [guinea] entrance, and boarders 30 guineas; schoolhouse stone and lime; number of pupils by the Protestant return: 18 Established Church, 22 Presbyterians, 1 Roman Catholic, total 41, all male; by the Roman Catholic return: 18 Established Church, 22 Presbyterians, 1 Roman Catholic, total 41, all male; associations none.

Crumlin, master Patrick Dogherty, Roman Catholic; annual income 30 pounds; schoolhouse: house in comfortable state, furniture in bad order, cost 31 pounds; number of pupils by the Protestant return: 4 Established Church, 19 Presbyterians, 7 Roman Catholics, 26 males, 4 females; by the Roman Catholic return: 4 Established Church, 19 Presbyterians, 7 Roman Catholics, 26 males, 4 females; [patron] the Reverend N. Alexander.

Crumlin, master William J. Moore, Protestant; annual income 28 pounds; schoolhouse the session house; number of pupils by the Protestant return: 8 Established Church, 28 Presbyterians, 2 Roman Catholics, 21 males, 17 females; by the Roman Catholic return: 9 Established Church, 28 Presbyterians, 1 Roman Catholic, 21 males, 17 females; associations none.

Ballydonaghy, master James Lunie, Presbyterian; annual income 14 pounds; schoolhouse stone and lime; number of pupils by the Protestant return: 8 Established Church, 9 Presbyterians, 7 Roman Catholics, 14 males, 10 females; by the Roman Catholic return: 8 Established Church, 9 Presbyterians, 7 Roman Catholics, 14 males, 10 females; connected with Kildare Place Society, the schoolhouse built by subscription, Lord Hertford gave 12 guineas.

Ballygeesy, master Michael Kerr, Roman Catholic; annual income 28 pounds; schoolhouse stone and lime, cost 70 pounds; number of pupils by the Protestant return: 33 Established Church, 3 Presbyterians, 18 Roman Catholics, 38 males, 16 females; by the Roman Catholic return: 33 Established Church, 3 Presbyterians, 18 Roman Catholics, 38 males, 16 females; connected with Kildare Place Society, Reverend E. Cripples [Cupples ?], Reverend I. McMullen, William Whitla Esq., Dr Murray, patrons; Marquis Hertford gave 35 pounds towards building schoolhouse.

Parish of Glenavy, County Antrim

Statistical Remarks by Lieutenant G.A. Bennett, October [1832 ?]

NATURAL STATE

Name, Situation and Extent

Glenavy is written in some ancient records Lynavy and Lanaway. The name may be derived from Glanna-obhin signifying "the pleasant glen", or from Glanamhann, "the glen of the river", for the position of the townlands of Glenavy along the glen through which the Glenavy river takes its course gives countenance to either of these etymologies.

It was anciently in the territory of Killultagh, in the south or Upper Claneboy and county of Down. It now is situated in the barony of Upper Massereene and county of Antrim.

This part of the union is bounded on the north and east by the parishes of Camlin, Tullyrusk <Tullyrousk> and Derryaghy, on the south by the parish of Ballinderry, Portmore Lough and Aghagallon, and on the west by Lough Neagh from Selshan harbour to the Glenavy waterfoot.

The figure of this parish is very irregular. The greatest length is from the south west extremity of the Deer Park to the north east of Ballymonimore at Knockaun bridge, which is nearly 8 and a half miles, whereas its greatest breadth from north to south is not 2 and three-quarter miles. It is divided up into 18 townlands, covering an area of 7,217 acres 33 perches British statute measurement.

Ecclesiastical Union

Glenavy is a vicarage in the diocese of Connor and archdiocese of Armagh, being episcopally united to the parishes of Camlin and Tullyrusk. It is a lay impropriation in the advowson of the Marquis of Hertford, who receives the rectorial tithes. The precise year in which the union took place is not known, but by a regal visitation book deposited among the records of the court of prerogative that there was a union so early as the year 1633. The present incumbent is the Reverend E. Cupples, who receives the vicarial tithes by an amicable composition with his parishioners. They vary from 6d to 10d ha'penny per acre.

The church is situated in this part of the union, on the banks of Glenavy river and a short distance north of the village. It is a plain neat edifice and there is a good glebe house in the adjacent parish of Camlin. There is a neat Roman Catholic chapel in Ballymacricket townland, situated near the road from Glenavy to Moira.

NATURAL FEATURES AND PRODUCTIVE ECONOMY

Surface and Soil

Near the south east extremity of this parish the ground is of considerable elevation, Crew hill (the highest in the parish) being 627 feet above the level of the sea, and it may be observed that the surface forms a gradual descent on approaching Lough Neagh and the valley along which the Glenavy river takes its course. Thus Carnkilly is 333 feet, Darachrean 189 feet and Lough Neagh 50 feet above the same level. Along the shore of the latter the ground is rich, fertile and gently undulating. Two-thirds of the soil in the parish is a heavy clay, capable of producing good crops. Along the banks of Lough Neagh it is sandy.

Agriculture

The kinds of grain chiefly cultivated are wheat, oats, barley and rye, and the mode of culture the same as in the adjacent parishes. Potatoes are considered the best preparation crop, the drill system being usually adopted in planting them and the ground allotted to them is generally the stubble of the third or fourth crop of oats. Wheat is sown in October or November, when the potato crop is taken away, or sometimes the ground is reserved after the latter for oats in the ensuing spring as it suits the convenience of the farmer. The following may be considered a good average produce per acre: of wheat or oats 15 cwt, potatoes 250 bushels. The manures are lime and the produce of the farmyard. The size of farms varies from 1 acre to 150. The highest acreable rent is not above 2 pounds and the lowest 8s.

MODERN TOPOGRAPHY AND PRODUCTIVE ECONOMY

Villages

The only village in this part of the union is Glenavy, which is pleasantly situated on the river of the same name. Besides the church, there has been lately erected a Methodist chapel. There are no fairs or markets held here. The population is 268, 122 males and 146 females. The nearest market is at Crumlin.

Fuel

There is no bog in this part of the union except some small patches in Ballypitmave and Ballynacoy which are nearly exhausted. Turf is the common fuel and it is obtained from the Montyaghs, called the Park moss, in Aghagallon parish. The expense of carriage is great to some parts of the parish. The bog rates from 7s to 24s per acre or, when sold by the stack measuring 3 yards by 12 yards and 20 rows high, from 35s to 3 pounds, according to the quality. There was formerly a considerable quantity of moss in the Deer Park, which is now converted into meadow.

Economical Produce and Price

There is no limestone in the parish, but the proprietor of the estate burns lime for the accommodation of all his tenantry, which may be had at 9d per barrel or laid down at 1s, including charge for conveyance. The farmers who have kilns prefer buying it by the load at 6d or 8d, containing about 15 cwt, and burning it themselves. The basalt is used for making and repairing roads and for building.

NATURAL FEATURES

Springs and Streams

There are several springs in this parish, many of which are impregnated with a calcareous matter which encrusts the kettles and other boilers and renders them unfit for the purpose of washing, but the waters in general are found salubrious; and the principal streams that water this parish are the Glenavy river that separates the parish from the united parish of Camlin, which rises in Derryaghy parish, and the Crew burn and Black burn, both rising in Ballypitmave.

MODERN AND ANCIENT TOPOGRAPHY

Roads

The principal roads are those passing from Antrim to Lurgan and from Antrim to Lisburn. The former enters at the Leap bridge and leaves it at Carroll's bridge; the latter enters at Glenavy bridge and, passing through the village at Glenavy, leaves it at Doinan's public house on the Crew hill. It is otherwise well intersected with by-roads branching off to Belfast, Stoneyford, Moira, the Montyaghs, Lough Neagh and Crumlin.

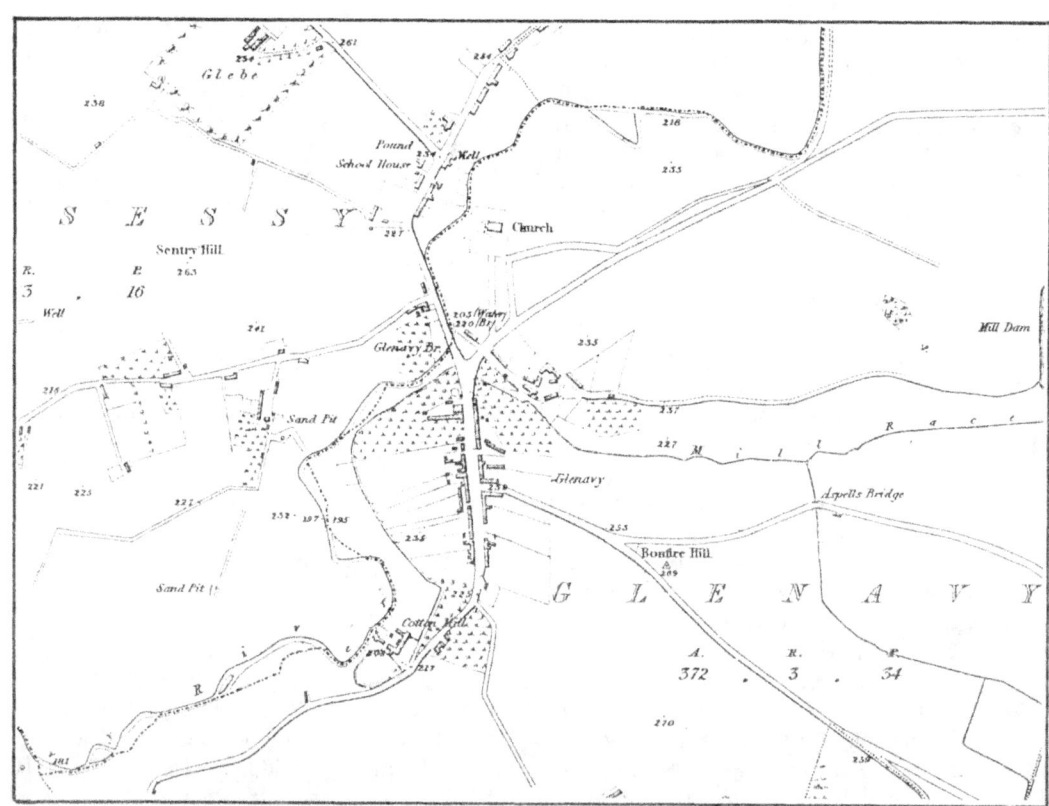

Map of Glenavy from the first 6" O.S. maps, 1830s

Parish of Glenavy

Antiquities

There are no very remarkable antiquities within this parish except some ancient forts which remain in a good state of preservation, the most remarkable of which is that called the Great Mound, situated in the townland of Ballynacoy, about 1 and three-quarter miles east of the village of Glenavy, its elevation being 514 feet above the sea.

Manufactories and Mills

Adjoining to the town of Glenavy there is a cotton factory in a very ruinous state and is seldom wrought. A few years ago there was employed 130 hands in it; and in the townland of Ballyvorally there is a bleach mill (with a green of 27 acres attached to it) that employs from 20 to 26 hands, and there is constantly between 5 and 6 ton of coals consumed weekly; and there is also a small corn mill in the town of Glenavy.

NATURAL HISTORY

Geology

The constituent rock of this parish is basalt, varying, however, from the granular to the compact, where every trace of the mineralogical character vanishes. The latter is the case at Ballypitmave. At the Crew hill it is of a dark, iron-grey colour which is associated with and varies into loadstone or amigdaloidal trap, being full of small interstices filled with calcareous spar, green and yellow earth. It also may be seen at Ballymacricket, where it is close grained and contains steatite, and at the bed of the Glenavy river and of other streams.

The minerals found in the parish are crystals of hornblends, calcareous spar filling the cavities of the basalt, sandstones containing quartz and mica, and the Lough Neagh pebble found near the shore. The latter vary in their colour, the most common being white, rarely red. They take a fine polish and resemble cornelian, a beautiful specimen of which is sent.

Along the shore of Lough Neagh fossil wood or wood coal (as it is called by the inhabitants) is found. By the poorer classes it is sometimes burnt for fuel, but it emits a very disagreeable smell.

SOCIAL ECONOMY

Schools

The schools are either established or temporary. The former are kept in houses built for the purpose by the inhabitants, of which there is one in each of the following townlands: Ballymonymore, Crew, Deer Park, Aghadolgan; and the latter or temporary schools by itinerant teachers in houses of their own providing, one of which are in each of the following townlands: Ballymoat, Ballymacricket and Glenavy.

Population

The population of this parish by a census taken in 1826 appear to be 3,297 souls, and in 1831 there was 3,376, which shows an increase of 79, besides a number who have since emigrated for America. By the census taken in 1826, there adheres to the Established Church 1,477, Dissenters 310 and Roman Catholics 1,510. The census of 1831 is as follows: families 634, males 1,664, females 1,712, males above 20 years 797, male servants 51, female servants 76, total 3,376.

Townlands

The content of each townland [proprietor the Marquis of Hertford] is as in the following table viz.

Aghadolgan, 336 acres 2 roods 3 perches.
Ballyminimore, 372 acres 3 roods 36 perches.
Ballymonymore, 146 acres 1 perch.
Ballynacoy, 694 acres 3 roods.
Ballypitmave, 580 acres 2 roods 19 perches.
Ballymoat, 406 acres 2 roods 16 perches.
Ballymacricket, 335 acres 3 roods 3 perches.
Ballyvorally, 487 acres 2 roods 18 perches.
Ballyvanen, 476 acres 21 perches.
Crew, 610 acres 2 roods 21 perches.
Deer Park, 1,103 acres 1 rood 5 perches.
Edenturcher, 144 acres 22 perches.
Fenmore, 369 acres 1 rood 7 perches.
Glenavy, 372 acres 3 roods 34 perches.
Lower Carnkilly, 132 acres 3 roods 25 perches.
Tullynewbane, 333 acres 1 rood 12 perches.
Tullynewbank, 241 acres 1 rood 27 perches.
Upper Carnkilly, 72 acres 1 rood 3 perches.
Area of the parish 7,217 acres 33 perches.

[Signed] G.A. Bennett, Lieutenant Royal Engineers, 12 October 1832.

Extracts from Draft Memoir by George Scott and Another, February 1835

NATURAL FEATURES

Lakes

Lough Neagh bounds the parish on the western

side, for a description of which refer to coast Memoir.

Rivers

The Glenavy river, forming the northern boundary of this parish, flows from east to west for 2 miles, when it turns at the footbridge in the townland of Ballynacoy and flows in a northern direction as far as Ballydonaghy bridge in the townland of Ballymoneymore. From thence it runs southerly to the town of Glenavy and from Glenavy falls east and west into Lough Neagh. It has its source at the Divis mountain. On this river there is 1 very pretty waterfall 40 feet over trap rocks, to which the surrounding trees add beauty and variety. With the exception of this waterfall, which is in the townlands of Ballyvollen and Ballyvorally, the descent of the water throughout the parish is gradual. It is of very little importance as a mill stream, but would supply more machinery with water than is at present erected on the river, to take advantage of which it is the intention of Mr Howe, who has a cotton manufactory in the townland of Glenavy, to erect a flax mill in the same townland next year (1836).

The average fall of the water is 28 feet in half a mile. This river in the winter season is subject to very sudden and great floods. During the times of such floods drains are cut to let off the water, which does not leave any deposits but is considered by the people more beneficial than injurious to the next year's crop, but the flood subsides as rapidly as it overflows.

This river does not facilitate nor could it afford any advantage to communications as it [is] mostly narrow and the bed is indiscriminately composed of sand, stones and small rocks.

The character <caracter> and scenery of its banks is various. In the parish of Tullyrusk, townland of Tullyrusk, and the townland of Ballymacward Lower, in the parish of Derryaghy, the banks are exceedingly steep, average height 30 feet, without plantations, and in some places uncultivated. From thence it runs to the townland of Ballymoneymore in the parish of Glenavy, through rather an open valley <vally> composed of small, irregular connected features, where the banks are again steep, average height 25 feet. The young plantations on these banks, surrounding W. Gregg Esquire's cottage, gives the country a picturesque <picturesk> appearance. From this point it flows mostly through broken ground. At times the banks are craggy and abrupt but of short duration and frequently through flat ground. In the parish of Glenavy, townland Ballyvorally, and the parish of Camlin, townland of Ballyvollen, it again becomes pretty on account of its steep banks, the waterfall and thick plantations.

Except this river there is not any other in the parish, but innumerable small streams flow into this river fertilising the soil in their progress. There are no mineral or hot springs in the parish. There are several springs in this parish, many of which are impregnated with a calcareous matter, but the waters in general are of a salubrious quality.

Woods

About 1,400 acres on the shore of Lough Neagh were held as a park by the Lords Conway. This park was stored with deer, pheasants, hares and a variety of game. About 50 years since, a considerable portion of it was leased to tenants and cleared of wood. The remainder, under the name of the Hogg or Little Deer Park, continued to be appropriated to the same purpose till about 32 years since, when it was also given up to cultivation and leased to tenants. Boate, in his *Natural history of Ireland*, says there were great forests in the county of Antrim, especially in Killultagh; some few vestiges still remain.

SOCIAL ECONOMY

Table of Schools

Ballymacrickett townland, 8 Protestants, 21 Catholics, 15 males, 14 females, total 29; this school was bought by a subscription raised from the parish; cost 15 pounds and is supported by the parents of the children, established 1825.

Crew townland, 31 Protestants, 5 Catholics, 23 males, 13 females, total 36; supported only by the parents of the children, established 1813.

MODERN TOPOGRAPHY

Village of Glenavy

The village of Glenavy is for the most part dirty and the houses, with a very few exceptions, are much out of repair. It is an irregular-built village, mostly cabins. It is not lighted at night. The footpaths are broken and bad. The only public building in the village is the church and it is situated a little off the road. It is but ill supplied with shops.

There was formerly a market held here the first Wednesday in every month, but has been discontinued for some years on account of the number of outrages which took place every market day. On the first Wednesday of this month, February 1835,

Parish of Glenavy

it was again revived, where the general supply of articles were offered for sale. In the evening some few fights took place, but not of any consequence.

It is a post town and the arrival of the post differs both half an hour from the Crumlin times. The Dublin letters are delivered at 8 o'clock a.m. and the northern letters at 5 o'clock p.m. [signed] G. Scott.

Glenavy is the only village in the parish. It is pleasantly situated on the river of the same name.

Public Buildings

It contains a church and a Methodist meeting house. The cost of the erection of this church amounts to 1,220 pounds, 450 pounds of which was furnished by the Board of First Fruits and the remaining 770 pounds was raised by presentment and subscription. It is a plain building and within the last few years has had an addition of a square turret, the corners of which are ornamented and consequently, from a distance, gives it the appearance of a handsome building. The church is a neat edifice erected in the year 1812. There are 47 seats in the aisle, would contain 288 persons; 15 seats in gallery, would contain 76 persons; dimensions 60 feet by 30.

The meeting house, erected in 1836, the expenses defrayed by general subscription, cost 100 pounds. There are 30 seats, would contain 90 persons, dimensions 33 by 23, supported by collections made every preaching night. It is an exceeding plain building much out of repair.

There is a neat Roman Catholic chapel situated near the road from Glenavy to Moira, in the townland of Ballymacricket; built in 1802. There are 17 seats in aisle, would contain 85 persons; in gallery 28 seats, would contain 140 persons; cost between 350 to 400 pounds, dimensions 68 by 33. The expense of the erection of this chapel was defrayed by generous subscriptions and collections. Built at various periods, the interior of this chapel is extremely neat. It is always decorated with ivy and over the communion table there is a picture of Our Saviour crucified (not a good one), but it gives a finished appearance to the place.

Bleach Greens

Ballyvorally townland; there is a bleach mill, the diameter of the wheel 30 feet, breadth of wheel 4 feet, fall of water 34 feet, overshot wheel. The quality <quallity> of the linen <linnen> depends much on the bleaching. All the linen is sent to New York. The process is as follows: the linen is boiled, then washed and dyed, next beetled and afterwards bleached and finished by lapping <laping>. The lapping is the only part of the business that requires any degree of skill and it is general for a person to serve several years of apprenticeship in order to get a knowledge of it.

Cotton Factory in Glenavy

Belongs to Mr Thomas Howe: diameter of wheel 26 feet, breadth of wheel 5 feet, fall of water 24 feet, breast wheel. There is a sufficient supply of water and it is intended that more machinery will be erected on this water next year. The usual wear and tear <tare> is 10 per cent. The decrease in the manufacturing of the articles is one-eighth. The men work 12 hours a day and master [?] finds and repairs tools. All the produce used for home consumption. The number of persons employed at present varies from 100 to 120.

Communications

The road from Antrim to Moira enters at Glenavy bridge, passing through the parish.

The road between Antrim and Lurgan passes through the parish for a distance of 1 and a quarter miles, average breadth 22 feet. The portion of road in this parish is nearly straight <strait> going over hills and valleys, made and repaired at the expense of the county.

The road from Antrim to Lisburn passes through the parish for a distance of 2 and a quarter miles and the road to Moira a distance of 1 and three-quarter miles (for information respecting the road vide Ballinderry Memoir). Otherwise this parish is well intersected with by-roads branching off to Crumlin, Stoneyford and Lough Neagh.

Gentlemen's Seats

Goremount, the residence of Mrs Gore.

SOCIAL ECONOMY

Trades or Callings

Grocers 3, grocer and spirit shops 2, whiskey shops 1, milliners 2, houses of entertainments for the poorer classes 2, saddlers 1, [signed] George Scott.

Local Government

There are no petty sessions held in this parish, neither are there any magistrates residing in it or police stationed in the village. No combinations exist to deprive workmen of the liberty of working as they please. No illicit distilling carried on in the parish. The houses are not insured. For more information, vide Ballinderry Memoir.

Habits of the People

The cottages are generally built of stone, many slated but thatch prevails, generally 1-storey; comfort and cleanliness much more adhered to than the more northern parishes. There are no remarkable early marriages [n]or have I seen any chief amusement or recreation. The time they are not employed in farming is generally spent weaving. The patron days seem to be almost forgotten. There is not any peculiarity of costume. The dress of the better description of farmers which inhabit this parish is good, but the lower order are not particular.

Memoir by James Boyle, January 1836

NATURAL FEATURES

Hills

This parish occupies the northern side of one of the features spreading out from the mountainous ridge in the more easterly parishes and terminating in a low and almost level beach along the eastern shore of Lough Neagh. Near the south eastern corner of the parish is Crew triangulation point (692 feet above the sea), its highest point, and from this point the ground inclines gradually towards the lake, its surface being, however, traversed by a succession of little ridges and winding valleys, the former gradually diminishing in elevation, their general direction being from north north west to south south east. Towards the north there is a general fall terminating in the steep bank along the Glenavy river. As it approaches its mouth this bank increases in height and forms one side of a pretty valley known by the name of Glenconway. The low tract along the west of this parish forms a portion of the great level district extending along the eastern shore of Lough Neagh from its northern to its southern extremity.

The principal points in this parish are Crew, 629 feet (at its south east corner), Cairn hill, 614 feet, Green Mound, 517 (at its east centre), Carnkilly Lower (near its centre), 336 feet, Darraghrean (near its west side), 189 feet and Lough Neagh, 50 feet above the sea.

Lough Neagh

Lough Neagh (at its centre 48 feet above the sea at low water) forms the western boundary of this parish, within the confines of which there are 9,213 acres 1 rood 23 perches of its surface included. Its depth in this parish varies from 3 to 30 feet, being shallow along the shore but soon deepening. In winter its waters rise generally from 5 to 6 feet above their summer level, but commit no injury except by the check they give to the discharge of the waters from the numerous streams flowing into it, thereby preventing the more speedy drainage of the adjacent country. Along the shore of this parish its beach, being pebbly and stony, is not susceptible of injury. Towards the water it becomes soft and of a muddy sand.

The eastern and southern sides of that part of the coast of Lough Neagh called Sandy bay are formed by the shore of this parish, which, receding considerably towards its northern side, extends due south for 1 and a half miles. It then strikes out westerly for 1 and a half miles, presenting an irregular and uneven line terminating at Tunny Point. From this it turns sharply southwards for 1 mile and again it pursues a due westerly direction for three-quarters of a mile, terminating in Lignaboy Point. Here it takes a south west turn to the extremity of Hog Park Point (is [a] cape extending for three-quarters of a mile from the general line of coast) and then it doubles, extending round its southern side which forms the northern of Bartin's bay, presenting a total of 6 and a half miles of coast.

Along the coast of this parish the scenery, both in itself and in the views from it, is exceedingly beautiful: its low shores running out into numerous little promontories which from a distance appear densely clothed with wood, while on 3 sides the view is bounded by lofty ridges of mountains.

Ram's Island

In that part of Lough Neagh included in this parish is the beautiful little island known by the name of Ram's Island, and so called from its resemblance in form to a ram's horn. It is 1 and a half miles west of the shore of this parish. Its extreme length is two-thirds of a mile and breadth 157 yards and its extent is 6 acres 3 roods 13 perches. It is but little more than 20 years since it fell into the hands of Lord O'Neill, to whom it now belongs and who has expended so much in rendering it the exquisite spot which it is at present.

Previous to the year 1810, this island was inhabited by a man named McIlrevy, who, from having occupied it for a long time, acquired a right to it and held it by prescription. It was bought from him by Mr James Whittle of Liverpool, who planted and improved it considerably, it having before been merely covered with brushwood and celebrated only for the ancient round tower which still stands on it. Mr Whittle gave McIlrevy 100 pounds for it and Lord O'Neill soon after gave Mr Whittle 1,000 pounds for it.

His lordship has laid it out in the most tasteful manner, the island being almost covered with the arbutus, the turf beautifully laid down and traversed by numerous walks. His cottage, which he also built on it, is considered a most curious and elegant structure, beautifully planned and constructed, the furniture, which is most costly, being perfectly rustic and in good keeping with the cottage.

The cottage is situated at the southern end of the island, the narrow tongue which extends northward being often all under water except a small portion of it known by the name of Duck Island, which is a little more elevated than the rest.

Ram's Island is a favourite spot for picnics and is much resorted to in summer by parties of pleasure from all the counties round the lake.

Portmore Lough

A portion of Portmore lough or Lough Beg is situated in the southern part of this parish, the remainder of it being included in the adjoining parish of Ballinderry. Its total extent is 626 acres 16 perches, of which 342 acres 2 roods 6 perches are included in this parish. Its distance from Lough Neagh at the nearest point is 4 furlongs and 27 perches, a low ridge about 18 feet at the highest point above these levels, which are similar, separating them. Its form is nearly circular and it seems to have been formed by the waters of the numerous streams which empty themselves into it. Its extreme length from north to south is 1 and a third miles and breadth from east to west 1 and an eighth miles. Its depth is very variable but in summer a man can touch its bottom with an oar. Its bed is a rich alluvium. It inundates the adjacent low meadows in winter and its drainage would be attended with much advantage.

An attempt was made in 1740 by a Mr Dobbs to drain it, by means of a windmill and buckets. This was one night frustrated by the water forcing its way back through the cut. It abounds with bream and eels and several other descriptions of fish are found in it. The seasons for taking the bream are at the blossoming and the colouring of the cherry. They then totally disappear and it is a curious fact they are never seen in Lough Neagh.

Rivers

The Glenavy river, which takes its rise in the more easterly parish of Derryaghy, at an elevation of 950 feet above the sea and 902 feet above Lough Neagh, after flowing westerly in a circuitous manner for 3 miles, descends to a level of 402 feet above the sea and, entering the east side of this parish, flows northerly for 2 and a third miles between it and the parish of Tullyrusk. It then turns sharply westward and, pursuing a west south west course rather circuitously for 4 and a quarter miles and passing through the village of Glenavy, discharges itself into Lough Neagh, 2 and a third miles west of that village. Its average fall is 1 foot in 85 feet, its average breadth 23 feet and its natural depth from 1 and a half to 6 feet. Its bed is in general gravelly, in some places it is sandy, and between the townlands of Ballyvollen and Ballyvorally, 1 and a half miles west of Glenavy vallage, its course is interrupted by a ledge of trap <trapp> rocks which, crossing it, produce a very fine waterfall of 40 feet perpendicular.

It is subject to very violent and rapid floods, which scarcely ever commit any injury to the country. In a few places the low holmes <hoames> are overflowed but, drains being cut, the water soon runs off without producing any effect. It is applicable to drainage and irrigation and is usefully situated for the purpose of machinery, but it is [in] but [insert alternative: only] 3 instances applied to that purpose, though capable of furnishing a much greater supply of water power. Towards the east of the parish its banks are very steep and average 30 feet high. They afterwards become varied, sometimes high and sometimes dwindling into level holmes. West of Glenavy they become interesting, being steep and prettily planted, and near the waterfall, where it flows through the narrow and pretty valley of Glenconway, where the banks are lofty, steep and thickly planted, the scenery is picturesque and pleasing.

There are numerous little brooks and rivulets which, flowing down the parish, irrigate the lands and afford a supply of water for domestic uses. In some of the more level and flat points of the parish the supply of water, particularly in summer, is scanty and pumps are therefore rather numerous.

Bogs

In the townland of Ballypitmave is almost the only patch of bog in the parish. It is very small and not worthy of notice.

Woods

About 1,400 acres on the shore of Lough Neagh were held as a park by the Lords Conway. This park was stored with deer, pheasants, hares and a variety of game. About 50 years since a considerable portion of it was leased to tenants and cleared of wood. The remainder, under the name of the Hog or Little Deer Park, continued to be appropriated to the same purpose till about 32 years since, when it was also given out to cultivation and leased to tenants.

This parish forms a portion of the great manor of Killultagh, noticed by Boate in his *Natural history of Ireland*, in which he says "there were great forests in Antrim, particularly in Kilultagh." The only remains of natural wood are now to be found in the old undisturbed hedgerows near the lake where holly, oak and hazel saplings or shoots with a few wild cherries are to be found. Some little petrified wood is also found in the land near the lake.

Climate

The climate is rather dry and very healthy and the air pure. From its exposed situation on the shore of Lough Neagh to the prevailing south west and westerly winds, it is not so mild as the more interior parishes and but for its high and bushy hedgerows it would suffer from these winds. Towards the east of the parish early frosts are often injurious. Its aspect is excellent and the seasons early. Wheat is sown in winter and reaped sometimes early in August. Oats sown in March, reaped during the end of August and the month of September. Potatoes are mostly planted during the first fortnight in May and raised in November.

MODERN TOPOGRAPHY

Town of Glenavy

The village of Glenavy is situated on the stream and at the northern side of the parish of the same name, in the barony of Upper Massereene, manor of Killultagh, diocese of Connor and north east circuit of assize. The village is built upon the main road from Antrim to Banbridge which crosses the summit of a little ridge, giving a smart fall to the street on each side. A small portion of the village extends across the river into the parish of Camlin, but will be included in this description.

The situation of Glenavy is cheerful and pleasing: the little valley intersecting the village being prettily wooded and watered by a tolerable stream and the surrounding country being richly cultivated and somewhat diversified. It merely consists of a straggling street extending for half a mile from north to south. In the village itself, except immediately about the bridge, there is nothing interesting. On the contrary, towards its extremities the appearance of the cottages is anything but neat, comfortable or interesting.

Origin of Glenavy

The origin of Glenavy is unknown but there is no doubt of its being a place of some antiquity. Its situation at the intersection of a river by a leading road, perhaps the only one then between Antrim and Banbridge, and the natural formation of the ground at this point, rendered it an eligible situation for the creation of a town. There are not, however, any traces of buildings which could indicate its having been used as a military position, nor are there any ruins in its vicinity.

Glenavy is said to have been created a fair and market town by a patent from Charles I but these fairs and markets are not now held. In 1690 it was garrisoned by the Queen's Regiment of Horse, commanded by Lieutenant-General Sir John Lanier, as is corroborated by a silver chalice presented by the officer of that regiment to the church of Glenavy, and an old 2-storey house in the village, now used as a public house, is said to have been their guardhouse.

The establishment of a post office in Glenavy is said to have been of early date.

Markets and Fairs

A large market was formerly held in Glenavy on the first Wednesday in the month. These markets were, however, the scenes of dreadful party riots which deterred the country people from attending them, and they were finally given up in consequence of one fight which took place there about 30 years ago.

An attempt has been lately made to establish fairs to be held in Glenavy on the first Wednesday in every month for the sale of horses, cows, sheep, pigs; and premiums to be given to the highest buyers and sellers at the February, May, August and November fairs have been offered. These fairs have been revived in October 1834 and are likely eventually to thrive, particularly as no riots now take place.

Streets and Houses in Glenavy

Glenavy consists of 1 straggling and irregular street containing 86 cabins and cottages and 15 2-storey houses, the former occupied by labourers

Parish of Glenavy

and a few mechanics, and the latter by dealers. There is no private gentleman residing in the town and the people are of the middle or lower class. The labouring class are rather poor and the business or dealing carried on by the rest is very trifling. There is not, however, any poverty or distress in the village, as the labourers never suffer from want of employment. In addition to their other business, the dealers also farm. All classes are quiet, civil and industrious.

The houses are built without regard to uniformity or regularity. They are built of stone. The 2-storey houses are roughcast and slated, some of them are very old-looking. The 1-storey cottages are, with 2 or 3 exceptions, dirty and comfortless-looking, mostly all thatched and few of them roughcast or whitened. The street is tolerably wide and cleanly and has a narrow footway on each side.

Public Buildings in Glenavy

The public buildings consist of a church, a Methodist meeting house and a bridge. The church is very prettily situated in the valley along the river and a little retired from the street. It is a very pretty village church with a neat square tower ornamented with 4 crocketted pinnacles and containing a good clock with 3 dials. The church measures 60 feet long and 30 feet wide, and contains accommodation for 400 persons. It contains a gallery and is very neatly and comfortably fitted up internally. It was erected in 1812 at a cost of 1,220, of which 500 pounds was given and 250 lent by the Board of First Fruits, 150 pounds presented at the vestry, 300 pounds given by the Marquis of Hertford and 20 pounds given by the Countess of Longford.

The Methodist preaching house was erected in 1830 at a cost of 100 pounds, defrayed by subscription. It is a perfectly plain building measuring 33 by 23 feet and containing accommodation for 100 persons. It is situated near the centre of the village.

The bridge over the Glenavy river is near the centre of the village. It is a plain substantial structure consisting of 3 semicircular arches and measuring 80 feet long and 24 feet wide.

General Remarks

Glenavy, though not increasing in size, is rather improving in the appearance of its houses. Should the fairs succeed, as they are likely to do, it certainly will improve. There are now 3 police stationed in it and it is now free from those quarrels which have hitherto retarded its improvement.

Mail

The mail from Dublin arrives at half past 7 a.m. and is dispatched from Dublin at 5 p.m. The mail from Belfast arrives at 5 p.m. and is dispatched for Belfast at half past 7 a.m. These mails are conveyed in a taxed cart, carrying only the driver.

MODERN TOPOGRAPHY

Roman Catholic Chapel

The other public buildings in the parish consist of the Roman Catholic chapel situated near the road from Glenavy to Moira, in the townland of Ballymacricket, and three-quarters of a mile south of the village of Glenavy. It was erected in 1802 on the ruins of the former chapel which was burned during the rebellion of 1798. It measures 68 feet long and 33 feet, and contains a gallery and accommodation for about 400 persons. It is plain but neat in its appearance, being roughcast and neatly whitened. The interior is as yet but partially seated. It has cost between 350 and 400 pounds, which was defrayed by subscription.

The interior of this chapel is tastefully decorated with evergreens and over the altar is a painting of the Crucifixion. This, however, is not a very masterly production.

Gentlemen's Seats

Goremount, the property of Mrs Gore, a neat 2-storey house, prettily situated in the midst of some planting in the townland of Ballymacricket, a quarter of a mile south of the village of Glenavy.

Mills and Manufactories

The manufactories in this parish consist of a cotton factory, a bleach green with its machinery and a corn mill.

The corn mill is situated in the village of Glenavy. The machinery is propelled by a breast water wheel 14 feet in diameter and 2 feet broad.

The cotton factory is within a short distance of the southern end of the village of Glenavy. It is in rather a dilapidated state, though at present at full work. The machinery is propelled by a breast water wheel 26 feet in diameter and 5 feet broad, and having a fall of water of 24 feet.

In Ballyvorally townland, and on the Glenavy river, is a bleach green extending over 27 acres. The machinery is propelled by an overshot water wheel 30 feet in diameter and 4 feet broad, and having a fall of water of 34 feet. This establishment affords constant employment to from 20 to 26 men.

The Glenavy river furnishes a regular supply of water to these manufactories and might be further applied to machinery.

Communications

This parish possesses sufficient facility of communication with the neighbouring towns and districts by means of the numerous roads traversing its surface, which, however, are not too numerous. The materials used in their construction and repair are trap and the different other species of basalt, either from the beds of the rivers or several quarries in the parish.

The old system of carrying roads over hills seems to have been strictly adhered to in this parish, as the diversity in the surface of this parish is such as to admit of many of the roads being constructed almost horizontally. The new roads, however, are better laid out and there is still much room for improvement in the construction of the old ones.

The main roads are: the main road from Crumlin to Moira through the village of Glenavy. This road traverses the centre of the parish for 1 and a half miles. It is very hilly and unnecessarily so, as a little glen or ravine runs almost parallel to it for a considerable distance and through this an almost horizontal road might easily be constructed. Its average breadth is 22 feet. It is not in good repair.

The main road from Crumlin to Lurgan traverses the western side of the parish for 1 and a third miles. Its direction is good but it is very hilly and might, but with much difficulty and by carrying it nearer the lake, be made less so. Its average breadth is 23 feet. It is in bad repair.

The road from Glenavy to Lisburn traverses the eastern side of the parish for 2 and a third miles. Its direction is pretty good but it is very hilly and some of the ascents are steep. It is not in very good order. These main roads are kept in repair at the expense of the barony.

The by-roads are very numerous and in the east of the parish almost too much so. They are in general pretty good, but not very well laid out, many of them being hilly. Their average breadth is 17 feet. Some of them are repaired by the manor, but most of them by the manor [county ?].

There are 5 small bridges over the Glenavy river and these, with the numerous pipes over the smaller streams in the parish, afford every facility to intercourse.

General Appearance and Scenery

In all parts of this parish the scenery and appearance of the country is interesting in the extreme, but particularly in its lower and westerly districts where the high and thick hedges and rows of trees, the groves of orchards and clusters about every house give it, even from a short distance, the appearance of a densely wooded district. The neat-looking farmhouses, peeping out from among the trees, and the shady roads and lanes resemble a rich English district and give the country a cheerful aspect. From the higher grounds and from its shores the views are most extensive and the scenery of the most exquisite description, combining all the beauty and variety of a landscape rich in wood, water, diversity of surface and a prospect terminated at almost every point by lofty mountains.

SOCIAL ECONOMY

Early Improvements

The parish of Glenavy forms a portion of the vast estates confiscated from the ancient family of the O'Neills and granted to that of Conway (now Seymour), the Marquis of Hertford, by Queen Elizabeth. On the coming of the Conways to this country they brought with them many followers both of English, Scots and Welsh <Welch>, with whom they colonised the country, and it is said that many of the soldiers in King William's army who were quartered in the village of Glenavy under [crossed out: Duke Schomberg and] General Lanier settled in this parish.

There are still some in the parish who, from their names, seem to be descendants of the aboriginal inhabitants and are members of the Roman Catholic Church. The names alluded to are those of McQuillen, O'Neill, Mulholland and McRory. The names usually met with those imply their being strangers, namely Bell (very numerous), McNiece, Ferris, Farr, Bickerstaff, Wickcliffe, Palmer, Gwyllan, Yarr, Killewry, Cardwell, Breathwait, Knairs, Patterson. Except Bell, Ferris and Palmer, none of these names are particularly prevalent, but they are given to show the different countries from which the colonists came.

The Roman Catholics are very few, and humbler in their stations than the others. The Christian name of Agnes, also called Nancy, is rather common, but besides their names there are many circumstances indicative of their not being originally natives of the soil. Among others are: their taste for gardens and orchards, there being scarcely a house without either or both of these appendages; their style of farming; and their peculiar cast of countenance, having very fine high and broad foreheads and general light hair, and the freedom from the Scottish accent or Irish brogue.

To the colonisation of this parish by an industrious and peaceable people it may be indebted for its present highly advanced state of cultivation and the independent state of its population. The Hertford family have been always excellent landlords, letting their lands at a reasonable rate and keeping up the practice of fining down the rent a quarter at the renewal of each lease, the calculation being that the tenant is allowed 6 and a half per cent for the purchase or fine paid. The leases are for 3 lives throughout this estate. This is usually considered an uncertain tenure and one on which a tenant rarely ventures to improve, but here it is not so, the tenantry having every confidence in their landlord, who, unless where arrears are unpaid, always renews with them.

Progress of Improvement: Cultivation

Their proximity to the very extensive flour and corn mills at Crumlin, where they can always procure a ready sale for their grain, is a great matter to the farmers. These mills were established in 1765 and in a great degree encouraged the cultivation of grain in this parish, which is almost entirely an agricultural district, the principal crops being wheat, oats and potatoes. The corn law of 1788 still further encouraged the cultivation of grain, and the opening of roads and facilitating the transportation of farm produce to Belfast materially benefited the farmer and held out further inducements for industry. To that market (12 miles distant from the centre of the parish) he takes his pork, milk, butter and potatoes and occasionally his grain, sometimes bringing back lime in returning.

Their orchards are profitable sources of emoluments to the farmers and, except in the south of this county, rather novel to the north of Ireland. Every farmer has an orchard of a greater or less extent, and on average this will produce him at the rate of 12 pounds annually per acre. The orchard is rented by an "apple man", who takes the fruit to Belfast and sells them to persons who export them. The quantity of fruit formerly exported from this district to England and Scotland was enormous.

A few of the working class are engaged in the manufacture of linen which they take to the important markets of Belfast and Lisburn, and some weave for employers.

The more general establishment of a better description of schools and the consequent diffusion of useful and religious knowledge has lately done much good in this parish.

The people are in a very prosperous state. Their rents are moderate and their tithes very low. Their industry is increasing and they are in the neighbourhood of good markets, and the prices of clothes and other necessaries of life have declined in a greater ratio than the prices for the commodities of the farmers.

Obstructions to Improvement

There are no obstructions to improvement in this parish but the farmer has serious obstacles to contend with in the distance he has to draw his turf and lime. The nearest bog is at the south west extremity of the parish, a distance of 6 miles from its northern side, and lime, which is procured from the kilns in Aghalee parish, is 5 miles from the western side of this one.

Local Government

There is no magistrate in this parish. The nearest is Charles Armstrong of Cherry Valley in the adjoining parish of Camlin. The residences of the neighbouring magistrates are not conveniently situated. This, however, is little felt here as this parish furnishes very little business for sessions or assizes, the trifling disputes of the farmers relating mostly to trespass or servants' wages, and these are settled at the Crumlin petty sessions, which are held on every alternate Tuesday.

This parish, as indeed the entire barony of Upper Massereene, is included in the manor of Killultagh, the manor courts and courts leet of which are held in Lisburn, the former once in 3 weeks and the latter once in 6 months; Fortescue Gregg Esquire, seneschal, the Marquis of Hertford, lord of the manor. The jurisdiction of this court is very great, as sums not exceeding 20 pounds are recoverable at it by civil bill and sums not exceeding 100 pounds by attachment.

There are 3 constabulary stationed in the village of Glenavy.

There is not any illicit distillation. Outrage or theft are unknown. There formerly were some party fights in the fairs in Glenavy, and one of these about the year 1805 was so serious that the fairs were then given up and only attempted to be renewed about a year and a half ago.

There are not any insurances.

Dispensary

Patients from this parish are admissible to the dispensaries in Crumlin and Lisburn, which have produced good effects on the health of the poorer class who, however, are but few and comparatively free from disease. Consumption is not unusual and measles are rather prevalent. Fever sometimes visits the lower districts of the parish, but none of these complaints can be called prevalent.

Schools

The improved description of schools of the present day are doing much good in this parish. Sunday schools have been particularly beneficial in their effects. The people evince their anxiety to have their children instructed in their willingness to subscribe towards the erection of schoolhouses and in availing themselves of their benefits.

Poor

In 1808 there were 36 poor on the books of the parish, but in these were included the poor in the 3 united parishes. There are now 30 poor in the union on the church books. Their only support is the collections in the different places of worship and the voluntary charity of the people, which is freely bestowed, either in a little meal or potatoes, and which is quite adequate to their support.

Religion

This parish is episcopally united to those of Camlin and Tullyrusk, and constitutes a vicarage of which the Reverend Edward Cupples is vicar. He resides in Lisburn. The vicarial tithes amount to 380 pounds per annum and the lay tithes to 101 pounds per annum. The vicar keeps but 1 curate, who resides in the parish of Camlin. The parish church is in the village of Glenavy.

The Methodist clergyman (who preaches in the Methodist meeting house in the village of Glenavy) is partly supported by his flock and by a certain salary and allowance for a horse and for each child, which he receives from the Methodist Society.

The Roman Catholic chapel in this parish serves also for the neighbouring ones. The priest is supported solely by his flock.

By the revised census of 1834 there are in this parish 1,589 Episcopalians, 282 Presbyterians and 1,484 Roman Catholics. There are also a few Quakers.

Habits of the People

An independent, respectable and enlightened class of farmers constitutes the mass of the population of this parish. Some of these, or rather their sons, are employed in weaving during the seasons when they are not engaged in the fields. But a small proportion are exclusively weavers. The agricultural labourers bear but a trifling proportion to the rest of the population and the remainder are made up of petty dealers in the village and a few kinds employed at the cotton mill and bleach green in this parish.

The farmers are a respectable class, comfortable in their circumstances, enlightened in their ideas, tasteful in their residences and notions, and very industrious in their habits. A drive through this district is quite sufficient to display their character to the traveller, as there is everything in the aspect of the country, whether as regards its very advanced state of culture, its extreme fertility, the substantial residences of its yeomanry, possessing all the neatness and comfort of appearance which cleanliness and their situation in a grove of orchards and shady trees can contribute, which must indicate a people possessing more than ordinary ideas of civilisation and improvement.

Their taste for gardens and orchards are strong indications of their English extraction. Their system of farming is anything but Irish, as potatoes are generally planted and moulded by the plough. Threshing machines are numerous, the hedgerows neatly trimmed, the lanes shady, the fields large and well laid down and squared, and the farms are generally from 30 to 40 acres in extent, though there are some of from 50 to 150 acres. The implements of husbandry are of an improved description: good iron ploughs driven by reins, and large farming carts drawn by draught horses of a suitable breed. All these circumstances, with the aspect and scenery of the country, give it more the appearance of a rich English district.

Food and Houses

The farmers are a hard-working industrious race, at the same [time] provident and comfortable in their living. They use a good deal of bacon and also cheese which they make. They get a good deal of fish, chiefly pullen and eels, from Lough Neagh and these articles, with baker's bread, some meal but less than formerly, potatoes and milk, constitute their food. Tea is much more generally used, chiefly owing to the cheapness of grocers' licences and the more general establishment of petty grocery shops. With the exception of animal food and cheese, the labourers live similarly to the farmers and in one respect the parish differs from most of others, namely in the

Parish of Glenavy

people living better than formerly. It should have been stated that they generally grow vegetables in their gardens for domestic use.

The houses of the farmers are in general 1-storey, thatched, roughcast, roomy and comfortable and cleanly. A good many, however, are 2-storey and some are slated. They are well furnished and each has a neat parlour with good chairs, a clock, cupboard and a mahogany table. Many of the farmers' houses are very old and evidently, from their oak floors and the oak timber in their high pitched roofs, have been built by the original settlers. Even the houses of the working class are superior in comfort and cleanliness, being roughcast and whitened, consisting of 2 apartments, thatched, well lit and suitably furnished.

Fuel

The great privation the working class suffer is the want of fuel, which, being so distant from the northern side of the parish, is very expensive. They therefore have recourse to brambles, bushes, mill seeds (the husks of the corn) and dry sods.

Dress

They dress well and with taste, a woman never being seen at worship without a bonnet, stockings, and mostly all the young women wear gloves. A neat cotton gown, straw bonnet, shawl or handkerchief, neat shoes and stockings and gloves is the usual dress of the country girls; dark blue coats with brass buttons, blue or drab trousers <trowsers>, beaver hats and coloured waistcoats that of the men. Umbrellas are indispensable and watches numerous. During the week, though cleanly, they are otherwise careless in their persons, but the children in the schools are particularly cleanly.

Longevity

They are a long-lived people. There are at present in this parish the following persons: Widow Russel, 103, Widow McCormick, 105 and Arthur Bell, 94 years of age, and persons of 80 and 90 years old are frequently to be met with.

They marry early: the females often at 15 and the males at 20. The average number in a family is 5 and a half.

Amusements, Morality and Traditions

They have very little amusement of any kind: a little dancing, less cock-fighting and some card-playing. All these are on the decrease and there are few parishes where there is less taste for recreation. They are peaceable and quiet but very fond [of] whiskey, and this, from the number of public houses, they have no difficulty in procuring.

They are in some respects very immoral, no greater proof of which can be given than that there are at present upwards of 40 illegitimate children of different ages in the parish. The farmers' servant-women are not proverbial for their chastity. But in almost every respect they are improving.

They keep up the customs of eating apples and nuts at Hallowe'en and a goose at Christmas <Christmass>, and there is an idle day at Easter. At Christmas there were formerly 13 idle days. Of late years, they have given up the custom of burning fires on Midsummer Eve.

Physical Appearance and Character

The people in this district are free from either the Scottish accent or the Irish brogue, and speak with a pure and agreeable accent. They have very fine high and broad foreheads, and generally light hair. Their countenance differs from that of the men of the northern districts in the county. The women are very comely and have smaller and finer features.

The manners of all classes are more agreeable than those of people of the county Antrim generally, being much more gracious, communicative and civil without being at all servile. They are a manly race both in their persons and in their manners.

Emigration

About 12 persons have annually gone to Canada since 1832, previous to which time there was a much greater spirit for emigration. They generally go in families who take more or less capital, the price of their farm, with them. Some few young men have returned, not finding the country to answer their expectations. None go to the English or Scottish harvests, the agricultural labourers not being more than actually sufficient for the cultivation of the soil.

PRODUCTIVE ECONOMY

Tables of Trades and Occupations

Apothecary and surgeons 2, constabulary 3, carpenter 1, grocers 3, houses of entertainment 2, innkeepers and publicans 3, mantua makers 2, postmaster 1, schoolmaster 1, sextoness 1, saddler 1, shoemakers 2, tailor 1, weavers [blank].

Glenavy Fairs

The fairs to be held on the first Wednesday in each month and the premiums to be distributed quarterly on the February, May, August and November fairs in the following manner, viz. horses: first premium 1 pound 10s, second premium 1 pound, third premium 15s.

Sheep: first premium 5s, second premium 3s, third premium 2s 6d.

Black cattle: first premium 10s, second premium 5s, third premium 3s.

Pigs: first premium 5s, second premium 3s, third premium 2s 6d.

Yarn: first premium 5s, second premium 3s, third premium 2s 6d; the premium for yarn to be given to the largest quantity spun at the residence of the seller and, should two or more articles be sold at one price, that the premiums for the respective classes be divided among the candidates (these premiums are given by the landlord). 25th October 1834.

Glenavy quarterly fairs: premiums will be distributed in future on the February and August fairs for horses and on February, May, August and November for black cattle, sheep, pigs and yarn in the following manner.

Horses: 1st, to the buyer of the highest priced horse 1 pound, to the seller of the highest priced horse 1 pound; 2nd, to the buyer and seller each 15s; 3rd, to the buyer and seller each 10s.

Black cattle: 1st, to the buyer at the highest price 10s, to the seller at the highest price 10s; 2nd, to the buyer and seller at the highest price, each 7s 6d; 3rd, to the buyer and seller at the highest price, each 5s.

Sheep: 1st, to the buyer at the highest price 5s, to the seller at the highest price 5s; 2nd, to buyer and seller at the highest price, each 3s; 3rd, to the buyer and seller at the highest price, each 2s.

Pigs: 1st, to the buyer at the highest price 5s, to the seller at the highest price 5s; 2nd, to the buyer and seller at the highest price 3s; 3rd, to the buyer and seller at the highest price 2s.

Yarn: 1st, to the seller of the largest quantity 5s; 2nd, to the seller of the largest quantity 4s; 3rd, to the seller of the largest quantity 3s; 4th, to the seller of the largest quantity 2s. Glenavy, 15th January 1836.

ANCIENT TOPOGRAPHY

Drawings

Sketch of chalice.
Plan of 12 forts; draft ground plan of 5 forts.
Standing stone in [?] Lisnaree with dimensions, 4 feet high.
Draft ground plans of 2 forts at Ballynacoy and 3 forts at Tullynewbank.

Note on Chalice

The chalice bears the following inscription: "This plate was given to ye church of Glenavy by the officers of ye Queen's Regiment of Horse, commanded by ye Honorable Major-General Sir R. John Lanier, in the year 1690, in honorem Ecclesia Anglicanae."

SOCIAL ECONOMY

Schools

[Table contains the following headings: name, situation and description, when established, income and expenditure, physical, intellectual and moral education, number of pupils subdivided by age, sex and religion, name and religion of master or mistress].

Sunday school, held in the Roman Catholic chapel in the townland of Ballymacricket, established 1823; income: local subscriptions among the people 2 pounds 12s; expenditure, salaries: 2 teachers [?] 1s per Sunday each for the summer half year, [total] 2 pounds 12s; intellectual education: spelling (Manson's book), reading, lesson book and Scriptures; moral education: managed by the priest, all versions of the Scriptures; number of pupils: males, 59 under 10 years of age, 62 from 10 to 15, 7 above 15, 127 total males; females, 68 under 10 years of age, 36 from 10 to 15, 9 above 15, 113 total females; total number of pupils 240, 60 Protestants, 180 Roman Catholics; masters Michael Mulholland and Daniel Donnelly, Roman Catholics.

Private school, in a house built for the purpose by subscription in the townland of Crew, originally established more that 20 years; income from pupils 19 pounds; intellectual education: *Manson's Spelling and reading book, Gough's Arithmetic, Murray's Grammar*, writing and book-keeping; moral education: visits from the Protestant clergy, Sunday school, Authorised Version of Scriptures daily, church catechisms; number of pupils: males, 9 under 10 years of age, 12 from 10 to 15, 21 total males; females, 8 under 10 years of age, 7 from 10 to 15, 15 total females; total number of pupils 36, 31 Protestants, 5 Roman Catholics; master John Neill, Protestant.

Private school, in a house built for the purpose by subscription and situated in the townland of

Parish of Glenavy

Ballymacricket, established 1826; income from pupils 18 pounds; intellectual education: *Manson's Spelling and reading book, Gough's Arithmetic, Murray's Grammar*, writing and book-keeping; moral education: visited by the priest, Authorised and Douay Version of the Scriptures daily; number of pupils: males, 8 under 10 years of age, 10 from 10 to 15, 18 total males; females, 9 under 10 years of age, 8 from 10 to 15, 17 total females; total number of pupils 35, 12 Protestants, 24 Roman Catholics; master Michael Mulholland, Roman Catholic.

[Totals]: males, 86 under 10 years of age, 84 from 10 to 15, 7 above 15, 166 total males; females, 85 under 10 years of age, 51 from 10 to 15, 9 above 15, 145 total females; total number of pupils 311, 102 Protestants, 209 Roman Catholics.

School Statistics

[Table contains the following headings: townland, name and religion of master or mistress, free or pay school, income of master or mistress, description and cost of schoolhouse, number of pupils subdivided by religion, sex and the Protestant and Roman Catholic returns, societies with which connected].

Ballyminimore, master Bernard Donnedy, Roman Catholic; pay school, annual income 15 pounds to 17 pounds; schoolhouse stone and lime, in bad repair, cost 20 pounds; number of pupils by the Protestant return: 10 Established Church, 20 Presbyterians, 5 Roman Catholics, 22 males, 13 females; by the Roman Catholic return: 12 Established Church, 23 Presbyterians, 9 Roman Catholics, 27 males, 17 females; associations none.

Aghadolgan, master Hugh Donnelly, Roman Catholic; pay school, annual income 20 pounds; schoolhouse stone and lime, cost 18 pounds; number of pupils by the Protestant return: 9 Established Church, 23 Roman Catholics, 20 males, 12 females; by the Roman Catholic return: 9 Protestants, 23 Roman Catholics, 20 males, 12 females; associations none.

Old Park, master William Craney, Protestant; pay school, annual income 13 pounds; schoolhouse stone and lime and thatched, cost 26 pounds; number of pupils by the Protestant return: 14 Established Church, 19 Roman Catholics, 15 males, 18 females; by the Roman Catholic return: 14 Established Church, 19 Roman Catholics, 15 males, 18 females; associations none.

Ballyvannon, master James McGanelly, Roman Catholic; pay school, annual income 20 pounds; schoolhouse stone and lime and thatched, cost 26 pounds; number of pupils by the Protestant return: 17 Established Church, 9 Roman Catholics, 17 males, 9 females; by the Roman Catholic return: 17 Established Church, 9 Roman Catholics, 17 males, 9 females; associations none.

Crew, master Francis M. Stevenson, Established Church; pay school, annual income 12 pounds; schoolhouse stone and lime, cost 25 pounds; number of pupils by the Protestant return: 21 Established Church, 3 Presbyterians, 11 Roman Catholics, 19 males, 16 females; by the Roman Catholic return: 21 Established Church, 3 Presbyterians, 11 Roman Catholics, 19 males, 16 females; the Marquis of Hertford gave 5 pounds 13s 9d towards building the schoolhouse.

Ballymoate, master John Loughan, Roman Catholic; pay school, annual income 20 pounds; schoolhouse the master's own house; number of pupils by the Protestant return: 11 Established Church, 4 Presbyterians, 5 Roman Catholics, 11 males, 9 females; associations none.

Glenavy, mistress Mary McGannity, Protestant; pay school, annual income about 11 pounds; schoolhouse: room in a private house; number of pupils by the Protestant return: 15 Established Church, 2 Roman Catholics, 17 females; associations none.

Lough Neagh

Statistical Survey by Lieutenant Thomas Graves, copied by C.W. Ligar, 1834

Memoir Writing

Memoir Writing

Received from Mr Ligar, 22 October 1834.

The following information has been given by Lieutenant Thomas Graves R.N., and is contained in a small manuscript, the materials of which he collected during the prosecution of a survey of Lough Neagh under the Right Honourable the Lords Commissioners of the Admiralty in 1831 to 1832, and which he is about to publish.

Natural State

Situation and Name

This lake, with the exception of Ladoga and Onega in Russia and Geneva in Switzerland, is the largest in Europe. It is surrounded by the counties of Antrim to the north and east, Armagh to the south, between which and Antrim a small portion of Down reaches its margin, Tyrone to the west and Londonderry to the north west. By means of the Newry and Belfast Canals it offers a great facility for introducing foreign importations and distributing them at a moderate expense throughout the province, as well as a ready issue for the exportation of the native produce of this improving part of the country. Its consequent utility therefore renders it an object not only of much local importance, but also of great national interest.

The ancient name of the lake was Echach or Eacha, which in the Erse language signified "divine" and loch "a lake", or "the divine lake." In the same language neasg or naasgh "a sore" might have alluded to its virtues in curing certain cutaneous disorders and have from thence been easily converted into Neagh or Neach. [Insert footnote: *Statistical survey of Armagh* by Sir [Charles] Coote].

History and Social Economy

Healing Properties of the Lough

A curious notice respecting its supposed healing qualities is in Boate's *Natural history of Ireland*, in a letter from Francis Nevil Esquire to the Lord Bishop of Clogher: "That there is some healing quality in the water of the lough is certain; but whether diffused through all parts thereof is not known nor pretended. There is a certain bay in it called the Fishing bay, which is about half a mile broad. It is bounded by the school lands of Dungannon, hath a fine sandy bottom, not a pebble in it, so that one may walk with safety and ease from the depths of his ankle <ancle> to his chin upon an easy declivity, at least 300 yards before a man shall come to that depth. I have been in it several times when multitudes have been there and at other times, and I have always observed that as I have walked the bottom has changed from cold to warm and from warm to cold, and this in different spots throughout the bay." [Insert footnote: This sensation is generally experienced by bathers in almost every lake and river].

"The first occasion of taking notice of this bay for cure happened to be no longer ago than in the reign of Charles II and was thus: there was one Mr Cunningham that lived within a few miles of the place, who had an only son grown to man's estate. This young man had the evil to that degree, that it ran upon him in 8 or 10 places. He had been touched by the king and all means imaginable used for his recovery, but all did no good and his body was so wasted that he could not walk. When all hopes of his recovery were passed, he was carried to the lough where he was washed and bathed, and in 8 day's time, bathing each day, all the sores were dried up and he became cured and grew very healthy, married, begot children and lived 9 or 10 years after. The natives thought it would not do well, but upon some particular time appropriated for that service, and now great crowds come there on Midsummer Eve, of all sorts of sick, and sick cattle are brought there likewise and driven into the water for their cures, and people do believe they receive benefit."

The bay above mentioned is now termed Washing bay. The warm springs, if ever there were any, are no longer to be found, and the only remains of its former celebrity are 2 fairs held on the Sunday before and after Midsummer, called Big Sunday, at which dancing, drinking and broken heads are much more prevalent than experiments on the virtues of the waters. Small groups, however, are to be seen bending their steps to take advantage of the healing properties of the small rivulet that falls into the bay, which they fancy has some good effect, and many are the cures ascribed to these ablutions, which would most probably be as efficacious if made at any other part of the shores of the lough. The rivulet has obtained the name of the Holy river and is much venerated.

Traditions of the Lough

Tradition has not been idle in assigning several causes for the formation of this lake, many of which are curious and seem to have been handed down from father to son from time immemorial and no doubt improved as they passed through each generation. That great favourite among the lower orders, and the hero of so many of their legendary tales, Fin McCool, the giant (Fingal of the Scotch), being exasperated at some act of indiscretion, or to show his great power, is said to have seized a handful of such size that the hollow caused by its removal formed the basin of the present lough. The earth being thrown into the Irish Channel formed the Isle of Man, which is gravely stated to be of exactly the same shape and size as the outline of the lake. It is also a prevalent belief that if a fire is not continually kept burning on the island, it would return to its former situation.

Another account is as follows: a well that stood in the centre of the space now occupied by the lough, the waters of which were supposed to possess some wonderful charm and to be under the influence of the fairies or, as they term them, "gentle spirits", was left under the direction of an old woman, probably a witch, with the injunction that she should close the wicket of the enclosure that surrounded it after any visitors to the well. The aged damsel, it appears, made too free with the "crathur" and neglected the command, upon which the water overflowed and followed the terrified witch so far as Toome, where she was thrown into it by the inhabitants and paid the forfeit of her life for her indiscretion. The overflowing then ceased and thus the lough was formed!

Some of the early writers affirm that Lough Neagh suddenly burst out in the reign of Lugaidh Raibderg in the 56th year of the Christian era and was then called Lion Mhuine. Lendrick mentions a singular circumstance, that the soundings were sometimes interrupted by trunks of trees standing in an upright position and these were most numerous near the mouth of the Blackwater. The idea of a town being buried under the waters of the lough is also prevalent and is noticed by Moore in his Irish melodies.

"On Lough Neagh's banks as the fisherman strays,
when the clear cold eve's declining;
he sees the round towers of other days,
in the waves beneath him shining."

In the course of the survey under the Lords Commissioners of the Admiralty in 1831 to 1832, the soundings in the neighbourhood of the Blackwater were found regular and no circumstance occurred that in any degree favour either of the above remarks. Lieutenant Graves, to show that the idea existed while he was prosecuting the survey, mentions that one of the seamen, when heaving the lead and finding a sudden alteration in the depth of the water, exclaimed facetiously: "By my soul, it's down a chimley, your honour!"

NATURAL FEATURES

Rivers, Water Level and Drainage

Although 8 considerable rivers, viz. the Moyola, Ballinderry, Blackwater, Upper Bann, Glenavy, Crumlin, Six Mile Water and Main Water discharge themselves into the lake, yet there is only one visible discharge at Toome Bridge over an extensive and shoal bar, having only 2 feet of water in it in the summer season, through a narrow channel which intervenes between it and Lough Beg; and joining the Lower Bann at New ferry, eventually issues into the sea at Coleraine and separates the counties of Antrim and Londonderry. "Before the autumnal season of the year, when the rains begin to soften the earth and swell the rivers, the water discharged at Toome is very inconsiderable, so as not to afford a depth greater than that which may reach to the knee of a person wading, and once it happened that a person taking advantage of an inblowing wind walked over dry shod; but at the same season the influx of water is inconsiderable." [Insert footnote: Appendix to Dr Barton's *Lectures on natural philosophy*, Dublin, 1751].

The Upper Bann, which may be supposed the greatest of the 8 rivers, for it gives a name to all the rest where they flow in one channel to the sea, being called the Lower Bann, has been frequently observed to have scarce any current [of] water in it, immediately before the falling of the great rains. At the conclusion therefore of the summer, supposing it a dry season, there is very little water flowing into the lough since the other rivers are singly inferior to the Bann in quantity of water. When the rains fall in abundance and the rivers swell above their banks and continue so during 5 months and sometimes more, there is a prodigious quantity of water, insomuch that the discharge at Toome being vastly less, the water of the lough usually rises from 6 to 9 feet perpendicularly and spreads over about 10,000 acres [insert marginal note: see Ordnance Survey] of land more than it does when it is at the lowest, when it covers [blank].

The discharge of water thus accumulated during the winter months from the rivers before mentioned, not having sufficient space to escape at Toome, causes a considerable rise on the shores of the lake and covers much land annually, and thereby renders it unfit for anything but grass.

Charles Brownlow Esquire, M.P., who has a large property near Lurgan and in the neighbourhood of the Upper Bann, has at an immense expense made embankments and has erected wind pumps and steam engines to endeavour to prevent the encroachments of the water, but as yet to no purpose. A very considerable tract of land lying between Toome and Castledawson, called the Creagh, is also annually inundated, besides many other places adjoining the lough, which, although separately not of so great extent as the 2 instances above mentioned, yet suffer from the same causes.

A prospectus is now in circulation and commissioners are now investigating the best means of lowering the lough to its summer level. Should this be effected, additional value would certainly be given to some of the land annually covered and an inconsiderable slip of coast on the borders of the lough would become exposed, that is, the difference between the now summer and winter levels, but this would probably be of little value as the shore is either large stones or sand.

A circumstance, however, which seems to have been insufficiently considered is the navigation of the lough, which if drained too much will be destroyed. Even now during the summer there is only 2 and a half feet of the water at the entrance of the Upper Bann where the Newry Navigation commences, and the canal into the Blackwater has not more than 3 feet at its entrance. It should therefore be ascertained if the land reclaimed or improved would compensate for the injury done to the inland navigation. A great objection to the draining of the lake would be the injury expected to be done to the fisheries. As a proof of the value attached to them, it may be mentioned that Earl O'Neill purchased within a few years the right of the eel fisheries at Toome from the Marquis of Donegall for 8,000 pounds, besides a yearly rent of 400 pounds.

Petrifactions

Persons residing along the shore of the lough all agree in stating that pieces of petrified wood of no very considerable size are often thrown up on those parts of the shore most exposed to the prevailing winds, which will comprehend the Antrim bay and all the eastern side of the lough open to the south west. The petrifying power of the lough is mentioned by Nennius, a writer of the 9th century, who says: "Est aliud stagnam quod facit ligna durescere in lapides. Homines autem fingunt ligna et postquam formaverint projiciunt in stagnum et manent in eo usque ad caput anni et in capite anni lapis invenitur et vocatur stagnum Loch Echach." English: "There is another lake which makes wood harden into stone. People cleave the wood into pieces and, when they have formed them, cast them into the lake and there they remain until the beginning of the year; and at the commencement of the new year a stone is found and the lake is called Lach Echach."

A general idea is that the change takes place in 7 years and holly is the favourite wood, but no experiments have been made that are now known to sanction such a belief; and as an argument against it, it may be mentioned that at Toome a large bed of timber, consisting of roots and branches partially imbedded in the sand and lying in the fairway of the only channel through which the lough discharges itself, although remembered to have been there as long as the oldest inhabitant can recollect, shows no signs of alteration or petrifaction, either above the soil in which it rests or below it. Neither have any of the posts which appear in so many parts of the lough, used by the fishermen to secure their boats to and dry their nets between, although many are half immersed, undergone any visible change. It appears, however, that a petrifying property exists in the vicinity and is rather to be ascribed to the soil than the water.

Dr Barton, in describing a series of specimens to illustrate the subject, mentions that the largest and most perfect petrifactions were found at some distance up the Crumlin river and Six Mile Water, when, on the contrary, those specimens found on the shores had evidently become rounded by the action of the water.

A large mass of petrifaction that required 8 horses to draw it, which appears to have been the root of a tree, is at present in the Honourable Colonel Pakenham's <Packenham's> garden at Langford Lodge and was removed by him in 1824 from its position below Glendarrah in the Crumlin river, a distance of 2 miles from the lake.

Islands in Lough Neagh

Of these, there are very few and none of any considerable extent. The largest is Ram's Island, situated in nearly the centre of Crumlin bay, and contains about 7 acres of ground capable of cultivation, but in a dry summer upwards of 20 acres are exposed. It formerly belonged to David McArevery, a fisherman, who disposed of it to Conway McNene Esquire for 100 guineas. It then passed into the hands of Mr Whittle, from whom Lord O'Neill, who is the present proprietor, purchased it for 1,000 pounds. His lordship has built a neat and handsome cottage on it. The grounds are tastefully laid out and the planting by which it is surrounded renders it one of the most picturesque spots on the lake. A round tower in tolerable preservation forms the most remarkable object on the island and confers on it a high degree of historical interest and antiquarian association. In some old maps it is called Enis or Innis Garden; when the change was made is not known.

The Three Islands, a name applied to the 3 islets lying off the parish of Duneane in the vicinity of Scawdy, are also the property of Earl O'Neill, who has planted them with trees of various descriptions and on the western one has erected another neat and retired cottage. From the centre island to the shore a spit of sand extends which in dry summers is wholly exposed.

Coney Island lies off the entrance into Maghera, is destitute of trees and on it are the ruins of some houses of modern date. The island produces a small crop every season and at a trifling expense might be made as picturesque and ornamental as Ram's Island.

History

Fisheries: History of Ownership

In May 1604, in the reign of James I, the Lord Deputy Sir Arthur Chichester received a grant of the fisheries of Lough Neagh and was appointed admiral and commander-in-chief thereof, with full powers and authority to dispose of all the shipping boats and vessels thereon. These grants were afterwards repurchased by government in favour of the London Society for a pension of 40 pounds sterling per annum, to Sir A. Chichester with liberty for him to fish.

When Charles I set aside the Corporation of London, the title of those persons became void. In the time of the Commonwealth, Cromwell granted to one of the Skeffington family the right of the eel fisheries on the River Bann in lieu of a certain pension which that family claimed for services rendered to the government. After the Restoration, the Corporation of London agreed to take out a new charter, but Sir A. Chichester, on whose pension great arrears were due, had the precaution 3 months before this event to obtain a patent dated 3rd July in the 13th year of Charles II, not only all his former possessions but also the right of the fishery from Lough Neagh to the rock or cuts about a mile above Coleraine.

The lease granted by Cromwell was given to Sir A. Chichester, but from the previous charter of King Charles the chief of the Skeffington family retains to this day the title of Baron of Lough Neagh.

In these charters the lake is termed Lachus Neachus alias Lough Sidney, alias Lough Chichester, in honour of the Lord Deputies, Sir Henry Sydney and Sir Chichester. The 2 latter have, however, been unable to supplant the more ancient appellation by which it continues to be known.

The most considerable and most important fishery is that at Toome, for eels, as may be readily inferred from the immense rent paid for it.

Productive Economy

Salmon and Eel Fisheries

As the salmon ascends to spawn in the lake, so the eel descends to bring forth its progeny in the sea. The latter, during the months of April and May, not thicker than a straw, may be seen making their way up the Bann in immense numbers. To assist them in passing the falls at the salmon leap near Coleraine and at Portna, ropes of straw are purposely placed, over which they may be seen climbing with great dexterity. Such is their anxiety to reach the lough that a log of wood or obstruction, from the shallowness of the river, will not impede their progress and at times persons are employed to assist them up with buckets.

The salmon fry are supposed to have left the fresh water by the beginning of June, at which time the eel fishery commences and continues until the end of February. August, September and October are considered the best months, both as to numbers taken and in respect to preserving them, for, as the season advances, the eels become strongly flavoured and tough.

There are 4 weirs close to Toome Bridge on its southern side, at the mouth of which nets in shape similar to a trawl are fixed every evening to intercept the eels in their descent to the sea. For it is remarkable and found from repeated trials to be the case that not an eel can be taken in the daytime except the weather be very dull and the river flooded, and even in a moonlight night scarcely any are caught. The wind blowing strong from south east at the beginning of the day and shifting towards the evening to the south west, with a dark night, is the time in which they are taken in the greatest quantities. Indeed so numerous are they when a concurrence of these circumstances take place, that it frequently happens nets are carried away, although well watched and emptied every 10 minutes. As many as 50,000 it is said have been taken in a night, but this a circumstance of rare occurrence.

The fishermen consider the decline of the moon after Michaelmas or, as they term it, "the Michaelmas dark" the most propitious part of the season.

Quantities of eels are daily sent to all the principal towns in the north of Ireland. Those not disposed of in that manner are salted and a ready sale for them is found during the winter, and they keep well until Lammas. The price varies from a ha'penny to 6d each, or about 2d per lb.

In answer to an inquiry as to whether the eel reached its full size, 4 or 5 lbs, in one season, a person who was formerly concerned in this fishery stated that such was the case: that he had made an experiment by tying a piece of silk through them as they ascended and that he caught the same fish full grown on their descent in the same season. This appeared proof positive, but another experiment made in a well near Toome was not so fortunate, for the fry, after remaining there upwards of 6 months, though apparently healthy, had scarcely increased in size. Probably the confined situation in the latter case might have been the cause of this difference. The specific name of the eel above mentioned is Anguilla vulgaris, common eel.

NATURAL HISTORY

Varieties of Salmon and Other Fish

The following notices respecting the fish found in Lough Neagh are extracted from a manuscript of the late Mr Templeton of Belfast, who devoted many years of his life to the study of the natural history of Belfast.

Salmo salar, salmon: these fish make their way to the lough to spawn. They vary much in shape, those in some rivers being much robust, in others more slender and apparently calculated for greater activity. Thus those in the Bann, a slow running river nearly throughout its whole course, are remarkably thick and strong made. The salmon of the Bush, a rapid running stream, are more slender in their form. The same variation of colour takes place in these 2 rivers. The Bann, with transparent waters, produces a bright clear-coloured salmon, while the Bush river, whose waters are tinged by the bogs in which it rises, produces salmon whose white parts are tinged more or less with brown. This change of colour produced by the water is very conspicuous in the common trout and eel. I have often seen trout and eels that lived in lakes and bogs that had their originally white belly tinged with a brownish yellow.

Salmo fario, gillaroo trout, Salmo lacustris <locustris>, the buddagh: I have ventured to consider the above as constituting but one species, having had many opportunities of examining and comparing trouts of various sizes, from the smallest specimens found in our rivulets to those very large ones found in Lough Neagh. And I have every reason to say that if any careful observer will notice all the intermediate sizes, he will often find as strong marks of distinction between 2 specimens of the same size as he can possibly find between one of 1 lb and one of 20 lbs.

By a careful perusal of authors who have described the Salmo lacustris, I find the chief characters dwelt upon are size and colour. Size I think scarcely worth attending to, and as to the tinges of colour, everyone who has caught fish in the Irish lakes and rivers knows how variable it is, fish inhabiting transparent waters having their bellies whitish and their colours clear and well defined. All the fish in Lough Neagh have their white parts tinged in some degree with reddish tawny. Mr Cox, in his *Tour in Switzerland*, describes the Salmo lacustris as having a conical head, larger in proportion than the salmon. The under-jaw in a full-grown fish ends in a blunt hook; the colour, so low as the lateral line, of a deep blue brightening as it approaches the line; beneath, that of a silvery white; and all the upper part spotted irregularly with black; dorsal fin 12-rayed, pectoral 14, ventral 12, anal 12.

The small trout of our rivers vary in shape and also in the proportional size of the head, in clear streams a dusky blue, sides with a slight bluish tinge and belly white. In bog water lakes these colours of the back and sides acquire a brownish tinge and the white of the belly is often ferruginous orange; the spots on the back, sides and fins vary also in number and size. The bright red spots usually seen, are in some, become brown or nearly obliterated. Our large trouts of Lough Neagh vary also in form and the upper jaw is often seen to project beyond the lower. The back is dusky blue; about the lateral line a little reddish tinge is observable. The belly has the same tinge with a shade of tawny. The spots are very irregularly shaped, black surrounded with brown on the sides. They appear as if several had imperfectly formed a junction. They are seen on the whole upper part of the body and even on the skin surrounding the iris. The tail is not more forked than in a small fish. The irregularity in the number of the rays in the fins does not enable us to fix on this as forming any precise character. The dorsal fin seems to be the one least variable in the number of the rays. It is generally 12-rayed, but varying from 11 to 12, pectoral 12, 13, 14, ventral 9, 10, 11, anal 9, 10, 11, canelal 24, 27.

It was long supposed that the gillaroo trout found in many of our lakes was distinct from the common one, but the late accurate examination of several individually of this kind proved beyond a doubt that the apparent distinction arises solely from their living more than is usually the case on the Helix tentaculata, Tellina cornea, by which their membraneous stomachs are increased in thickness so as to assume the appearance of the gizzard of a fowl, whence the name of "gizzard trout."

In Ireland every running stream may be said to abound with this fish, no stream too rapid, nor indeed does any cataract of moderate height retard their progress in ascending the rivers before their spawning time. At this period, the month of October and November, the large trout of Lough Neagh, in attempting to ascend the Main Water and the Six Mile Water, are caught in large quantities. On the 12th September 1811 there was taken in the pound at Mr Ledlie's mills near Antrim 7 cwt of Lough Neagh trout.

Salmo alpinus <alpinous> or charr of Lough Neagh, whiting: "reddish white with a dusky back, ferruginous spots, very minute scales and the pectoral and ventral fins red ferruginous."

While endeavouring to trace the history of Lough Neagh whiting, I have found considerable difficulty in determining its identity with any hitherto described species of the genus. That which seems most to approach is certainly the lean charr of the Westmoreland lakes and indeed, there is scarcely more disagreement than what might arise from the tingeing property of the water. Those of Lough Neagh are generally from 12 to 14 inches long, though some are met with 15 inches in length.

Salmo wartmanii: Lough Neagh pullan; Esox lucius: pike; Petromyzon fluviatilis: lesser lamprey; Petromyzon branchialis: pride.

I have often observed it about Belfast and other parts of the county Antrim (about May), on the gravelly fords where 5 or 6 appeared to unite their efforts to excavate a place wherein to deposit their spawn. They are said never to conceal themselves under the stones but lodge in the mud, and that they are never observed to adhere to anything as the other species do.

Gasterosteus aculeatus: stickleback, found in the rivulets running into Lough Neagh.

Cyprinus erythropthalmus <erythrophalinus>: rudd or red eye, a native of Lough Erne and many other lakes and most probably of Lough Neagh, being found in the Lagan river.

Cyprinus brama: bream, common throughout the lough.

Perca fluviatilis: perch.

List of Shells found in Lough Neagh

Named according to Turton's last work: Cyclas cornea, Anodon cygneus, Unio margaritiferus, Vitrina pellucida, land shell, Helix niteus, land shell, Helix radiata, land shell, Clausilia rugosa, land shell, Bulimus [Bulinus] lubricus, land shell, Tuccinea amphibia, Planorbis cannatus, Planorbis vortex, Planorbis contortus, Limneus pereger?, Limneus glutinosus, Limneus fossarius or palustris, Physia fontenalis (found by Messrs Hyndman and R. Patterson, members of Natural History Society, Belfast), Valvata obtusa, Paludina impura, Aneylus fluviatilis.

Birds of Lough Neagh

Birds noticed on or near Lough Neagh: Sparrow hawk, kestrel, barn or white owl, long-eared owl, hood crow, rook, jackdaw, magpie, common starling, cuckoo, woodpecker, common creeper, kingfisher, swallow, martin, swift, thrush, fieldfare, blackbird, redbreast, water ousel, wren, red wagtail, grey wagtail, yellow wagtail, whinchat, meadow pipit, titlark, woodlark (mistaken by many for nightingale), great titmouse, blue titmouse, long-tailed titmouse, common bunting, yellow bunting, reed <rede> bunting, snow bunting, bullfinch, house sparrow, chaffinch, goldfinch, ring dove, partridge, quail, plover, pewit, coot, corncrake, sandpiper, jack snipe, common snipe, curlew, bittern, grebe, golden plover, teal, wild goose, gull, widgeon, golden eye, shag, woodcock, water hen, gannet, grey goose, duck.

Parish of Magheragall, County Antrim

Fair Sheets by Thomas Fagan, July and August 1837

MODERN TOPOGRAPHY AND SOCIAL ECONOMY

Magheragall Church

Magheragall church, on the leading road from Lisburn to Ballinderry and about 2 and a half miles from the former town, is an oblong building, 1-storey high and slated, and measures 56 by 28 feet inside, walls 3 feet thick; and attached to the west end a very handsome tower, 3-storey high and measuring 17 feet 3 inches by 16 feet 9 inches on the outside, and on the third storey a moderate sized bell in rather decayed state, its surface bearing date 1672. The corners, pinnacles <pinicles> and all other ornaments of the tower are cut freestone, as is also the base and corners of this church. The entrance door opens from the tower to the body of the church, and a small side door from the vestry, which is attached to the church on the north side and stands 1-storey, slated and 7 and a half feet by 7 feet inside.

The interior of the church is spacious and well lighted by 3 windows on the south and 2 on the north side, and a large window on the east gable, all which are Gothic shape, and ventilation afforded by small funnels up through the breast or seat of each window. There is a neat gallery constructed against the gable in the west end of the church and supported in front on 2 timber columns, and the stairs ascending to it made of timber. The roof of the church is chiefly of metal and the doors and windows cased with cut stone. The alley is laid with cut freestone and the pews boarded, and in the middle of the church a neat metal stove.

The communion table stands on the east end and on the south side of it the pulpit, which is elevated some feet above the floor, and beneath it a baptismal font of cut stone. On the north side stands a handsome reading desk. Pews on the ground floor 32: 30 of these average 11 feet 3 inches of seats each and will hold 7 persons each pew, total 210; 2 of these average 22 feet of seats and will hold 14 persons each pew, total 28; 11 pews on the gallery, each 11 and a half feet of seats and will hold 7 persons each pew, total 77; 4 pews on the gallery, 7 and a half feet of seats each and will hold 5 persons each pew, total 20; total accommodated in the church 335, allowing 1 and a half feet to each sitting.

The interior is well finished, well ventilated in the order before stated and all its furniture neatly done and well arranged; and in the south side wall a very handsome monument of marble slabs erected to the memory of the late Richard Houghton of Springfield, Esquire, who died 1828 aged 78 years.

In the north side of the tower, cut in a circular stone outside, date of erection as follows: "1830, Paul McHenry, builder", and cut on stone on the south side over the entrance door: "This is the [chi-rho sign] victory that overcometh the world, even our faith."

The cost of erecting this church was 1,000 pounds and the materials of the old church in addition, the above sum given by the First Fruits and only a small part refunded. It stands on a handsome eminence and for the greater part on the ground of the old church. The burial ground is enclosed partly by a stone and lime wall and partly by a quick fence, sheltered on the north and east by a plantation, and in the interior several lofty forest trees. Entrance by a neat wrought iron gate. Divine service in summer at 11.30 a.m. and at 5.30 p.m., and in winter at 11.30 a.m. only. No glebe or glebe house in the parish. 5th and 6th July 1837.

Collections for Poor

Annual collection about 13 pounds, which sum is quarterly distributed to 40 persons on the poor list. Deserted children on the parish: 1835, 1836 and 1837 2 only.

Income and Residence of Vicar

The Reverend John Mussen is vicar of Magheragall. Benefice 72 pounds 10s, grant from First Fruits 46 pounds, total 138 pounds 10s. Of the above sum, the vicar gives to a parish schoolmaster annually 2 pounds. Mr Mussen lives beside the church in a thatched cottage 1-storey high. No curate in the parish. Information obtained from the Reverend John Mussen, vicar of Magheragall.

Congregation

Attendance at the above church on Sundays, of dry or fine weather, from 200 to 300 persons. Informant as above.

Parish of Magheragall

Magheragall Churchyard

In the churchyard stand several handsome raised tombs and neat headstones. At the east gable of the church stands 3 raised tombs erected to the following persons: (1) To Robert Redman of Springfield, Esquire, who died 1788 aged 68 years; (2) To James Watson of Brookhill, Esquire, who died 1772 aged 77 years; (3) To Elizabeth Boyes, wife of James Boyes Esquire, who died 1794 aged 62 years, and their respective families.

The following embrace the principal names and surnames on family tombs. Male names: Alexander, Edward, George, James, John, Joseph, Hugh, Henery, Thomas, William, Patrick, Robert, Richard.

Female names: Allice, Ann, Barbara, Elizabeth, Isabella, Mary-Ann, Maudlin, Mary, Jane, Sarah, Margaret, Elenor.

Surnames: Adair, Beshaw, Brown, Ballentine, Campbell, Crossey, Clark, McCollom, McDonnell, Dawson, Ewart, Fisher, Garrett, Younghusband, Greer, Higginson, Higgins, Heaveron, Horner, Johnston, Larmor, Mears, McMurlin, McNaught, McKinstrey, Singleton, Rogers, Thomson, Whitla, Wear, Watson, Wakefield. Several stones not legible and several familes not having tombs or headstones. The oldest legible stone in the yard is 1713.

MODERN TOPOGRAPHY

Seceding Meeting House and Fort

Magheragall Seceding meeting house stands about 3 and a half miles from Lisburn and is situated in the townland of Ballycarrickmaddy. It is 1-storey high, slated and measures 38 feet 6 inches by 17 feet 9 inches inside, walls 2 feet thick. It has 1 door and 8 oblong windows, floor partly boarded and partly made of lime and sand. The pulpit stands in the south side of the house, elevated some feet above the floor. Pews in the house 14: each has 16 feet of seats and will hold 10 persons each pew, total accommodated with seats in the house 140, allowing 1 and a half feet to each sitting. Average attendance on Sundays 60 to 100 persons; divine service at 11.30 in the morning. Collections are made amounting to about 5 pounds annually, which go to repairs on the house.

The Reverend John S. Brown is minister of this congregation and gets average annual stipends 18 pounds, royal bounty annually 50 pounds, total annual income 68 pounds. This house was originally a thatched house, erected by the Seceding congregation themselves above 50 years back. But in 1816 it was rebuilt and slated by subscriptions from benevolent persons of different creeds, cost about 80 pounds. The site or ground is held on lease under Lord Hertford at a small annual rent and is enclosed by a quickset fence, entrance is by a good iron gate.

There is a session house, 1-storey high and slated, joined to the west end of the meeting house, and on the grounds a fort approaching to oval, 35 by 30 yards and occupied partly by burials and partly by forest trees. Part of the parapet, which was made of clay, is now destroyed, but the existing part averages 6 feet high and 16 feet wide, and is faced with quicks. The parapet and exterior of the fort was planted with a variety of forest trees about 10 years back. They at present form an ornament and shelter, and render the area of the fort a handsome but very rare burial ground attached to a place of worship.

The first person that have been interred in this new burial ground was James McCollom, who died 1815 aged 75 years. Names on headstones there at present: Alexander, David, James, Thomas, Elizabeth, Rebecca; Montgomery, Galway, Kelso, Kennedy, Orr. Information from Alexander Larmor and others. 7th July 1837.

Wesleyan Methodist Preaching House

Wesleyan Methodist preaching house in the townland of Knocknadona, 2 and a half miles from Lisburn on the leading road from the latter town to Glenavy, stands 1-storey high and thatched, and measuring 31 by 19 and a half feet inside, walls 2 feet thick. It has 1 door and 8 windows, floor made of clay. The pulpit stands in the east end of the house, elevated some feet above the floor. Seats in the house 16, each 8 feet long and will hold 5 persons each seat, allowing 1 and a half feet to each sitting; total accommodated with seats 80. Divine service at 11 o'clock in the morning, average attendance 30 to 50 persons. Preachers: Reverend William Armstrong and Henery Giles of Lisburn. Their annual salary is given on Lisburn Fair Sheets. This preaching house accommodates a day and Sunday school. It was built by subscription above 40 years back, cost of erection not at present known.

Springfield

Springfield, the seat of Captain Houghton, stands about 3 miles from Lisburn, on the leading road from the latter town to Ballinderry. The house is a very neat oblong house, slated and stands 1-storey high. There is a fruit and vegetable garden containing about 2 English acres, enclosed partly by a stone and lime wall and partly by a quickset fence. Entrance from the above road by a neat wrought iron gate, at which stands a neat porter's lodge, and in front of the house a large lawn interspersed by a variety of forest trees. The demesne, which consists of about 87 English acres, is bounded to a great extent by plantations and divided into well-arranged fields, which are enclosed by good quickset fences and iron gates to each. The house and demesne is in good order and eligible for a gentleman's seat.

The house was originally an ordinary farmhouse, but about 60 years back the place passed into the hands of the late Edward Wakefield Esquire, who rebuilt the house and resided there for several years, till the tenure expired about 1811, at which period the late Major Houghton got a new lease of the situation and subsequently made several improvements on the house and demesne. The present proprietor has also improved the place to some extent since his father's death. Informants John McGrath and Moses Watson. 12th July 1837.

Brookhill

Brookhill, the seat of Captain Watson, stands 4 miles from Lisburn, north east of the leading road from the latter town to Ballinderry. The house is commodious, stands 2-storey high and slated, with 2 bows in front, 1 on either side of the hall door, and a wing to the rear, nearly as large as the front house and standing equal height. There is a most beautiful garden containing about 4 English acres, enclosed partly by a stone and lime and partly by a brick wall, and in front of the house a small but handsome lawn. The demesne, which consists of 340 English acres, is bounded to a great extent with lofty plantations and several acres of the interior occupied with wood and groves of different kinds of timber, including a few scattered remnants of native wood. The fields vary in size from 6 to 45 acres and are enclosed with quickset fences and iron gates.

The entire of the ground is occupied by Mr Watson annually as follows: 50 acres under oats, 50 acres under wheat, 50 acres under green crops, 50 acres under hay and 50 acres under grazing, exclusive of plantations. 6 beasts are annually stall fed and 12 fattened on grass. Mr Watson keeps, constant, from 20 to 30 blood horses including young and old, also 28 couple of dogs for hunting, which afford great amusement in the neighbourhood during the hunting season. For these dogs he has an accommodating kennel contiguous to his dwelling house and supports all at his own expense.

Brookhill is a very handsome residence for any gentleman. The original house was erected above 100 years back by the late James Watson Esquire, grandfather of the present Captain James Watson, now the proprietor, but the house was overhauled by the latter gentleman 42 years ago, when he enlarged it by adding the rear wing and the 2 bows in the front to it, roofed the old house in the new, with other improvements at a very considerable expense, though the place is held on lease under the Marquis of Hertford.

Brookhill Ancient Castle

Local tradition says that Brookhill, the residence of James Watson Esquire, was a seat of great antiquity and also of an ancient castle, said to have been inhabited, or at least in the possession of, Sir John Rawdon, but who the founder of the castle was is not known at present. However, the site of the castle stands opposite Mr Watson's present house and constitutes a part of his garden. There is no account of the size of the castle, but at present there remains in the garden wall several yards in length of the old parapet wall that surrounded the castle and is still called the Castle Wall. It was built of stone and lime and stands 7 and a half feet high and 2 and a half feet thick, and seems to be cemented together by grout similar to other ancient buildings.

There is also in the neighbourhood of Brookhill House a field of ground called the Horse Park, and said to be anciently called so in consequence of being formerly occupied for exercising a troop of horse belonging to the proprietor of the castle in it. However, taking into account the vestiges above described, together with the ruins of an ancient church and burial ground which stands contiguous to Brookhill, and 4 forts still existing on the demesne and 2 destroyed, as also a giant's grave, part of which still remains, they proved to a certainty that it was truly a seat of antiquity. Besides, there have been urns of bones, ancient coin, human bones and subterraneous <subteranious> vaults discovered beneath the surface contiguous to the site of the old castle.

Local tradition also says that there was a battle fought at Brookhill in 1641 between a party of the rebels, or of Phelim O'Neill's forces that was retreating that way from the memorable battle of Lisburn alias Lisnagarvey, and a party of the loyalists that stayed <staid> guarding Brookhill. However, O'Neill's party is said to have defeated

Parish of Magheragall

the former and consumed the place by fire, as also value to a large amount. The proprietor, in razing old ruins in Brookhill at some former period, discovered a large quantity of human bones beneath their surface.

Brookhill, with 7 townlands attached to it, is said to have been formerly the property of the Rawdon or Moira family, and that it passed into the hands of the Hertford family by marriage connection. Information obtained from James Watson Esquire, Moses Watson and others. 19th and 20th July 1837.

Magheragall House

Magheragall House, now occupied by James Higgins, was built about 100 years back by the late James Watson of Brookhill, Esquire. It is a good 2-storey house, slated, 24 English acres in the demesne and a good garden enclosed by a quickset fence. It was for many years occupied by Mr Hull, son-in-law to Mr Watson. Informants James Watson Esquire, Brice McKenna and others. 17th and 18th July.

Streamvale

Streamvale, the seat of the late Reverend Francis Patton and now occupied by his daughters, the Misses Patton, stands about 3 miles from Lisburn, north of the leading road from the latter town to Ballinderry. The dwelling house is a beautiful thatched cottage, 1-storey high. The garden contains about 1 English acre, stands in very neat order and enclosed by a quickset fence, and in front of the cottage a small fish pond. The demesne consists of about 60 English acres, all laid off in fields of moderate size, enclosed by quickset fences and iron gates, and in several of the fields small plantations of various kinds of forest trees. The Misses Patton occupy the entire land in tillage and grazing and have their farmyards and office houses in neat order.

The chief part of these improvements have been made by the above Mr Patton, who was for many years previous to his death vicar of Magheragall parish. This family is of the Knockmore Pattons, who settled in this neighbourhood shortly after the 1641 war, and who have since retained a respectable rank in society. Information obtained from James Campbell and others. 20th July 1837.

Garretts Burn

Garretts Burn, the seat of Henery Garrett Esquire, stands about 2 and a half miles from Lisburn, on the old road from the latter town to Ballinderry. The house is a neat 2-storey house, partly slated and partly thatched. The garden, 1 English acre, is enclosed by a quickset fence and handsome iron gates to it and the yards and fields. The farm consists of 75 acres of arable land and a small portion of it under plantations. The house was built about 80 years back by the late Henery Garrett of Garretts Burn, Esquire.

Cattle Pound

Magheragall pound is enclosed by a stone and lime wall 5 feet high, a small iron gate to the entrance and a stream of water passing through it. Informants Henery Garrett Esquire and others. 29th July 1837.

Corn Mill

Magheragall corn mill is occupied by John Larmor. It is 2-storey high and roofed with tiles. There are 2 water <whater> wheels in it, one for grinding and the other shelling the corn, and both breast wheels: diameter of the grinding wheel 15 feet, breadth of the grinding wheel 4 feet; fall of water between the trough and bucke[t]s scarce observable; diameter of the shelling wheel 14 feet, breadth of the shelling wheel 2 feet 3 inches; fall of water from the trough to the buckets 1 foot. Supply of water limited in June, July and August of dry or hot summers.

Of the date of erecting this mill there is no local account, but the walls are of stone and lime, grouted similar to ancient buildings and seated on logs of oak, the site being low and the natural foundation soft and uncertain for building on. The present roof and covering of tiles was put on 90 years ago and has undergone no alteration since that period, save repairs. It is thought to be one the oldest corn mills in the above county and to have been rebuilt at the instance of one of Lords Hertford. Besides the quantity of corn manufactured for the public, the occupier purchases grain himself and keeps a constant supply of meal for the accommodation of the poor, who can only purchase small parcels. Information from the occupier and others. 6th July 1837.

Roads

The leading road from Lisburn to Ballinderry averages 20 feet wide clear of banks or fences, all within the above parish, and is kept in repair by presentment.

The leading road from Lisburn to Glenavy averages 21 feet wide clear of banks or fences, all within the above parish, and is kept in repair by presentments.

The leading roads from Lisburn to Ballinderry and Antrim, Glenavy, and passing through the above parish, is partly kept up by presentments and partly by a 5 years contract; but a small portion of the latter engagement in Magheragall parish. Breadth of these lines of road is already given on Fair Sheets.

The by-roads through the parish vary in their average breadth, but are chiefly from 14 to 17 feet wide between banks and fences, and all kept in repair by county presentments. These are locally called by-roads, open in both ends, that is to say that they pass from one leading road to another, and is in consequence kept up by the county. But there are several other by or accommodating roads in different parts of the parish that are made and kept up from the proceeds of court leet assessment. These are locally called "lonins" or "lonin ends" very commonly. However, they are communications open from either a leading road or a by-road to accommodate farmers residing in the interior or other parts of the townlands where public roads are not sufficiently accommodating. The landholders of the different townlands through which these lanes or bridle paths pass cess themselves at courts leet held twice a year in Lisburn, to keep them in repair for their own accommodation; and the repairs of them are presented for at the courts leet the same as the repairs of public roads are presented for at the assizes. On the whole the parish is well accommodated with public and private roads. Informants John Anderson, Ralph Jefferson and others. 2nd August 1837.

The old road from Lisburn to Ballinderry averages 20 feet wide clear of banks or fences, all within the above parish. Repairs on it is neglected since the new line of road was opened by Magheragall church.

MODERN AND ANCIENT TOPOGRAPHY

Flax Mill and Forts

Magheragall flax mill is situated in the townland of Mullaghcartin and occupied by John Larmor. It is thatched and stands 1-storey high. The water wheel is breast, diameter 15 feet, breadth of breast wheel 2 feet 10 inches, fall of water from the trough to the buckets scarce observable. The supply of water to this mill is limited in dry or hot summers, the same as at the corn mill, both having the benefit of one and the same watercourse. Both belong to one farmer and stand on his own land.

This flax mill was erected above 40 years ago and is situated on one side of the ruins of a Danish fort.

The fort seemed to have been a circular fort, 40 yards in diameter and made of clay, but it is now destroyed and the site occupied partly by the mill and partly by grazing.

There was another clay fort in the above farm, but it is now destroyed and the site under a wheat crop. Informant John Larmor.

ANCIENT TOPOGRAPHY

Ancient Church and Round Tower

In Ballyclogh, and holding of Moses Watson, there stands the ruins of an ancient church. Of the north side wall there is at present standing 17 feet in length and 8 feet in height. Its original thickness was 3 feet and built of rough stones cemented together with grout similar to other ancient buildings. The remainder of the church walls have been remodelled and turned into a barn and stable. From the portion of the old building at present to be seen, it appears that the church stood 50 feet long and 13 and a half feet wide in the interior. It was roofed with Irish oak and the floor made of clay. It had 2 large entrance doors which were also of oak. Attached to the east end stood a round tower about 40 feet in height and about 7 feet in diameter inside, and hollow to the top. It appeared to have been designed for a bell as there was no stairs or other building to lead to the top, either inside or outside. Its walls was built of well dressed stones and stood about 4 feet thick, permanently bound by grout.

The first dilapidation of the tower occurred about 60 years back, when it was brought within 7 feet of the surface and the stones brought to rebuild Springfield House. The latter part of it was razed to the ground in 1816 and the stones used in other building. The church is thought to have been burnt down in the 1641 war, but the walls remained for many years after without much dilapidation.

Mr Moses Watson's dwelling house, which stands contiguous to the old church, is also thought to have been burned along with the church, as in rebuilding the house about 100 years ago there was discovered in the walls, which were built of stone and lime, several oak uprights or columns in a half-burned state. From the situation of these timber columns in the walls it would appear that the roof of the house mainly rested on them and that they suffered by the conflagration. It is likewise thought that this house was a residence for the clergy belonging to the church or parish.

Parish of Magheragall

Attached to the church stood a small burial ground. It is now destroyed and the site occupied as a garden. In destroying the burial ground from time to time within the last 80 years, there was large quantities of human bones lifted, both out of it and out of the church also. Several of the skulls and other bones were of extraordinary strength. There were also raised several pieces of freestone supposed to have been parts of headstones. There was also found in the ruins a small copper coin of Charles I's reign. The human bones were buried adjoining the old graveyard.

This old church stood on an eminence about the centre of the parish, north of the leading road from Lisburn to Ballinderry and in the neighbourhood of Brookhill House. Information obtained from Moses Watson, John and Henery Holmes and others. 10th and 11th July 1837.

Fort and Stone Columns

In Ballyclogh and holding of Moses Watson, and about 100 yards north west of the aforesaid ancient church, there stood 3 ancient stone columns, varying in height from 3 and a half to 6 and a half feet and of great thickness. They were situated in a Danish fort, but have been sunk beneath the surface in 1806 and nothing remarkable got about them. The fort, which was made of clay, is now destroyed and the site under tillage.

Giant's Grave in Ballyclogh

In the above townland, and demesne of James Watson Esquire, there stands a giant's grave composed of 4 large stones lying prostrate and occupying 10 and a half by 7 and a half feet of ground, and rising about 3 and a half feet above the surface. In labouring the ground in the neighbourhood of this grave in May last, there was discovered about 1 and a half feet beneath the surface, deposited in circular stone buildings, 5 ancient earthen urns containing each a quantity of calcined bones and ashes or moist earth. They were situated on and covered with flat stones, but much destroyed by the hurry of the labourers in lifting them out, supposing at first view that they contained treasure of more value than decayed bones. However, what could be saved of the crocks and bones were sent to Belfast Museum by John Wakefield Esquire. Informants Moses Watson and Mr McKenna, the land steward, who assisted in lifting the crocks. I have lifted a specimen of the crocks and bones from one of the little tombs, which I forward to Mr Boyle for inspection.

Ancient Coins

Beneath the surface in Brookhill demesne there have been discovered at different periods several ancient silver and copper coins. One of the copper coins I have procured from the land steward and forward to Mr Boyle.

Moses Watson of Ballyclogh has at present 3 copper and 1 silver coins of old coinage. One of these he found in the ruins of the old church and the others in different parts of his land. The silver coin seems to be of Queen Elizabeth's coin and one of the copper coins of Charles I's coin.

Urn of Bones

James Maharry, in quarrying stones in Magheraliskmisk limestone quarry in 1834, got about 1 and a half feet beneath the clay surface an earthen urn containing a quantity of calcined bones and ashes, and also an urn of small size beautifully carved on the surface. It was narrow at the mouth and bottom and wide in the middle. Whether it contained anything or not could not be observed as the large urn was turned down on the mouth, over it and the bones and ashes, and all resting on the surface of the limestone rock. The large urn was much decayed. It and the bones crumbled to dust on being removed, but the small urn was tolerably sound and remained for some time in James Clark's, of the above townland, but subsequently fell to dust. Informants James Maharry and William Clark.

Ancient Boat

In 1816 there was discovered, about 8 feet beneath the surface of a bog in the townland of Ballynadolly, an ancient boat about 8 feet long, 5 feet wide and 4 feet deep, with seats along the sides and ends of it, also lying inside of it 2 small oars. It was constructed of staves nearly similar to modern boats and in a tolerable state of preservation when lifted out of the bog, but it has since split and fallen away by the air and sun. Information obtained from George and John Right.

Fort

In Knocknadona, and holding of John O'Connor, there stands the ruins of a fort nearly circular and 50 yards in diameter. It is under potato crop at present. The parapet was of clay and stones but much destroyed at present. The existing part of it stands from 4 to 6 feet high and in some parts 10 feet thick. The moat is from 10 to 19 feet wide. There are houses built on one side of this fort.

Grey Stone in Knocknadona

In the above townland, and holding of Robert Fergusson, there stands an old stone column 3 feet above the surface, 2 and a half feet broad and 1 and a half feet thick. It is in a sloping <sloaping> position. This column is locally called the Grey Stone and said to be the ruins of an ancient grave. At the distance of 6 feet from it there stood another column similar to the one above described, but it was taken away for building about 15 years back.

Forts

In Ballymave, and holding of Joseph Hide, there stands the ruins of a circular fort, 40 yards in diameter and enclosed by 2 moats each 13 feet wide and about 3 feet deep. The terrace between the moats is 40 feet wide. It and the area of the fort is under a crop of corn. If there had been a parapet round this fort at any period, it was destroyed ere this time. There are a few ancient thorns standing on the fort.

In Ballycarrickmaddy, and holding of William Burrows, there stands the ruins of a clay fort approaching to circular shape and 30 yards in diameter. The existing part of the parapet is 5 feet high and 20 feet thick. There is part of the moat still remaining and averages 6 feet wide. The area of the fort is under a potato crop.

In the last-mentioned townland, and holding of George Dawson, there stood a clay fort, but now totally destroyed and the site growing corn.

In Ballycarrickmaddy, and holding of Richard Dawson, there stood 2 forts that were made of clay, but they are at present destroyed and the site under tillage. In demolishing them at a former period there was fire hearths and forge dross got beneath their surface. Informants Richard Dawson, William McClure and others. 8th July 1837.

Forts

In Ballycarrickmaddy, and holding of Samuel Larmor, there stands the ruins of a fort. It is nearly destroyed and fences run through it. As near as can be at present judged, it was circular and 50 yards in diameter. A small part of the moat remains and averages 10 feet wide. The entire is under grazing.

In Ballymave, and holding of Samuel Larmor, there stands the ruins of a fort under grazing. It approaches to circular and 40 yards in diameter. The parapet is of clay and varies from 4 to 9 feet high and from 8 to 16 feet wide. The moat averages 9 feet wide. Informants John Holmes and others. 11th July 1837.

In Brookhill demesne there stands a fort approaching to oval shape, 60 by 45 feet on the top. Its summit stands 30 feet above the moat encircling it. The original width of the moat seems to have been 20 feet, but it is at present greatly disfigured, as is also a sort of clay parapet that stood outside of it. The fort itself appears to be made chiefly of clay, though odd stones appear through its surface. The sides of it are studded with forest trees of different kinds. It stands 25 yards north of the road from Lisburn to Ballinderry and measures 150 yards round the base. There is no appearance of any steps being to ascend to its summit.

20 feet east of the above fort stands the ruins of a three-angle fort. It measures 50 feet in length on either side of the 3 sides and stands about 14 feet high, and planted on the sides with forest trees. It was made chiefly of clay and stands as an outpost to the former one. It was also surrounded by a moat and parapet which are now nearly levelled.

These forts differ in construction from most of others and are locally called mounds.

In Brookhill demesne there stands a fort approaching to oval shape, 40 by 35 yards and growing a plantation of different kinds of forest trees in an advanced state of growth. The parapet was made of clay and stones, but is greatly altered by the planting. It stands from 4 to 14 feet high above the field and 18 feet thick in several parts. There is a modern fence made round the fort and the old moat destroyed.

A short distance from the above stands a circular fort 30 yards in diameter and growing a plantation of forest trees. It is enclosed by a parapet of clay and stones from 4 to 7 feet high and the moat levelled.

In the above demesne there stands the ruins of a circular fort 36 yards in diameter and under grazing. The parapet was made of clay and stones but is now nearly destroyed. The existing part of it varies from 6 to 10 feet high and 15 feet thick. The moat is at present destroyed.

There was another clay fort in the above demesne but it is totally destroyed and the site under potato crop. There was in the whole 6 forts in this demesne.

In Magheragall townland, and holding of Captain Houghton, there stands the ruins of a fort now under grazing. The existing part of the parapet is 4 feet high and from 4 to 8 feet wide, and made of clay and stones. The existing part of the moat is 10 feet wide.

Parish of Magheragall

In the above townland, and holding of James Higgins, there stood a fort of clay, but it was destroyed totally many years back. The site is at present under crop.

Forts and Ancient Urn

In Moneybroom, and holding of James Maherg, there stands the ruins of a fort approaching to circular shape and 50 yards in diameter, and at present under grazing. The parapet was made chiefly of clay and has undergone dilapidation to some extent. As it at present stands it averages 7 feet in height above the bottom of the moat, but nothing above the area. The moat varies from 10 to 15 feet wide. The face of the parapet is grown over with scrog of old wood. The gate stands on the south side of the fort and 10 yards east of it.

There was raised in 1835 an ancient earthen urn which was neatly carved on the surface. If it contained anything there is no local account of it. However, it was deposited in a stone building about 3 and a half feet beneath the surface in the edge of the parapet and was lifted in the night time by persons who dreamt of money being contained in it. They left the urn in small pieces on the site where raised. They also destroyed or carried off anything it might have contained. There was old stone querns and Danes' smoking pipes got beneath the surface of this fort. Informant William Maherg. 24th July 1837.

In Moneybroom, and holding of James Maherg, on the west and about 7 yards distant from the fort described [above], there stood 2 forts of about 7 yards in diameter each and seemed to serve as outposts to the former. These latter forts are totally destroyed and the site under grazing. Informant William Maherg.

Forts

In Kilcorrig, and holding of the Reverend Joseph Kelso, there stands the ruins of a fort approaching to circular shape and 30 yards in diameter, enclosed by 2 moats and 1 parapet. The inside moat varies from 10 feet to 15 feet wide and the outside moat from 6 to 10 feet wide. The parapet was of clay and stones but it is destroyed to a great extent. The existing part of it is from 4 to 10 feet high and 20 feet thick at the base. The area of the fort stands 4 feet above the bottom of the moat and is at present under meadow.

In the last-mentioned townland, and farm of Widow Collins, there stood a fort, but it is at present destroyed and the site under oat crop.

In Knocknadona, and holding of Bernart McGarry, there stood a fort which is now totally destroyed and the site under crop. In demolishing this fort in 1835 there was a circular pit covered by 3 flat stones got beneath its surface, but nothing of interest got in the pit. Informant Robert Grey and others.

In Magheraliskmisk, and holding of Vallentine Tullerton, there stands the ruins of a fort approaching to circular shape and 35 yards in diameter. It is at present under grazing. It was enclosed by a moat and 2 parapets, all which are destroyed to some extent. The inside parapet is 17 feet thick at the base and 6 feet high. The outside parapet is 15 feet thick at the base and 3 feet high. These parapets were of clay and stones. The moat is 15 feet wide.

7 yards south of this fort stands the ruins of an oblong fort 35 by 25 feet and enclosed by a moat and parapet. The parapet is of clay but nearly destroyed. It stands 2 feet high and 9 feet thick. The moat is 11 feet wide.

On the east side, and about 15 yards from the above large fort, there stood a fort of small size, but at present totally destroyed and the site under grazing. These 2 small forts seem to stand as outposts to the large one first described.

In the above holding there stood another fort which is at present totally destroyed and the site under tillage.

In the above townland, and holding of William Clark, there stood a fort of clay and stones, but so disfigured at present by modern fences and bridle roads passing through it that no idea can be formed of its original shape. Whatever remains of it is under grazing. Informant William Clark. 25th July 1835.

In Magheraliskmisk, and holding of Richard McQuillan, there stood a fort which is at present totally destroyed and the site under potato crop. In destroying this fort there was a few Danes' smoking pipes got beneath its surface.

In Ballynalargy, and holding of Joseph McQuillan, there stood 2 forts which are now totally destroyed and the site under tillage.

In Magheraliskmisk, and holding of Alexander Hall, there stood a fort which is at present totally destroyed and the site under tillage.

Forts and Human Bones

In Ballynalargy, and holding of Nathaniel Hall, there stands the ruins of a fort approaching to circular, 35 yards in diameter and under meadow. The parapet was of clay. The remaining part of it is 5 feet high and 6 feet thick. The moat is levelled.

In Moyrusk, and holding of John Wardle, there

stood a fort which is at present destroyed and the site under meadow.

John Anderson, in removing part of the remains of bog in the last-mentioned townland in 1830, got, about 4 feet beneath the surface, what he supposed to be 2 skeletons of human bodies, all except the skulls. These he did not find. The bones were in utter decay and crumbled to dust on being dug out to the air. Informant John Anderson.

Forts

In Mullaghcarton, and holding of Richard Tullerton, there stood a fort which is now destroyed and the site under grazing.

In Drumsill, and holding of John Anderson, there stands the ruins of a fort approaching to circular shape, 40 yards in diameter. The parapet was of clay. The remaining part of it is 4 and a half feet high and the moat levelled.

In the last-mentioned townland, and holding of Samuel Johnston, there stands the ruins of a fort approaching to circular and 30 yards in diameter. The parapet was of clay and stones, 17 feet thick and 6 feet high and the moat 11 feet wide. This fort is under grazing and destroyed in shape by modern fences through one side of it.

In Ballycarrickmaddy, and holding of Thomas Belshaw, there stands the ruins of a fort approaching to circular and 60 yards in diameter, and at present under grazing. The parapet was of clay and stones, 15 feet thick at the base and from 5 to 10 feet high. The moat is 15 feet wide. There was a second parapet of clay and stones round this fort. It was 15 feet thick, but at present demolished. The existing parapet was faced up and planted with whitethorn at some former period.

Fort and Antiquities in Mullaghcarton

In the above townland, and holding of John Larmor, there stands the ruins of a fort approaching to circular shape and 35 yards in diameter. It is at present under barley. The parapet was of clay and stones, and stands from 4 to 9 feet high and from 5 to 10 feet thick. The moat is nearly destroyed.

In demolishing part of this fort in 1800 there was a small stone hammer about 6 inches in length found beneath its surface. It had a handle in the centre similar to any iron hammer, save that this hammer, with its attached handle, was hewn out of 1 stone. The handle was about 5 inches long. There was also found in the same place a brass battleaxe having a socket to embrace a handle. These articles have been subsequently destroyed. Informants Alexander Larmor and John Stewart. 27th July 1837.

Forts

In Ballycarrickmaddy, and holding of George Right and others, there stands the ruins of a fort, nearly square, 42 by 40 yards, but greatly disfigured by a public road that runs through it. The parapet was of clay and stones, and stands 18 feet wide and from 3 to 8 feet high, and the moat 13 feet wide. This fort is occupied partly under meadow and partly by the road and fences.

In the above townland, and holding of Hugh Weir, there stood a fort which is now utterly destroyed and the site under wheat. In the last-mentioned holding there was a second fort commenced to be made but never finished. The part made of it is also destroyed and the site under tillage.

In Moneybroom, and holding of John Taggert, there stood a fort which is now destroyed and the site under oats.

In Moneybroom, and holding of Edward Davis, there stands the ruins of a fort. It was circular, 40 yards in diameter and is at present under oats. The parapet was made of clay and stones. It stands at present 5 feet high and 6 feet thick. The moat is levelled. Informant John O'Connor. 28th July 1837.

Ancient Oak Trunks

In sinking the foundations of Magheragall church in 1829, there was 2 oak trunks found about 5 feet beneath the surface. They were constructed out of a solid piece of oak timber and was about 4 feet in length and 6 inches in depth in the clear each, and about 4 inches thick. The lids were decayed, as was also anything they might have contained. These trunks mouldered away by being removed and exposed to the air. They were oblong shape.

Bog and Fort

In the townland of Knocknarea there were several acres of black bog, but at present there is nothing more than its remains to be seen, the greater part of which is reclaimed <recleamed> and growing crop. This bog was tolerably deep and contained some oak blocks, but no other kind of timber.

In the above townland, and holding of John Pattison, there stood a fort which is now destroyed and the site under tillage.

Battleaxe

In Ballynadolly, and holding of Joseph Lewis,

Parish of Magheragall

and about 2 feet beneath the surface of new land, there was found in 1822 an ancient brass battleaxe much resembling a saddler's cutting knife and 9 inches in length. It was subsequently sold at a small price in Lisburn. Informants John Lewis and others.

SOCIAL ECONOMY AND ANCIENT TOPOGRAPHY

Dubourdieu Family

Shem Dubourdieu of Knocknadona, farmer and son to the late Shem Dubourdieu, formerly surgeon in the Longford militia, is grandson to the late minister of that name that formerly preached to the French Huguenots <Hugonots> that settled in Lisburn. He and his children, consisting of 4 sons and 6 daughters, are the only descendants of the above foreigners that at present exist in Lisburn or its vicinity, though they were at some former period numerous in the latter town. The present Shem Dubourdieu and his children hold a small tenement under the Marquis of Hertford, by which they partly support themselves and partly by cotton weaving, and also by labouring in a limestone quarry in the above townland. This man is not locally said to have been lawfully begotten.

McQuillan Family

Richard, Joseph and Isaac McQuillan of Magheraliskmisk and Ballynalargy, farmers, are offspring of the Dunluce family of that name. Their ancestor settled in Magheraliskmisk at some period before the 1641 war and his offspring remain here to the present.

The above Richard McQuillan resides at present in a stone and lime house built by his ancestor previous to the aforesaid war. The roof is of old oak and supported on oak columns. It stands 1-storey and thatched. His great-grandmother was obliged to employ black cattle to plough her land in the absence of horses, taken from her during the above war. Informants Richard McQuillan, Shem Dubourdieu and others. 26th July 1837.

NATURAL FEATURES AND PRODUCTIVE ECONOMY

Bog in Magheragall

There was a small bog in the above townland, but it is all cut away and its remains brought to a state of cultivation. It was a black quality of bog but not of great depth. Informant James Campbell.

Discoveries in a Bog

In the townlands of Ballynadolly and Aghacarnan there is between 150 and 200 acres of nearly cut-out bog, not more at present than from 2 to 4 feet in depth, and a large portion of it cut out altogether. The subsoil is partly of whitish and reddish sand and partly a blue clay. No other than baked turf to be got in this bog at present, though at a former period there were several feet of slane or spade turf cut over the present remains, and some good oak and fir timber got imbedded in the exterior, but nothing at present except a few oak blocks. The portion of the bog that the Marquis of Hertford holds in his own hands is annually let in small lots to the public and the remainder of it attached to different farms adjoining its shores.

At the depth of from 6 to 10 feet beneath the surface of this bog there have been discovered at different periods within the last 40 years a large quantity of oak planks varying in length, breadth and thickness, but all evidently dressed and brought to shape for some particular purpose, many of them morticed and wooden pins through each end. Some of this latter timber is still extant on Thomas Thompson's of Ballynadolly and other houses, but changed in form and converted to other uses. There was also large quantities of decayed nuts found. Also a quantity of decayed wheat was found in 1834 at some depth beneath its surface. It is called the Wolf bog, and is said to have been formerly inhabited by wolves. Informants Thomas Thompson, Daniel McKeown and others. 5th August 1837.

Lime-kilns

There are 4 lime-kilns constantly burning lime in Knocknadona, which lime is sold to the public from 10d to 1s 3d per barrel. There were others, but are discontinued for the present. Tax yearly on each kiln burning lime in this parish 10 guineas. This sum is paid to Lord Hertford for the quarry. Informants William Maherg, Thomas Thompson and others.

Quarries and Lime Works

In Magheraliskmisk and Ballynalargy there are limestone quarries extensively wrought throughout the year and the limestone brought to different parts of the counties of Antrim and Down. These quarries and limeworks are gaining concerns to the owners and also to a large number of labourers constantly employed at them. The bowels of the soil in several parts of the parish is pregnant with the above valuable mine.

Social Economy

General Remarks on Houses

In this parish there are several respectable and commodious 2-storey houses, part of which are slated and others thatched. About three-fourths of all the farmhouses in the parish is whitewashed inside and outside, and have good sash windows in front which afford ventilation by lifting or letting down one of the sashes occasionally. Their yards are large and in many instances enclosed by stone and lime walls or neat quickset fences, and good iron or wooden gates to the entrances and gardens. Where open springs or good streams are not convenient, the wealthy farmers have good metal or wooden pumps in their yards. And in most of their houses, handsome clocks in the parlours or kitchens, and the house well furnished in other respects.

They seem to hold furniture of the old fashion in great respect, as in many of their houses are to be seen oak presses with carving and various devices on their shutters and the old 2-armed chairs of the same taste, as also a service of the old pewter <puter> dishes and plates. Of these, they are very careful. Their gardens are generally sheltered with lofty trees, and more or less of fruit trees in many of them. Many of the cottier houses, though small, are whitewashed inside and outside, and their household clean looking. Farmers and cottiers seem to be honest, industrious, inoffensive and anxious to wear decent apparel on public business, and also to afford their growing children intellectual and moral education and other useful pursuits. Informants John Larmor and others. 1st and 2nd August 1837.

Habits of the People

In this parish there are several farms from 50 to 80 acres English, and many from 2 to 10 English acres, but the majority of the farms are from 10 to 30 English acres. The generality of the landholders seem to live comfortably as to food and raiment. Food chiefly used is potatoes, flesh meat, oat and wheat bread, milk, butter and vegetables. Some, or at least many, use tea daily with all its necessaries. The humbler class use little flesh meat or tea, except tradespeople. Their fuel is partly coal, turf and branches of different kinds of wood. In the latter the poor are limited almost at all seasons.

Many of the landholders in the parish carry on linen and cotton weaving. Cottiers also weave linen and cotton, but either class of people are not so numerous, or at least so many of them making a livelihood by weaving, as there are in Blaris parish. But since the failure of prices of weaving cotton took place, a greater number are employed at weaving linen cloth in Magheragall than in Blaris parish. Farmers or cottiers don't altogether depend on weaving for their support. The farmer has one part of his family at the farm, which he considers the surest pledge for rent and food, and if those employed in weaving meet the purchase of clothes and other taxes and casualties, he feels happy. One or more of the cottier's family labour when they can get employ and weave occasionally. Informants Thomas Thompson, Daniel McKeown and many others. 4th August 1837.

Census

Census of the population as taken in 1831 and classed into different denominations in the above parish in 1834: Protestants of the Established Church 2,042, Presbyterians of the Synod of Ulster 646, Roman Catholics 350, Dissenters 63, Quakers 12, total 3,113; taken from the enumerator's original book. In this parish there is no Roman Catholic chapel situated.

Tithes

The rectorial tithes of Magheragall, 200 pounds per annum, is received by Edward Johnson of Ballymacoss, Esquire; his father, the late Revd Phillip Johnson, former vicar of Derryaghy, having leased the aforesaid tithe from the Bishop of Down and Connor at some former period and which lease is not yet expired. The tithe of Magheragall is 300 pounds per annum; 100 of it goes to the vicar of the parish and the other 200 to Mr Johnson.

In this parish there are 5 publicans.

Lodges

There was 3 Orange lodges in the parish, but these are discontinued altogether for some time past. There are 2 Mason lodges still in existence in the parish. Ribbon lodges dare not be held in the parish. Informants Thomas Thompson and others.

Emigration

None have emigrated to America from this parish during the years 1835 or 1836. 2 families have gone out in June 1837. They were persons that held small farms and, at the request of some of their friends who had been previously in America, sold those farms and went with those friends, who encouraged them and were again returning to

Parish of Magheragall

America. It is seldom that any leave the parish to other countries.

Migration

Migration to the Scotch harvest: from Ballynadolly 2, from Ballynalargy 1, from Ballycarrickmaddy 1, from Ballyclogh 1, from Drumsill 1, total from the parish 6. Finished 7th August 1837. Informants Thomas Hill, Robert Johnstone and others.

Magistrates

Magistrates in the parish: James Watson of Brookhill, Esquire and Richard Haughton of Springfield, Esquire. No peace or revenue police in the parish.

Customs and Traditions

No legendary tales or stories or peculiar customs or costume in the parish.

Amusements

The principal amusement in this parish at present is afforded by Captain Watson of Brookhill, who keeps a good pack of hounds with he hunts regularly in the hunting season. Bullet playing, which consists in rolling a heavy iron ball along the surface, was so extensive in this and Blaris parish at a former period that the 2 parishes often contested for bets of 10 guineas a side, to be decided by the above play. Common play, which consists in playing or throwing <trowing> a round wooden ball on the surface and sticking at it with long sticks crooked in one end, and forcing it away from the opposing party, was also practised here, as was also dancing, leaping <leping> and jumping contested. All these are relinquished many years back and practised now by little boys only. Informants John Anderson, Thomas Thompson and others.

Longevity

Allice McCreanen of Mullycartin is now in the 90th year of her age. Her hearing, sight, memory and appetite is tolerably good. She can walk about occasionally by the assistance of 2 small walking sticks. She has still a few of her teeth and can eat oat bread. Information from Allice McCreanen and others.

Table of Schools

[Table contains the following headings: name, situation and description, when established, income and expenditure, physical, intellectual and moral education, number of pupils subdivided by age, sex and religion, name and religious persuasion of master or mistress].

Mullaghcarton national school, 4 miles from Lisburn on the old road from the above town to Ballinderry; house thatched and stands 1-storey, 21 by 14 feet inside, 1 door, 4 windows, school requisites in good supply, established 1830; income: from the Education Board 8 pounds, 13 pounds from pupils; intellectual education: books published by the Education Board; moral education: no visits from the clergy, all catechisms taught on Saturdays; number of pupils: males, 29 under 10 years of age, 10 from 10 to 15, 1 over 15, a total of 40; females, 30 under 10 years of age, 19 from 10 to 15, 1 over 15, a total of 50; total number of pupils 90, 77 Protestants, 4 Presbyterians, 6 Roman Catholics, 3 other denominations; master James Lewis, a Presbyterian. 4th July 1837.

Magheragall parish school, 2 and a half miles from Lisburn and contiguous to Magheragall church; house slated, stands 1-storey, 30 by 16 feet inside, 1 door and 6 windows, and school requisites in good supply, established 1824; income: from the rector 2 pounds, 10 pounds from pupils; intellectual education: books published by the Society for Discountenancing Vice; moral education: visits from the Protestant clergy and the catechisms of the Church of England are taught; number of pupils: males, 15 under 10 years of age, 14 from 10 to 15, a total of 29; females, 11 under 10 years of age, 5 from 10 to 15, a total of 16; total number of pupils 45, 41 Protestants, 4 Presbyterians; master Richard Scott, a Protestant.

Knocknadona private school, 2 and a half miles from Lisburn on the leading road from Lisburn to Glenavy; it is held in the Wesleyan Methodist preaching house of Knocknadona and school requisites are in good supply, established 1837; income from pupils 20 pounds; intellectual education: books published by the Kildare Place Society; moral education: visits from the Methodist preachers and all catechisms taught; number of pupils: males, 34 under 10 years of age, 6 from 10 to 15, a total of 40; females, 17 under 10 years of age, 5 from 10 to 15, a total of 22; total number of pupils 62, 42 Protestants, 13 Presbyterians, 1 Roman Catholic, 6 other denominations; master Samuel Collier, a Protestant.

Ballycarrickmaddy national school, 4 miles from Lisburn and situated contiguous to a by-road passing through Ballycarrickmaddy; house slated, stands 1-storey, 28 feet by 16 feet inside, 1 door and 4 windows, school requisites in good supply, established 1827; income: from the Education Board 8 pounds, from pupils 17 pounds; intellectual education: books published by the Education Board; moral education: visits from the Protestant and Presbyterian clergy and all catechisms taught; number of pupils: males, 50 under 10 years of age, 40 from 10 to 15, a total of 90; females, 58 under 10 years of age, 12 from 10 to 15, a total of 70; total number of pupils 160, 90 Protestants, 57 Presbyterians, 3 Roman Catholics, 10 other denominations; master Thomas Begly, a Presbyterian. Visited these schools from 2nd to 5th August 1837.

Sunday Schools

[Table contains the following headings: name, situation, when established, superintendents, number of teachers, number of scholars subdivided by religion and sex, books read, hours of attendance, societies with which connected, observations].

Magheragall parish Sunday school, held in the day schoolhouse, established 1824; superintendent Reverend John Mussen; 3 male teachers, a total of 3; number of scholars: 90 Protestants, 4 Presbyterians, 6 Roman Catholics, 55 males, 45 females, a total of 100, 60 Sunday school scholars; books read: Bible, Testament tracts and *Dublin Spelling book*; hours of attendance: open from 9 to 11 a.m. and from 2 to 5 p.m., none in winter; societies with which connected: Sunday School Society for books; opened by prayer, no expenditure last year.

Knocknadona Sunday school, held in the Wesleyan Methodist preaching house, established 1837; superintendent Samuel Collier; 6 male and 4 female teachers, a total of 10; number of scholars: 60 Protestants, 18 Presbyterians, 1 Roman Catholic, 20 other denominations, 52 males, 47 females, a total of 99, 84 Sunday school scholars; books read: Bible, Testament tracts and Sunday school spelling books; hours of attendance: open from 9 to 11 a.m. and from 3 to 5 p.m., none in winter; societies with which connected: Sunday School Society for books; no prayer or singing.

Ballycarrickmaddy Sunday school, held in the day schoolhouse, established 1825; superintendent Thomas Begly; 6 male teachers, a total of 6; number of scholars: 80 Protestants, 30 Presbyterians, 3 Roman Catholics, 8 other denominations, 70 males, 51 females, a total of 121, 48 Sunday school scholars; books read: Bible, Testament tracts and Sunday school spelling books; hours of attendance: open from 9 to 11 a.m. and 2 to 5 p.m., none in winter; societies with which connected: Sunday School Society for books; no prayer or singing.

Sheepwalk Sunday school in Ballynadolly, held in a small thatched house, established 1826; superintendent Thomas Hill; 3 male teachers, a total of 3; number of scholars: 40 Protestants, 32 Presbyterians, 8 Roman Catholics, 20 males, 60 females, a total of 80, 70 Sunday school scholars; books read: Bible, Testament tracts and Sunday school spelling books; hours of attendance: open from 7 to 9.30 a.m. and 3 to 6 p.m., none in winter; societies with which connected: Sunday School Society for books; no prayer or singing.

Mullaghcarton Sunday school, held in the day schoolhouse, established 1830; superintendent James Lewis; 6 male teachers, a total of 6; number of scholars: 40 Protestants, 2 Presbyterians, 8 Roman Catholics, 29 males, 21 females, a total of 50, 30 Sunday school scholars; books read: Bible, Testament tracts and Sunday school spelling books; hours of attendance: open from 8.30 to 10 a.m. and from 2.30 to 5.30 p.m., none in winter; societies with which connected: Sunday School Society for books; no singing or prayer. Visited from the 1st to the 5th August 1837 [signed] Thomas Fagan.

Draft Memoir by G. Scott and Another

MODERN TOPOGRAPHY

Public Buildings

Magheragall church is a neat edifice 60 feet by 30. There are 33 seats in the aisle, would contain 264 persons, and 11 seats in the gallery, would contain 88 persons; total 352 persons. Erected in the year 1830, cost 1,000 pounds, which was advanced at first by the Board of First Fruits, to be repaid by instalments.

Corn Mill

Magheragall corn mill, situated in the townland of Moneybroom: it is well supplied with water. It has a double wheel: diameter of largest 14 feet 6 inches, of small one 13 feet 6 inches, breast of each 2 feet 6 inches. They are breast wheels with a fall of 14 feet. No mills being on the stream, there are no regulations respecting the use of water.

SOCIAL ECONOMY

Table of Schools

[Table contains the following headings: name of townland where held, number of pupils subdi-

Parish of Magheragall

vided by religion and sex, remarks as to how supported, when established].

Knocknarea, number of pupils: 44 Protestants, 1 Catholic, 27 males, 18 females, total 45; under the Association for Discountenancing Vice; the master receives 7 pounds from this association and is also partly supported by the parents of the children; established 1828.

Mullaghcarton, number of pupils: 42 Protestants, 4 Catholics, 27 males, 19 females, total 46; the National Board of Education pays 8 pounds per annum and it is partly supported by the parents of the children; established [?] 1834.

Ballycarrickmaddy, number of pupils: 81 Protestants, 5 Catholics, 56 males, 30 females, total 86; the National Board of Education pays 8 pounds per annum and it is partly supported by the parents of the children; established 1828.

Table of Schools

[Table contains the following headings: name of townland where held, name and religion of master or mistress, free or pay school, annual income, description and cost of schoolhouse, number of pupils subdivided by religion, sex and the Protestant and Roman Catholic returns, societies with which connected. All are paying schools].

Knocknadowney, master Thomas Grier, Protestant, Established Church; income 20 to 24 pounds; schoolhouse: held in the Methodist preaching house; number of pupils by the Protestant return: 45 Established Church, 10 Presbyterians, 5 Roman Catholics, 32 males, 28 females; by the Roman Catholic return: 38 Established Church, 4 Presbyterians, 34 males, 8 females; associations none.

Mullicarton, master James Montgomery, Presbyterian; income 14 to 25 pounds; schoolhouse: [a] thatched house, cost 15 pounds; number of pupils by the Protestant return: 25 Established Church, 2 Presbyterians, 1 Roman Catholic, 23 males, 5 females; by the Roman Catholic return: 20 Established Church, 1 Roman Catholic, 21 males, 5 females; the schoolhouse built by subscription.

Ballycarrickmady, master Thomas Biggly, Protestant, Established Church; income about 20 pounds; schoolhouse: held in the session house of the Seceding meeting house; number of pupils by the Protestant return: 22 Established Church, 24 Presbyterians, 3 Roman Catholics, 25 males, 24 females; associations none.

Parish of Magheramesk <Magheramisk>, County Antrim

Statistical Remarks by Lieutenant G. Boscawen, May 1832

NATURAL STATE

Situation, Boundaries and Extent

This parish is situated in the barony of Upper Massereene, county of Antrim and province of Ulster, and is bounded on the north by the parishes of Ballinderry and Magheragall, on the east by the parish of Blaris, on the south by the parish of Moira and a very small portion of Hillsborough, and on the west by the parish of Aghalee. The mean distance from north to south is about 2 miles and from east to west 2 and three-quarters. It is divided into 11 townlands, covering an area of 3,147 acres 3 roods 5 perches British statute measurement.

Ecclesiastical Union

Magheramesk is a vicarage in the diocese of Connor and archdiocese of Armagh, and is united to the parishes of Aghalee and Aghagallon. It is a lay impropriation in the gift of the Marquis of Hertford, who receives the rectorial tithes. The vicarial tithes are paid by an agreement between the parishioners and present incumbent, the Reverend John Corkin, who receives 8 and a half [s?] per acre. The church belonging to the union is at Soldierstown in the adjacent parish of Aghalee.

NATURAL FEATURES

Surface, Soil and Produce

The highest ground is at the north portion of the parish, which consists of a range of undulating hills broken by transverse valleys, of which Balmer's glen is a remarkable instance. The greatest elevation is 335 feet above the sea. The southern portion may be denominated as flat and is terminated by the River Lagan, which forms a considerable portion of the boundary between this and Moira parish.

The soil in this parish is very fertile. On the hills it is a loose reddish clay and, when the immediate substratum is limestone, it is very productive. On approaching the Lagan it is more sandy. The mode of culture is the same as that adopted in the adjacent district. The low ground is usually laid out for pasture on which the farmers graze their cattle. Though all kinds of grain are cultivated, yet wheat and oats form the chief proportion. The grasslands are broken up for potatoes, to which succeeds wheat, barley or oats. A fair average produce of wheat or oats would be from 15 to 18 cwt, and of potatoes 250 bushels. The grasses raised are rye, timothy and clover.

Bog

There is no turbary in this part of the union except a few small patches which are nearly cut out and reclaimed. The inhabitants obtain their fuel from the Montyaghs in Aghagallon parish. The respectable farmers in general have a bank which is paid for according to its quality, and find their own conveyance.

MODERN TOPOGRAPHY

Villages and Markets

Villages: none in this part of the union.

The nearest markets are at Lisburn and Lurgan, the former about 4 miles from the east portion of this parish and the latter about 5 miles from the western extremity.

NATURAL HISTORY AND NATURAL FEATURES

Geology

This parish is by no means uninteresting to the geologist. It appears to be nearly the termination of the great basaltic area, though this rock projects some distance into the county Armagh. The limestone in Magheramesk is often divested of its covering of basalt, and in these instances the soil is remarkable productive. It is frequently quarried.

At the extensive quarry at Magheramesk, on the road from Moira to Glenavy, the basalt is sometimes incumbent on the limestone. The latter is usually white, but there are varieties of yellow and sky-coloured beds. It is very hard, returning a ringing sound when quarried. It contains numerous beds of flints, often coming out in large pear-shaped masses.

At Balmer's glen there is a bed of ochre <ocre> which appears to be the decomposition of the basalt, and here the flints are very fine and would answer well for gun flints.

A thin strata of fuller's earth is here apparent at the bed of a stream dividing the townlands of

Parish of Magheramesk 113

Ballynelargy and Derrynish, and blocks of gypsum (sulphate of lime) have been taken away.

The quarry at Magheramesk has some appearance of having been traversed by a whin dyke, but it is in a decomposed state. Quartz crystals and sandstone of quartz and mica are found in the fields, but there are no metallic minerals.

The organic remains are not numerous. They consist of fossil shells found general in the flints and a specimen of radiating spar has been found in the limestone.

The limestone in this parish is burned for lime at the quarry and is sold to the tenantry in the estate at 9d or 10d a barrel, but is in general purchased by the load of about 15 cwt at 6d or 8d and burned by the farmers at their own kilns. The basalt is used for making and repairing roads, for building, and the clay at Inisloughlin and other places is used for making bricks.

Springs

There are several spring wells which issue in general from the bottom of the limestone hills. The most remarkable ones are at Turtle's orchard, at Laurel Grove and at Magheramesk. The small streams serve as feeders to the summit level of the Belfast Canal, which passes through the south west part of the parish.

MODERN TOPOGRAPHY

Roads

The coach road from Moira to Lisburn and Belfast passes through the south extremity of the parish, and that from Moira to Glenavy through the west portion. This latter has a difficult ascent and is left in very bad order at the quarries.

An old road from Soldierstown to Lisburn passes through the north portion. It is otherwise well intersected with by-roads.

A new line of road has also been lately laid out passing through the centre of the parish.

ANCIENT TOPOGRAPHY

Antiquities

In Trummery are the ruins of an old church and round tower. The latter a few years ago was of considerable elevation. A short distance to the north of these ruins is a remarkable fort or mount. These remains of antiquity have nearly all been effaced by agriculture, though the outline of several of them may be traced in Lisnabilla. The only ones that remain to be mentioned are Spence's Fort near Maghaberry and Inisloughlin Fort, commanding a view of the Kilwarlin hills. The domestic and military antiquities are very numerous, such as coins, brass spears.

SOCIAL ECONOMY

Religion

Chapels: none!

There is a Quakers' meeting house situated in Ballynelargy, and a considerable proportion of the inhabitants of the parish are of this sect.

Schools

There is 1 schoolhouse in this part of the union, at Maghaberry, the rates of tuition being from 3s to 8s per quarter. It is now supported by the farmers and receives no endowment.

Manufacture

It is considered that above 100 persons are employed in the manufacture of linen and cambric, and about 40 in the retail trade and handicraft. Agriculture is, however, the chief occupation.

Tradition

The only tradition is one relating to the ancient church at Trummery. It is stated to have been destroyed in the civil wars during the Protectorate in the following manner. A strong house, standing where Trummery House is now built, was occupied by a party of Cromwell's soldiers to overawe the neighbouring country. To counteract this plan a detachment of the Irish army took post in the church by night, that they were attacked and dislodged by Cromwell's soldiers, who set fire to the church for this purpose.

Population

The number of inhabitants in this parish amounts to 1,700. [Table contains the following headings: townland, proprietor, area, numbers of families, males and females, total population].

Ballynelargy: 274 acres 3 roods 14 perches, 19 families, 44 males, 39 females, total 83.

Carnlougherin: 301 acres 1 rood 16 perches, 18 families, 60 males, 53 females, total 113.

Creenagh: 414 acres 25 perches, 71 families, 193 males, 210 females, total 403.

Derrynisk: 119 acres, 4 families, 11 males, 13 females, total 24.

Gortnacory Lower: 46 acres 3 roods 32 perches, 16 families, 48 males, 50 females, total 98.

Gortnacory Upper: 97 acres 36 perches, 11 families, 37 males, 36 females, total 73.

Inisloughlin: 363 acres 1 rood 38 perches, 38 families, 120 males, 134 females, total 254.

Lisnabilla: 87 acres 2 roods 34 perches, 9 families, 26 males, 24 females, total 50.

Maghaberry: 353 acres 3 roods 25 perches, 31 families, 81 males, 77 females, total 158.

Magheramesk: 498 acres 1 rood 10 perches, 31 families, 86 males, 86 females, total 172.

Trummery: 593 acres 2 roods 23 perches, 50 families, 127 males, 145 females, total 272.

[Totals] 3,149 acres 2 roods 13 perches, families 298, males 833, females 867, population 1,700; proprietor the Marquis of Hertford. [Signed] George Boscawen, Lieutenant Royal Engineers, 6th August [? 1832].

Draft Memoir by M.M. Kertland [before June 1835], with additions from another Draft Memoir, 1835

NATURAL FEATURES

Hills

There are no very striking forms in the features of this parish. The general form of the ground is a series of easy sloping ridges, whose direction is from north west by west to south east by east, the western extremities being the most elevated, as may be expected from the course of the Lagan river which, taking its rise in Lough Neagh, flows into the sea in the same direction. Towards the north boundary of the parish the ground rises rapidly into the parish of Ballinderry. The highest point within the boundary is 358 feet.

[Insert addition: The following are a few of the principal elevations with their height above the level (sea): Maghaberry <Magheraberry> 338 feet, Ballynaghten 228 feet, Magheramesk 263 feet, Spence's Fort 266 feet. The lowest level is about 100 feet above the sea].

The upper stratum of these ridges seems to be almost all limestone which is quarried to a great extent, and these excavations, from their great whiteness, strike the eye from a considerable distance. The lime is almost all burnt on the spot and consequently the kilns are very numerous.

Lakes and Rivers

There are no lakes in the parish.

The Lagan river, in some places dammed up and transformed into a spacious canal, forms the south boundary of this parish. It rises in or flows out of Lough Neagh, at a distance of about 20 miles from the sea, and discharges itself into Belfast Lough, the tides of which materially affect it for some distance. This river is navigable for lighters drawn by horses for a great way, by its natural bed being in many places dyked up and assisted by art. Within about a quarter of a mile of Boyle's bridge, on the road from Moira to Lisburn in this parish, the river ceasing to be naturally navigable, an entirely artificial canal has been substituted, by which the lighters are brought into the lough.

This parish is well supplied with water which, from the operation of the limestone strata through which it rises, is beautifully clear. Wells and pumps are not uncommon on the farmyards. There are no mineral or hot springs. The River Lagan has no mills, being too calm and slow for water power.

Bogs

There are in the parish a few small tracts of uncultivated low ground, which more properly deserve the name of marsh than peat bog. In winter they are partially covered with water. They are very inconsiderable.

[Insert addition: There are only 4 small patches of bog in the parish, 3 of which are situated towards the centre and the fourth near the southern boundary].

Woods

The little wood in this parish consists in a few trees round the farmhouses.

Climate

The low grounds in this parish, being partly shaded by the high ridges on the other side of the Lagan from the prevailing south west winds, are sheltered and warm.

NATURAL HISTORY

Botany

Ivy seems to be extremely luxuriant in this parish: every ruined cottage or deserted wall or kiln has a thick covering of it.

MODERN TOPOGRAPHY

Public Buildings

Neither town nor village in the parish. The only public building in this parish is a Quakers'

Parish of Magheramesk 115

meeting house in the townland of Ballinalargy. It was built in the year 1827, contains 300 persons, cost 300 pounds, was built by subscription of the attendants. The style of building is a simple oblong square.

There is also 1 small school, as follows: Maghaberry townland, males 38, females 16, Protestants 52, Catholics 2, total 54; partly supported by National Board of Education. The schoolroom pretty large and commodious.

No gentlemen's seats in this parish.

Mills

There is only 1 corn mill in the parish, in the townland of Gortnacor Upper. The diameter of water wheel is 16 feet, breadth 20 inches, fall of water 9 feet, breast wheel. The supply of water is uncertain in summer.

Communications: Roads

The main roads from Moira to Crumlin and from Moira to Lisburn pass through this parish. About a mile of the former and 4 miles of the latter are contained within the boundary. The road to Crumlin is very bad; it passes over very rough hills and is itself full of holes. Its average breadth is about 26 feet.

There are 2 roads to Lisburn, the old and the new. The latter is very broad, well laid out, level, macadamized and about 36 feet in average breadth. It is contracted to be finished in June next (1835) and will communicate with the county Down by a bridge to be built over the Lagan Canal.

The old road to Lisburn, which is still the coach road until the new one is opened, was very injudiciously laid out, up and down a ridge of little hills along the course of the river. It is full of holes and has not been repaired for some time, as the authorities having spending [sic] all the funds on the new line. Its average breadth is 30 feet. There are quantities of neat cottages and farmhouses all along this road.

[Insert addition: The road from Moira to Belfast through Lisburn traverses the parish from east to west for 2 and a quarter miles. The road which communicates between Moira and Glenavy extends through the eastern portion for 1 and a quarter miles].

Canal

The Lagan Canal is navigated by lighters drawn by horses which convey timber from Belfast harbour into Lough Neagh and thence to the opposite shores of Tyrone, Derry and Armagh. This canal is in part formed out of the Lagan river, with which it is now identified, under the name of the Lagan Navigation, and in this sense it is about 20 miles long, average breadth about 20 feet and average depth [blank]. For detailed accounts of this canal, see paper on Lagan Navigation.

Bridges

There are 4 bridges over the Lagan in this parish: Lady's bridge, on the road from Moira to Crumlin, has 1 arch, not of great span; is built partly of red freestone and partly of brick. It would not admit of 2 carts abreast.

Boyle's bridge, on the old road to Lisburn, is built of the same materials with 1 arch, but is extremely narrow and rises very high in the middle.

Spence's bridge, on a crossroad to the county Down, has 3 small arches and is built of stone.

There is another small bridge of 3 arches on a crossroad to Hillsborough. There is to be a fifth, of 1 arch, on Mr Stevenson's new road from Moira to Lisburn.

General Appearance

The first thing which strikes a stranger in this parish is the great quantity of lime quarries and kilns, the former of which, from the great whiteness of the lime, are visible from a considerable distance and break the smooth regularity which the ridges of ground present to the eye. The parish consists, generally speaking, of a great bank with a southerly aspect and a fertile appearance, but not much wooded.

ANCIENT TOPOGRAPHY

Antiquities

There exists near the south boundary of the parish, a few hundred yards to the right of the road from Moira to Crumlin, the ruin of an old church, to which was formerly attached a round tower about 60 feet high, crowned with a cupola. This tower, which was built in a great measure of red freestone, fell about the year 1828 and there is now hardly a vestige of such a thing having existed near the church. The church was an oblong square 48 feet long by 13 inside. The west gable, with a high pointed window almost choked with ivy, still remains entire. Tradition says this church and tower were reduced to ruin by some soldiers who had a barrack in Soldierstown in the year 1641, by means of cannon.

Social Economy

Early Improvements

The extensive lime quarries in this parish may be considered as some cause of its prosperity, as they afford work to a great many labourers, besides which the opening of the canal from Belfast and the high road passing through to Lisburn are all advantages to farmers who send the produce of their crops to those markets.

Obstructions to Improvement

As the greater part of this parish belongs to Sir Robert Bateson, who seems to be considered a good landlord although not resident on the spot, there appears to be no visible obstruction to improvement.

Local government: see parish of Blaris.

Dispensaries

None in the parish. The parish contains no almshouses nor mendicity institutions.

Religion

The Roman Catholics are not numerous, Presbyterians <Presbytery> seems to predominate; there are some Quakers and Methodists, the latter of whom have a meeting house in the adjoining parish of Blaris.

Habits of the People

The people in this parish appear very comfortable. There is a vast number of snug whitewashed farmhouses, particularly along the line of the road to Lisburn. They are almost all 1-storey houses, but extremely neat and clean inside. It is to be remarked that the people in this neighbourhood speak with much less brogue than in almost any other part of Ireland and in general appear very well informed, that is in comparison with the north of the county.

Emigration

Emigration is not near so frequent as further north.

Fair Sheets by Thomas Fagan, November and December 1837

Natural State

Description and Situation

The parish is well situated with regard to spring and river water. There is little bog or native wood in the parish and no mountain whatever. The greater portion of the parish is fertile and well cultivated.

It is bounded on the south and south west by the parishes of Blaris and Moira, and on the west and north west by Moira, Aghalee and Ballinderry, and on the east and north east by Magheragall.

Union

It is one of a union of the 3 parishes of Magheramesk, Aghalee and Aghagallon, of which the Reverend Robert Hill is vicar. Information obtained from John Crangill, John McSwain and many others. 11th December 1837.

Natural Features

Bogs in Inisloughlin

In the above townland there was above 60 English acres of bog, which is now cut out except a few scattered spots of no importance. There was some fir and oak timber got imbedded in it, but of little value. The greater part of the remains of these bogs is now reclaimed and growing the rotation of crops common in the parish. Informants John McSwain, James McAreavy and others.

Bogs

In Magheramesk there stood about 2 acres of bog which is now nearly cut out. Valuable marl was found in this bog but no timber. Informants John Turtle, John Spince and others.

In the townland of Derrynisk there was about 8 acres of bog which is at present nearly cut out and the remains reclaimed. There was oak and alder got included in this bog from time to time, but of little value. Information obtained from Francis Turner and others.

Modern Topography

Quaker Meeting House

Maghaberry Quakers' meeting house, on the old road leading from Lisburn to Ballinderry and situated within 2 miles of Moira, is a plain oblong edifice 1-storey high and slated, 51 by 23 feet 10 inches inside, walls 21 inches thick and floor boarded. It affords a fireplace in each end and is lit by 7 large oblong windows, entrance by 1 door. It is divided into 2 divisions, one of which is devoted exclusively to the female part of the congregation, who occasionally repair to it to arrange their temporal affairs. Both apartments are furnished alike and can be thrown into one in cases of monthly meetings, as the division is formed by a movable partition of boards.

There are 38 seats in the house: 16 of these average 10 feet long each and will accommodate 7 persons each seat, total 112; 17 seats average 9 feet long each and will hold 6 persons each seat, total 102; 2 seats is 6 feet long each and will hold 4 persons each seat, total 8; 1 seat is 7 feet long and will hold 4 persons; 1 seat is 17 feet long and will hold 11 persons; 1 seat is 20 feet long and will hold 13 persons; total of persons accommodated with seats in the house 250, allowing an average of 1 and a half feet to each sitting.

The house and furniture, though of a plain construction, is in clean order. Divine service is commenced at 11 o'clock in the morning on the first and fourth days of the weeks. The congregation is respectable and the average attendance at ordinary meetings about 100 persons and 200 at monthly meetings.

Attached to one end of the meeting house stands a small thatched house for the carekeeper's dwelling, and on the grounds a good stable, also a park, for the use of the horses occasionally brought there by members of the congregation.

The yard is tolerably large and affords a burial ground. It is enclosed by a quickset fence, sheltered and ornamented by a variety of forest trees. Entrance from the aforesaid road by a good iron gate. The first buried in the graveyard was a soldier who died in the neighbourhood.

The site was the gift of a Mr William Richardson, one of the Friends, above 60 years ago. The grounds are now held under Lord Hertford at an annual rent. Quakers and several Protestant families bury here, but neither have tombs or headstones over their graves. The meeting house was built at the expense of the Friends above 60 years back and enlarged and newly roofed in 1826, cost 280 pounds, which sum was also defrayed by the Quakers themselves. They don't accept contributions from any other religious sect under any circumstance. The above Mr Richardson, who gave the site of the graveyard, was subsequently in jail for non-payment of tithe and kept there till he died. He is now interred on the above site beside the soldier, in accordance with his own directions previous to his demise. The Reverend Lemuel Mathews was incumbent of the parish at that period and the person at whose instance Mr Richardson was incarcerated as above stated. Information obtained from Jacob Green and Robert Watson, Quakers. 13th November 1837.

Lord Conway's House

In Carnloughrin, and contiguous to the turnpike road leading from Lisburn to Moira, stands a house locally called Lord Conway's House and said to have been for some time occupied by the Conway family, after their getting possession of the territory of Killultagh, now the property of Lord Hertford. This house stood 1-storey high and thatched, and measured 21 feet wide on the outside. Length could not be accurately judged as the house has been overhauled. The entrance door was made of oak, very thick and was closely studded with broad-headed nails. The roof of several of the office houses was of stone and lime, similar to the arch of a bridge. There was handsome enclosed gardens, but are now destroyed by the above road. The offices are also demolished. One of the old pear trees still remains in the garden. The dwelling house is now occupied by John Smyth, a publican. Informants Robert Watson, John Smyth, John McSwain and others.

Trummery House

Trummery House, the seat of Mr Robert Dunlap, is situated about 5 and a half miles from Lisburn and contiguous to the turnpike road leading from the latter town to Moira. The house is an oblong building 2-storeys high and slated, with wings attached in the rear. There are good offices and enclosed yards in the rear. The garden and orchard is enclosed by good quickset fences and sheltered by forest trees. The demesne, about 122 English acres, is laid off in large and well enclosed fields, and is the seat of young and grown plantations of forest trees. It is likewise the seat of a good limestone quarry, also of an ancient church and burial ground, and is well accommodated with public and by-roads passing through it.

The house stands on a handsome eminence south of the above road and commands a fine prospect of a wide extent of the surrounding neighbourhood. It was built by the late Brent Spincer Esquire above 90 years back. It was enlarged by his son, the late Conway Spincer Esquire, about 60 years ago. Trummery House was the only gentleman's seat of eligibility in the parish and was for a series of years occupied by the Spincer family, who were the proprietors of several townlands in its neighbourhood. They have been succeeded in Trummery House by different gentlemen. Informants Robert Dunlap, Francis Turner and others.

Lady Bridge

The Lady bridge, across the canal and situated partly in the county Antrim and partly in county Down, stands in the neighbourhood of Moira and accommodates a leading road from the latter town to Antrim. This bridge has 1 half-circle arch, span 22 feet 6 inches. Breadth of the road on the bridge 15 feet 6 inches, breadth of the road at either end of the bridge 23 feet, average height of parapets 5 feet, thickness of parapet 1 foot 6, length of parapets on either side of the road 40 yards. The arch affords a horse track 6 feet wide for the accommodation of horses employed in drawing the canal lighters.

The bridge is in good order. It was built about 46 years back by the canal company, engineer Mr Owens, who was also engineer of canal. The arch and cornices is of cut freestone. 5 feet high of the parapets above the road is of brick and the remainder under the road of a blue quarry stone. Detached from the bridge stands a small arch that accommodates a feeder to the canal.

Coal and other lumber for Moira is discharged at the Lady bridge, it being the nearest landing place to the above town. There is no quay made for that purpose. There is a second landing place to accommodate Moira some distance south east of the Lady bridge, but the latter bridge is the nearest to the town. Informants Adam Hull and others. 24th November 1837.

Bridge and Roads

The Hertford bridge over the canal is situated on the turnpike road leading from Lisburn to Moira and has 1 half-circle arch, span 25 feet 6 inches. Breadth of the road on the bridge 39 feet, length of the bridge 30 feet, average height of parapets on the bridge 3 feet 6, thickness of parapets 1 foot 6. This is a handsome bridge built 1835 by the trustees of the Ulster turnpike roads, engineers Andrew Stephenson and Company. The arch affords a track 6 and a half feet wide for the accommodation of the horses employed in drawing the lighters. The chief part of the work is of black dressed quarry stone, arch faced and parapets corniced with a hard whitish cut stone. The body of the arch is turned with dressed freestone. The name of the bridge and date of erection is cut on a neat corniced stone in each parapet thus: Hertford bridge, 1835.

The above turnpike road averages 40 feet wide clear of banks or fences, including a footpath along one side of it, and is kept up from the proceeds of the toll-gates situated on the line. It was opened for access between Lisburn and Moira in 1836, engineers the aforesaid Andrew Stephenson and Company.

Bridge and Road in Inisloughlin

Spincer's bridge across the Lagan river, on the leading road from Hillsborough to Moira and partly situated on the above townland and parish, has 3 half-circle arches: span of centre arch 22 feet, span of each of the outside arches 21 feet, average breadth of the road on the bridge 21 feet 6, average height of parapets 4 feet, thickness of parapets 1 foot 6, length of parapets on either side of the road 355 yards, length of the bridge 30 yards. Detached from the bridge on the county Down side stands 3 arches to accommodate in cases of high floods in the river. These arches stand at some distance one from another. The span of the west arch of these is 12 feet, span of each of the other two is 7 feet.

On the county Antrim side of the bridge also stands 2 arches to serve as above, span of each 10 feet. These small arches are turned or rather faced with rough quarry stones and the large or bridge arches faced with cut freestone. The remainder of the work including the parapets is built of quarry and land stones. The main bridge seems in a permanent state of repair. The other arches and the parapets has suffered partial dilapidation.

This bridge is said to be old, but no accurate account here of the cost, date of building or who the engineer of it was. It is said to be erected at the expense of the 2 counties of Antrim and Down, in which it is equally situate. Information obtained from John McSwain and others.

That portion of the leading road from Hillsborough to Moira by Spincer's bridge, and situated in the above parish, averages 17 feet wide clear of banks or fences and is kept up by presentments.

Roads

That portion of the old road leading from Lisburn to Moira by Maghaberry averages 19 feet wide clear of banks or fences and is kept up by presentments, but much neglected since the turnpike road was opened and other level lines also. Informants John Turtle, John Spince and others. 21st November 1837.

That old line of road leading from the Halfpenny gate, Broomhedge, to Ballinderry, and locally called the Glen road, averages 17 feet wide clear of banks or fences and is kept up by presentments. This line of road was formerly paved with stones, all within the above parish.

Parish of Magheramesk

That portion of the leading road from Moira to Antrim by the Lady bridge, and situated in the above parish, averages 20 feet wide clear of banks or fences and is kept up by presentments. There have been several alterations made on this line in latter years, to evade hills over which it formerly passed. It was formerly paved with stones and locally called the Dublin road, it being the main leading road between the latter city and Belfast. There are pieces of the paved road still extant and useful to the farmers in such places as the above alterations were made.

That portion of the old leading road from Lisburn to Moira, and situated in the above parish, averages 27 feet wide clear of banks or fences, including a footpath along the one side, and is kept up by presentments; but since the new turnpike road was opened between the above towns, the old line was much neglected and is now in bad order. Information obtained from Jacob Green and others.

Public Roads and other Communications

This parish is well dissected and accommodated with public and by-roads passing through it from east to west and from north to south. The canal also joins it for a considerable distance on the south and south west, and passes through a portion of the south west side of the parish in the neighbourhood of Moira. The Lagan river also joins it for a considerable distance on the south side, or rather the south end of the parish. The turnpike road passing through the parish from east to west is 40 feet wide, including a footpath on one side of the line, and is kept up from the proceeds of the toll-gates situated on the line between Moira and Lisburn. The other public leading roads passing through [the] parish vary from 19 to 24 feet wide, including footpaths along some of the lines. They are kept up by presentments or grants from the county grand jury.

The by-roads, kept up by the county or grants from the county grand jury, vary from 16 to 21 feet wide. But there are several by-roads, or lanes as they are locally called, which are kept up by grants from the courts leet, held twice a year in Lisburn for the manor of Killultagh, in which this parish is situated. These lanes are chiefly for the accommodation of the landholders. These accommodating lanes, which open a communication from public leading roads and from by-roads also into the interior of townlands where farmers in many instances have their dwellings situated, are considered of great advantage and of little expense after they are first made. They vary from 10 to 14 feet wide. 2nd December 1837.

Quarries and Limeworks

This parish is the seat of extensive limestone quarries. There are 7 kilns kept burning lime constantly for public sale in the parish and several others that occasionally burn for the same purpose. Besides being a gaining concern to the owners of these kilns, it likewise gives employ to a large number of the working class resident in the parish. Each burning kiln is charged 11 guineas annual tax, which sum goes to the Marquis of Hertford who is lord of the soil. The lime is sold here at the same price as stated for Magheragall or Derryaghy parishes. Information obtained from Robert Dunlap, Joseph Hull and many others.

Bleach Green

In the townland of Magheramesk there was formerly a bleach green, latterly occupied by the late Henry Hammond Esquire. It was situated in that part of the above townland locally called Saggony bog, but it has been disused above 70 years back and the buildings belonging to it subsequently destroyed. The grounds are now held by different farmers. On the above bleach farm there stood a fort which is now destroyed.

Corn Mill

Broomhedge corn mill, situated in the townland of Gortnacor, Lord Hertford proprietor, John Bennett, tenant. This mill is 2-storeys high and thatched. The water wheel is undershot, diameter 12 feet 10 inches, breadth 2 feet 6 inches, fall of water 5 feet. This wheel is wood and drives 1 pair of stones. The mill is idle for want of water from the 1st May to the 1st October, in consequence of the site of the main dam being meadow grounds in the occupation of another farmer, who causes the water to be drawn off on the 1st May and let on again on the 1st October, the intervening months being necessary for the growing and saving of the hay crop. This mill is said to be of old standing, but was overhauled about 35 years back, being previously burnt by accident <accidence>.

ANCIENT TOPOGRAPHY

Querns and Stone Hatchets

Jacob Green, in demolishing a fort in his holding in the townland of Creenagh, found beneath its surface an ancient quern, circular shape, 18 inches in diameter, and in another part of his farm a quern of the above description. The latter is now situated in his kitchen fire hearth. He also found an oval quern of rather rude construction. These are not extant. He likewise found 2 stone hatchets in shape similar to others before described. One of these was taken to Dublin; the other is in his house in the above townland at present, but in an imperfect state.

Ancient Urns

In Creenagh and holding of Robert Watson, and contiguous to a small rivulet, stood a piece of ground supposed to have been an ancient burial ground. In labouring this piece of ground in 1834 there was discovered beneath its surface, at a depth of 2 feet, an ancient earthen urn, carved on its surface, burned bones in a decayed state, black earth, timber cinders, dross and parcels of burned soil resembling brick or crockery, all under a quantity of stones of different sizes and large flat stones over the latter. In another part of the farm he found a second urn of the above description. Specimens of the above antiques are at present at Mr Watson's dwelling in the above townland. Informants Robert Watson and James Strahan. 14th November 1837.

Discoveries in a Fort

In Inisloughlin, and holding of George Crooks, there stood, surrounded by bog, a fort which is at present destroyed and the site under tillage. In demolishing this fort at some former period there was found beneath its surface a cannon-ball 3 lbs and 12 oz. weight, also a brass battleaxe, brass spurs and other articles of old construction. These articles were found by Thomas English, who has subsequently emigrated to America and disposed of the above previous to his going.

Ancient Coin and Mill in Inisloughlin

In different parts of the above townland, and at sundry periods, there were several pieces of ancient and copper coin found beneath the surface, many of which have been sold in Belfast, some sent to Dublin and others brought by emigrants to America.

In the above townland and holding of George Crooks, and contiguous to the Lagan river, there stood an ancient corn mill, but the period of its being erected or disused is not known by any of the local inhabitants.

Ancient Building and Well in Inisloughlin

In the same townland and holding, and contiguous to Inisloughlin main fort, there stood an ancient building, supposed to have belonged to some of the O'Neill cheiftains but latterly inhabited by the Spincer family, once the proprietors of the above townland. The cellar, in which stood a draw-well, was visible to a late period, but the occupier of the farms in which it is situated closed it up and has the site now under tillage. There was a pipe constructed of brick extended from the cellar to the Lagan river, a distance of about 150 yards. It was permanently built and some feet beneath the surface. Its design would appear to be either to convey water to the draw-well in the cellar or to draw water from it. However, in latter years when a flood occurred in the Lagan the aforesaid well filled up with water, which passed from the river through the pipe, and when the floods fell in the river, the water sunk in the well also. The pipe remains undisturbed, but being some depth beneath the surface cannot be inspected. 16th November 1837.

Ancient Burial Ground

In Carnloughrin, and holding of John Smyth, there stood an ancient burial ground locally called Carnloughrin burial ground. In reclaiming it from time to time there was black earth and small bones found beneath its surface. The site is now under tillage and nothing to denote the burial ground but an ancient thorn bush that stood on the site.

Ancient Standing Stone

On an eminence in Derrynisk, and holding of Thomas Green, there stands an ancient stone column locally called the Grey Stone. It forms 4 irregular squares and stands 3 feet above the surface, and is said to be above 3 feet beneath the surface. It measures 3 feet 3 inches long by 3 feet 3 inches broad. It is situated south of the leading road from Lisburn to Moira and contiguous to the ruins of a Danish fort. On its smaller square appears something approaching to a rude burst [bust ?]. Its dimensions on the top is greater than at the surface. Informants John [Smyth ?] and others.

Forts and Burial Ground

In Maghaberry, and holding of John Spince, there is a fort approaching to oval shape, 40 by 35 yards. The parapet is of earth and stones and varies in height above the bottom of the moat from 9 to 14 feet, from 4 to 6 feet above the area of the fort and from 20 to 30 feet thick at the base. The moat is from 10 to 15 feet wide. This fort is now under grazing but nothing of interest to be seen about it.

In the above townland and holding there stood an ancient burial ground, now occupied by a limestone quarry. In destroying this old burial ground from time to time, there was found beneath its surface an ancient earthen urn, carved on the surface and containing a quantity of calcined bones and ashes, also a number of human skulls and every description of human bones. Several of the jaw-bones retained the teeth. The skulls were larger than those commonly raised in modern graveyards. These articles were found at different periods within the last 40 years and again buried in the earth thrown off the quarry.

In the above townland, and holding of Thomas Hammond, there stood a fort which is now destroyed and the site under tillage.

Quarry and Burial Ground in Magheramesk

In the above townland stands a limestone quarry, situated on the site of an ancient burial ground. In working this quarry from time to time there were several skulls and a large quantity of every description of human bones found beneath the surface of the topsoil. Some of these bones were found 1836. They have been all again buried beneath the soil in the remains of the quarry.

It is locally said that there was a great battle fought on the site of the burial ground. On the site is now growing a sort of board-tree timber called dwarf alder, and said only to grow where human blood was shed in combat. It grows about 4 feet high and blossoms and bears small berries similar to other board-trees. It is also said to cure many diseases, such as dropsy, tumours, bodily pains, inward biles, and is commonly brought to different and remote districts for the above purposes. Informants John Cossley, John Hamill and others. 22nd November 1837.

Ancient Spring and St Patrick's Footstone

In Magheramesk and holding of John and William Cossley, and in the immediate neighbourhood of the old burial ground described [above], there stands an ancient spring well which was formerly visited by sick people from different districts. At the base of the well stood a large stone, having on its surface the print of a human foot, and said to be that of St Patrick's foot. However, the patients who visited this spring and stone performed some religious ceremony, after which they drank of the spring or applied the water to the disordered parts and affected themselves to be thereby relieved from the disorders of which they previously complained. The above stone was removed from the well at some former period and used in modern building by the late Henry McConkey. It was thought by some to have been one of the ancient inaugurating stones.

In the above townland, and holding of Thomas Reyford, there stood a fort which is now destroyed and the site under tillage.

Ancient Gold Gorgets

In sinking beneath the surface a large stone that formerly stood in the townland of Carnloughrin, and holding of the late John Bennett, there was found at some depth beneath its surface 3 gold gorgets, beautifully ornamented on the surface along their edge with various devices. They were of equal size and thickness, and rolled round each other when found. There was 2 labourers and the above Mr Bennett at the finding of them but Bennett, as being then the occupier of the farm on which they were found, claimed them from the labourers, at the same time promising them a legal portion each man of what proceeds the sale of the articles would bring. However, he subsequently sold the gorgets, it is thought in Belfast, but the proceeds of the sale he never acknowledged. He gave to the late James Campbell, one of the above labourers, 20 guineas as his portion of the amount brought by the sale of the gorgets but to Henry Crangill, the second of the men present at finding them, he never gave any portion of the money or value for which they sold.

These gorgets was about the thickness of a common sheet of tin and had small buttons on each corner, by which they could be fastened when worn. They were formerly used as armour to save the throats <froats>. Informants John Smith, John Spince and Henry Crangill, one of the finders of the above.

The ancient gold gorgets alluded to is, according to local account, the same size and shape as the one found in county Derry, the draft of which Mr Ligar gave in the Memoirs of Desertmartin parish, situated in the latter county. 23rd November 1837.

Urn of Bones and Fort

In Ballynalargy, and holding of Alexander Tolerton, there was discovered in a stone building beneath the surface, and covered with a flat stone, an ancient earthen urn carved on the surface and containing a quantity of calcined bones and ashes. These antiques were found in 1827 but have been subsequently destroyed.

In the above townland, and holding of John Watson, there stood a fort which is now destroyed and the site under tillage.

Ruins of Native Wood

In Derrynisk, and holding of the late Francis Davis, there stands about 1 and a half acres of ruins of native wood. There are a large number of alder and some oaks of partial height and thickness still remaining, and some underwood. This wood formerly extended into Ballynalargy and other townlands, and was called Ballynalargy wood.

Ancient Well and Religious Ceremonies

Beside the above wood stands an ancient spring well that was formerly visited by hundreds of persons from various districts, and who laboured under sundry diseases. These persons came at Midsummer Day and performed some ancient religious ceremonies for relief or cure of the different disorders under which they suffered, and next applied the water taken from the spring to the parts complained of, which application and ceremony is said to have cured many. This practice is relinquished many years ago. Informants James Graham, Richard Turner and others.

Fort and Urn of Bones

In Magheramesk, and holding of Edward Hull, there stands a fort approaching to oval shape, 45 by 40 yards and about 5 feet above the surface of the field in which it is situated. It was enclosed by a moat and parapet which are now levelled. The breast of the fort is studded with thorns and scrog, and forms the present fence. The area forms a convex. At some depth beneath the surface of this fort there was a stone and lime building resembling a pipe observed but not explored. There was an earthen urn containing bones and ashes and carved on the surface found in the fort, also arrowheads and Danes' pipes, all within the last 30 years, but subsequently destroyed. Informants John McClure, Adam Hull and others.

Grey Stone

In the townland of Magheramesk, and contiguous to the canal, there stood for centuries back a stone of extraordinary size and locally called the Grey Stone. The farm in which it was situated is still called the Grey Stone farm. This stone stood above 7 feet high and above 20 feet in circumference. It was much regarded by the local inhabitants as being very gentle and the scene of fairy amusements, which is said to have been frequently observed about it in times gone by. This respected monument of antiquity was blasted with powder about 46 years ago and used in building the Lady bridge across the canal in that neighbourhood, by the late Mr Owens, engineer. Informants Adam and Joseph Hull. 25th November 1837.

Brass Battleaxe and Spear

In Trummery, and holding of John Hull, there was found beneath the surface in 1836 a brass battleaxe about 6 inches in length. It was subsequently given to John Rogan, an antiquarian residing in that neighbourhood. He also got flint arrowheads and ring stones found in the last-mentioned townland.

There was also found in Trummery in 1829 a brass spear, which has been subsequently given to Welsh, another antiquarian residing at Dromore <Drumore>.

Ancient Burial Ground

On an eminence in the townland of Magheramesk, and holding of Anthony Hull, there stood an ancient burial ground, the site of which is at present occupied by dwelling and office houses, yards and gardens. In sinking the foundations of these house at some former period there were skulls and other human bones discovered 5 feet beneath the surface. A rude and unlettered description of tombstone have been frequently found in the same place, also graves from 4 to 6 feet deep and small carns of stones also beneath the surface. It is locally considered that this place was the seat of an ancient church.

Some years back, in labouring one of the above gardens, there was discovered at some depth beneath the surface several feet in length of a strong wall composed of stone and brick. This wall has been raised and the materials of which it was composed converted to other uses. The skulls and other bones above mentioned were buried again on the site where found.

Battle at Magheramesk

In the above townland, and contiguous to the burial ground now described, there was a great battle took place between the English and Irish armies about 1688. This battle commenced in

Ballinderry parish, on an eminence called the Scout hill, and situated a short distance north of Magheramesk. James' army were defeated on the Scout hill by those of William. The former retreated southward to Magheramesk, where a second combat ensued in which James' army were again defeated and obliged to retreat, but experienced great slaughter.

Contiguous to the site of the latter combat there have been large quantities of every description of human bones found beneath the surface, in labouring the land from time to time, also several weapons of war, such as sheep-head swords etc. These weapons have been brought away to other districts, but the bones were interred again where found.

In view of the place where this battle was fought there stood an ancient thorn bush, to which Lord Blany (then commanding in the English service) hanked his horse during the engagement. It was in consequence called Blany's Bush. It subsequently decayed [and] the local inhabitants planted another thorn in its stead, which is also called Blany's Bush, and denotes to the curious the site of the aforesaid event.

The people of that neighbourhood is by tradition quite familiar with the foregoing events. It is also stated in that place that those battles occurred in the harvest time and that William's troops let loose their horses on a field of corn which they in a short time utterly destroyed. However, that, without being seeded on the following season (this field which is now occupied by John McClure), grew a luxuriant crop of black oats. Informants John McClure, John Hamill and others. 27th November 1837.

Trummery Ancient Church

Trummery ancient church, which is at present a pile of ruins, is locally said to have been founded by St Bridget. This venerable edifice is situated nearly in the centre of the above parish, on a handsome eminence north east of the turnpike road leading from Lisburn to Moira, 5 and a half miles from the former town and within 1 and a half mile of the latter. It was an oblong building 50 and a half by 13 feet 10 inches in the clear, walls averaging 2 feet 10 inches in thickness, built of grey land and quarry stones, and run together by grouted lime similar to other ancient buildings. The west gable is nearly in its original shape, with a large Gothic door or window in its centre. It is mantled over with ivy which gives it a venerable appearance, but the work is much disfigured in consequence of the well shaped corner and outside stones having been picked out and brought to modern buildings in its neighbourhood. Nearly one half of the side walls have been carried away altogether and the remaining part disfigured as above, and under similar circumstances.

It would appear from the situation of the existing part of the side walls that their original height above the outside surface was between 9 and 11 feet, but the interior is raised to a great extent by graves and soil. An entrance door of Gothic shape is said to have been on the south side of the church. The top part of this door is visible a few feet above the surface, but much disfigured by dilapidation. Within 2 feet of the top of the side walls, and 3 and a half feet distant one from another, there was a row of oblong holes seemingly designed for beams or joists <joices> to support a gallery. The walls were roughcast with lime outside and plastered inside. The east gable is nearly demolished. It does not appear that much freestone was used in any part of the building, or any cut stone whatever. 28th and 29th November 1837.

Trummery Round Tower

Joined to the north east corner of the church stood a very handsome round tower, built with the same materials as the church and the walls about the same thickness as the church walls. The east corner of the north side wall and the north corner of the east gable was grafted in the tower, thus: [small ground plan]. The blank in the tower wall shows the doorway opening into it on the south side. It stood between 30 and 40 feet high, quite circular and from 7 to 10 feet in diameter inside but occupied to a great extent by winding stairs of stonework that ascended nearly half its height. On the south side stood the entrance door and over it, at about half the height of the tower, stood a second door seemingly designed as an entrance to a loft or gallery. At about three-quarters of its height stood 4 oblong but narrow windows. They were directly opposite to each other on the north, east, south and west points. Near the top stood a fixture of oak joists, as if designed to support a bell. The top of the tower was closed in by masonry of limestone.

It was for many ages past mantled over with ivy, which gave it a majestic and venerable appearance, but at sundry periods within the last century the under part of it was disfigured and injured by people picking out the well shaped stones occupied in the walls and carrying them off to other buildings. They at length left the bulk of the tower depending on a mere skeleton at the foot. The durability of the materials with which it was built, combined with the interwoven mantle of ivy with which it was covered, is said to form its chief support and keep it standing for a series of time past. However, about 8 years ago this beautiful and venerable monument of antiquity yielded to dilapidation and time its hitherto lofty pride. About November 1828 or 1829 it fell to the ground, to the great surprise of the local inhabitants who deemed it an almost unrivalled piece of antiquity.

Nothing at present remains to denote the existence of this tower but the crumbles of its ruins and tradition of the local inhabitants. The situation it occupied, attached to the church as before stated, at once denotes the great antiquity of both, for it is rare to find a tower attached to the east end, or north east corner of either ancient or modern churches. The tower is said to have been the haunt of the late celebrated robber Redmond O'Hanlon for many years.

Trummery Graveyard

Attached to the east gable of the church on the south side stood a vault, said to have been erected by the Spincer family above 100 years back. It is at present, except the south gable, in ruins as well as the tower. The entrance to this vault opened from the body of the church through the east gable, and since its erection. From it the entrance opened into the tower, as the north end of it was grafted on the tower and embraced the tower door within its compass. The graveyard is enclosed by a quickset fence; entrance to it from a road passing east of it by a small iron gate. There is a handsome raised tomb on the north side, erected by the Guckin family, and on its surface several devices engraven.

The following are amongst the names and surnames on the tombs and headstones. Christian names of male and female: Roger, Henry, John, David, Dennis, Edward, Samuel, Mary, Ann-Jane, Elizabeth, Grace, Cathrine, Patrick, Thomas, George, Joseph, Francis.

Surnames of families who have tombs and headstones in Trummery: Gattney, Hill, Gilmore, Guckin, Grann, Bennett, Briggs, Davis, Hanlon, Atcheson, McClure, McIllreavey, McCorry, McCree, McCord, Moore, Connor, Neilson, McClure, Smyth, Spence, Burrows. The oldest stone legible in the yard was a tomb erected to the Burrows family, 1684. There are several tombs and headstones in the yard which cannot be read, the letters being defaced by time.

The Irish cry accompanied the funerals of Roman Catholics to this place up to about 1806. Since that period this class of people commenced burying at the neighbouring Roman Catholic chapels. Hymns now supersede the Irish cry with their funerals.

There is little local account of the destruction of the church, save that of its falling a victim to Oliver Cromwell's <Olover Crumwell's> hands, like many other ancient edifices. Informants James Graham, John and Sareah Crangill, John Hamill and many others.

Trummery Fort

About 75 yards north of the graveyard stands a fort approaching to circular shape, 24 yards in diameter on the top, which forms a sort of concave shape. It is composed chiefly of earth and varies from 15 to 24 feet of a sloping height above the level of the field in which it is situated. It was enclosed by a moat and parapet which have been levelled above 14 years back. There are 4 old lime trees standing round its base. Tradition says that the lime trees were planted on the fort by the late Brent Spincer Esquire of Trummery House. He is also said to have carried soil and stones to the fort, and to have thereby raised it several feet above its original height, to form an ornament opposite to his hall door. It is likewise said that he experienced some calamity in person and chattels subsequent to his intrusion on the fort, and that he and others alleged these misfortunes to the above trespass on the work of antiquity.

The fort is now under grazing. Local report says that there are artificial excavations and money beneath its surface. However, it has not been explored for either. Its size and vicinity to the old church contribute much to the antique appearance of the place. Informants John Crangill, Robert Dunlap and others.

Forts in Lisnabilla

In Lisnabilla, and holding of Richard Bell, there stands the ruins of 2 forts of circular shape, each 40 yards in diameter. They were enclosed each by a moat and parapet, all which are now nearly destroyed. The existing part of the moat is 15 feet wide, but the parapets are entirely destroyed. The ruins of these forts is much higher than the level of the field in which they are situated. The only separation between the two was the moat and parapets by which each was enclosed. They are now disfigured and under tillage, and their south breast forming a sort of fence averaging 5 feet

Parish of Magheramesk

high. Informants Joseph Hull, John McClure and others. 26th November 1837.

In Lisnabilla, and holding of Samuel Bell, there stood a fort which is now destroyed and the site under tillage.

Forts

In Ballynalargy, and holding of William Clark, there stood a fort, which [is] now destroyed and the site under tillage. There was nothing of interest got about it. Informants John McSwain and John McAreevy.

In Derrynisk, and holding of Isaac Bell, there stood a fort which is also destroyed and the site under tillage.

In Magheramesk, and holding of Jacob Douglass, there stood a fort which is now destroyed and the site under tillage.

In Trummery, and holding of Wesley Grey, there stood a fort which is also destroyed and the site under tillage. Informants James Graham, William Cossley and others.

In Gortnacor, and holding of John Bennett, there stood a very handsome clay fort which is now nearly destroyed and the site under tillage. In destroying this fort there was nothing of interest found. Informants James Strahan and others. 1st December 1837.

Inisloughlin Forts

In the townland of Inisloughlin and holding of James McAreavey, and on an eminence contiguous to the Lagan river, stands the ruins of Inisloughlin main fort, once occupied as a strong garrison by the noble O'Neills of Killultagh, and said to be one of the last fortresses they possessed in this part of the country during the war of 1641. It is likewise said that a most formidable battle took place here between the Irish army commanded by Maginnis and O'Neills, and the English army commanded by Cromwell's subofficers, one of whom was a Major Spincer, who signified himself by warlike exploits on the above occasion. However, the discoveries subsequently made in demolishing this fort and labouring the grounds in its immediate vicinity proves to a demonstration that a combat took place there, at the above or some other period.

In the fort and adjoining grounds there was a large quantity of every description of human bones found, which were again interred on the site, also several round metal balls, weighing from 8 to 28 oz. each and many of them supposed to have been fastened or coupled together by slings or chains. Many of these balls have been used in bullet play and were since lost, others were carried away to different districts. In and about it was also found several ancient silver and copper coins, gold rings, bronze weapons, and bronze medals of circular shape, also several small bronze saucers. The size and shape of one of the latter will be seen on [Drawings of Antiquities].

On the fort have also been found several flint arrowheads, some of which are still extant in the neighbourhood. Nearly about the middle of the area stood a large stone, pyramid-shape <piramid>, about 6 feet in length and 6 yards in circumference. It is now sunk beneath the surface. In the area of the fort also stood a fine draw-well, which is now closed up. This fort stood exactly square, 40 yards every way in the interior. It was enclosed by a moat and parapet. The former is totally destroyed. The parapet was very strong and chiefly composed of earth but is now destroyed except a skeleton of the north east and south east squares which average 40 yards long, 5 and a half feet high and 6 feet thick. At each corner of the fort stood a bastion of earth and stones, with a large thorn bush on each bastion. The ruins of the south east bastion still remain and the ancient thorn also. Whatever might have been the original dimensions of these bastions, the present ruins of the one above stated is 28 by 21 feet on the top, in some parts, and 7 feet high. These bastions contribute much to the strength of the fortress. It was at a former period nearly surrounded by bog and morass.

About 200 yards north east of it, in a bog, stood a small circular fort, said to be a great strength and almost inaccessible. The latter is totally destroyed. On the south and west sides likewise stood small forts, which are also destroyed. These small forts were considered outposts to the main fort.

On the whole it was considered to be one of the strongest fortresses in the north (of the same description) and the most difficult to be taken, as it was defended on the south by the Lagan river, which stands a short distance from it, and nearly surrounded on the east, north and north west by bog and morasses, all which, combined with the outpost forts before mentioned, rendered the main fort a strong fortress. However, the Irish are said to have been routed from it with great slaughter.

A short distance on the south west of the fort stood a castle or other strong building, once the seat of some of the O'Neill chieftains but subsequently overhauled and inhabited by the Spincer family. The latter family are said to have obtained from Elizabeth or Cromwell a grant of Inisloughlin townland for ever, in consideration of valour and loyalty during the 1641 war. They were of English extraction and came over with Cromwell at the above period. They held the above townland for a series of years, but at length made an exchange with the Hertford family between it and Trummery, with some other neighbouring townlands. Of these they obtained a good lease which expired some years back, but would not be renewed on the former conditions. 4th and 5th December 1837.

In Inisloughlin, and holding of Robert McCord, there stood a fort which is now destroyed and the site under tillage.

In the above townland, and holding of Thomas Dobbin, there stood a fort which has been demolished many years back. The site is at present under tillage. In demolishing the latter fort there was Danes' smoking pipes and flint arrowheads found beneath its surface, but nothing got about the former.

Tobar Dooney

In Inisloughlin, and holding of James Cahoon, there stands an ancient spring well locally called Tobar Dooney. This well was formerly visited by hundreds of persons from various districts, who laboured under various diseases and performed some ancient ceremonies for the relief of these diseases, but the practice is relinquished. Informants John McAreavey, George Crooks, John Hamill and many others.

Drawings of Antiquities

The undermentioned antiques [drawings of copper coin, 3 flint arrowheads] are at present in the possession of Mr George Crooks, Inisloughlin, and were found in the neighbourhood of Inisloughlin fort. There was also some circular metal balls about 10 oz. weight each found in and about the fort. They seemed to be fastened together in couples by chains. These balls have been lost in bullet play.

The annexed draft [drawing with inscription: "This plank is 8 and a half feet in length, 14 inches broad and 4 inches thick, and plain on both sides"] represents the size and shape of an oak plank found beneath the surface of a small fort constructed in a bog about 200 yards north east of Inisloughlin main fort. This small fort seemed to be an outpost to the former. The enclosed dotted stripe shows a gutter along in one edge of the plank and contains a row of circular holes as above shown. The far stripe shows a half gutter on the other edge of the plank. The dot above the dimensions shows 1 circular hole on the side of the plank.

The above antiques [drawings of 8 flint arrowheads, brass antique, 2 brass saucers, 2 sections of sword hilt and brass battleaxe] were found partly in Inisloughlin Fort and partly in other parts of the parish, and are at present in the possession of John Rogan at Lady's bridge near Moira.

These arrowheads [drawings] were found in the above parish and are in John Rogan's with the others shown [above]. 6th December 1837.

The stone hatchet above shown [drawing] is at present in William McConnell's house at Broomhedge and was found in the above parish.

Collection of Antiques

The following drafts represent the shape and size of antiques found beneath the surface in the townland of Creenagh, preserved and now in the possession of Robert Watson in the above townland [drawings of stone hatchets, flint arrowheads and part of a carved ancient urn]. He has also a collection of ancient silver and copper coin, many of which have been found within the above parish. Amongst them are Robert Bruce's, Edward IV's, Elizabeth's, Anne's, Henry VIII's, James I's, James II's and all the Georges, and all in a good state of preservation, and free to be inspected by any visitor connected with the Irish Ordnance Survey. Informant Robert Watson. 15th November 1837.

Ancient Stone Ornament

The annexed draft [drawing] represents the size and shape of an ancient ornament, blackish stone, found at a fort in Lisnabilla and holding of Samuel Bell. It is at present in his house in the above townland. The blank stripe shows a hole through the stone.

Curious Stone

The latter drafts [drawings] represent the size and nearly the shape of a very curious stone at present in Joseph Hull's house, townland of Magheramesk, and found beneath the surface in that neighbourhood some years back. These drafts show both sides of the stone but it seems to be natural and not artificial.

SOCIAL AND PRODUCTIVE ECONOMY

Floods in the Lagan

On the south and south west the Lagan river joins

Parish of Magheramesk

the above parish for a considerable distance. The floods which occasionally occur in this river, in cases of deep snow or heavy rain, inundate the valleys along its shore to a wide extent and in a more or less degree injure any crops either growing or remaining unremoved on their course. These valleys are chiefly under pasture, meadow, early potatoes or flax, the latter being the only crops ripe or fit for use in time to be removed before the inundations, which sometimes occur from middle of autumn. Very often hay or meadow is obliged to be cut down before it is fit for cutting in order to have it removed before the coming of these harvest floods, as they generally leave behind them on the grass sand and other sediments which, when dried upon the hay, render it indigestible and unsafe fodder, and often bring disorders on cattle, which in some instances prove fatal. In the main time these floods enrich the soil. In many instances several weeks elapse before they are completely fallen. Informants John McSwain, John Crooks and many others. 7th December 1837.

Farms

The farms in this parish vary from 3 to 150 English acres, but few of the latter size. The majority of them average from 10 to 40 English acres. The generality of them are well fenced with good hedges.

Farmhouses

About three-fourths of the farmhouses in the parish are commodious, well lit with large sash windows, whitened with lime outside and inside, and the interior in all other respects neat and well furnished, and the majority of them furnished each with a good clock. The yards are clean and spacious and in many instances well enclosed. In many of them are either good pumps or draw-wells. The gardens are chiefly well enclosed with quickset fences and sheltered with forest trees, and the majority of them well stocked with fruit trees of different kinds. The offices are in general in good order. About one-third of this class of the farmhouses are slated and about the same proportion of them 2-storeys high, including thatched and slated houses [insert marginal note: Reverend Robert Hill].

Amongst these are several Quakers' dwellings, which from their general order and cleanliness, externally and internally, at once denote the superior taste of the aforesaid class of people who inhabit them. The remainder of the farmhouses within the parish are in many respects tolerably comfortable, but not so generally whitened with lime inside or outside as those of the same class in Magheragall or Blaris. 8th December 1837.

Cottier Houses

The greater part of the cottier houses in this parish are well lit with small glass windows and in other respects tolerably comfortable, but not so generally whitened with lime outside or inside as those of the same class in Magheragall.

Fuel

Turf is the chief fuel with all classes in the parish. There are a few scattered remnants of bog in the parish, but turf is chiefly procured from the Montiaghs, distance from 5 to 7 miles.

Food

Their food chiefly consist of oat and wheat bread, porridge, potatoes, flesh meat, salt and fresh fish, milk, butter and vegetables. The wealthy farmers and tradespeople very commonly use tea, morning and evening. To the latter almost all classes in this parish are very partial, but the lower class of farmers and cottiers live chiefly on potatoes, porridge, milk, butter and vegetables. In these too they are often very limited and consequently seldom have tea in any shape.

Clothing and Ancient Costume

The parishioners in general have great taste for good clothing. On Sundays and market days their top apparel consists chiefly in shop goods. Their linen and stockings are principally of their own manufacture. The poorer class, who cannot purchase shop goods, generally purchase second-hand clothes at the market stalls. Brogues, a sort of coarse strong shoes made only by brogue makers, is partially worn in the parish and is the only remnant of ancient costume retained.

Linen and Cotton Weaving

About one-fourth of the parishioners, including farmers and cottiers, carry on cotton weaving. A few carry on linen weaving too, but the former is the most prevalent amongst them. By these trades a large portion of the working class make their chief support in this parish and live tolerably comfortable themselves and families, particularly when the cotton business is brisk and in good demand. Consequently, the farming class who carry on the trade, and whose chief support does not altogether depend on their earning in that way, are enabled thereby to live much more comfortable than they otherwise would. Of the above there [are] many instances of evident proof, for when a slackness occurs in the cotton business, those whose chief employ is cotton weaving suffer much privation and distress till the business again revives, more particularly the cottier class whose chief support that trade is.

SOCIAL ECONOMY

Character and Morals of the People

The parishioners in general are said to be industrious, honest, peaceably disposed, and to live on good neighbourhood with each other. In the parish there is only 1 place of public worship (the Quaker meeting house). 9th December 1837.

In religious or moral pursuits there is no class of people so zealous in this parish as those of the neighbouring parishes before described, neither have they within the parish an advantage of moral institutions of any description to inculcate religious or moral practices to old or young as they have in most of other parishes, and which is so essentially necessary for the temporal and eternal welfare of all persons.

Moral and Intellectual Education

There is no resident clergy in the parish, or day schools but 2, the one a national school. To this school all religious denominations have access for intellectual and moral instructions on weekdays. The other school is exclusively for the maintenance and general education and agricultural instruction of Quaker descendants who, or their parents, have hitherto adopted other religious creeds and who are now encouraged by this institution to return to their mother religion. At this Quaker agricultural school moral instructions are afforded on Sundays to the pupils, and also to any others who chose to attend. The average attendance is from 20 to 30 on each Sunday. There is no other Sunday school in the parish.

Temperance

Temperance is not advocated to any extent by the parishioners, nor have any temperance societies [been established] in the parish.

Religious Worship

Protestants worship at Soldierstown <Sogerstown> church. Presbyterians worship at Moira meeting houses. Quakers worship at their own meeting house, which is situated within the parish. Roman Catholics worship at Hillsborough Roman Catholic chapel and pay stipend to the parish priest of the latter parish. This class of people is limited in number in Magheramesk.

Jurisdiction

There is no resident magistrates in the parish or peace preservation. All disputes arising within the parish is decided at Lisburn petty sessions. There is no revenue police in the parish, nor smuggling or illicit distillation practised.

There is no private or professional gentlemen resident in the parish. The parish is situated in the manor of Killultagh. Consequently all small money debts and disputes of that nature is decided at the manor court held in Lisburn on every third Wednesday, William Gregg Esquire, seneschal.

Medical Aid

There is no dispensary in the parish. The poor of the parish receive advice and medicine at the county of Antrim infirmary situated at Lisburn.

Societies

There is no money clubs of any description in the parish, no reading or debating societies in the parish, no combinations among tradespeople or labourers in the parish.

There is no Orange or Ribbon lodges in the parish at present. There was none of the latter at any period. There is 1 Masonic lodge at present in the parish. 9th and 11th December 1837.

Amusements and Ancient Customs

Bullet play is partially practised by the youth of the parish. It is the only amusement of any account now extant among them. There is no ancient customs or costume of any account extant at present in the parish. Amongst the parishioners of Magheramesk there is no taste for legendary tales or stories.

There are 8 publicans or spirit dealers in the parish at present.

Table of Schools

[Table contains the following headings: name, situation and description, when established, income and expenditure, physical, intellectual and moral instruction, number of pupils subdivided by age, sex and religion, name and religion of master or mistress, date on which visited].

Parish of Magheramesk

Brookfield agricultural school for Quaker descendants; this school is situated contiguous to the turnpike road leading from Lisburn to Moira, 5 miles from the former town and within 1 and a half of the latter; the new schoolhouse built for the purpose is 2-storeys high and slated, 40 by 20 feet in the clear, lit by 14 oblong windows, entrance by 3 different doors, all school requisites in good supply, for details see [below]; established 1836; income: funds raised by the Society of Friends, from the managing committee 30 pounds, lodgings, food and fuel in addition; intellectual instruction: books read the Bible, Testament, English reader, English grammar, *Pinnock's Catechisms*, *Butler's Spelling books*, agricultural books, all procured from the school funds; moral instruction: [Authorised] Version of Scripture read, no visits from the clergy; number of pupils: males, 4 under 10 years of age, 4 from 10 to 15, 2 over 15, total 10; females, 3 from 10 to 15 years of age, 1 over 15, total 4; total number of pupils 14, all of other denominations; master William Shannon, a Quaker; visited 17th November 1837.

Maghaberry national school, situated on the leading road from Maghaberry to Moira and within 1 and a half miles of the latter town; the schoolhouse is 1-storey high and slated, and measures 20 feet 4 inches by 17 feet 2 inches in the clear, and is lit by 4 good windows, school requisites in moderate supply; attached to the school stands a house for the teacher's dwelling; established 1812, under the Education Board 1834; income: from the Education Board 8 pounds, from pupils 20 pounds; intellectual instruction: books published by the Education Board; moral instruction: visits from the clergy of the Established Church and all catechisms taught if required; number of pupils: males, 20 under 10 years of age, 27 from 10 to 15, 1 over 15, total 48; females, 11 under 10 years of age, 16 from 10 to 15, 3 over 10, total 30; total number of pupils 78, 30 Established Church, 5 Presbyterians, 8 Roman Catholics, 40 other denominations; master Francis Turner, a Protestant; visited 20th November 1837.

Agricultural School

Brookfield agricultural school, situated in the townland of Inisloughlin and contiguous to Trummery House, was established 1836 by the Society of Friends, for the intellectual and moral education, and also for instructing in the various branches of agriculture and industry, and likewise to give such trades to the male and female pupils as the committee of the school consider best calculated to render them useful to themselves and to the neighbourhood in which they may reside. None to be admitted into the school but the descendants of Friends or Quakers who are now poor and in humble circumstances, and who have a claim on the society as being the offspring of Quaker ancestors. Though their parents may belong to other religious sects, at present, does not interfere with the children's access to this school.

The school is yet in its infancy but it is contemplated to take in 30 boarders, 20 male and 10 female, who are to be lodged, fed, educated and clad in the school as above stated. It is also in contemplation, if there be sufficient funds, to admit 30 day scholars who will get instructions as above, or any of the branches their parents deem useful for them. These must also be the descendants of Quakers.

At present there are 14 boarders in the school, 10 males and 4 females, who are all Quakers: males above 15 years of age 2, above 10 and under 15 years 4, and under 10 years 4; female, above 15 years of age 1, above 10 and under 15 years 3; total male 10, total female 4, total pupils 14. Books read the Bible, Testaments, English readers, *Butler's Spelling books*, *Pinnock's Catechisms*, English grammar and agricultural books, all procured from the school funds. Teacher in the school William Shannon, who is assisted by Mrs Shannon, his wife; salary for both 30 pounds per annum, lodgings, food and fuel in addition. Female pupils, in addition to intellectual and moral education, are taught plain needlework and knitting.

The school is at present held in a thatched house 1-storey high. The schoolroom 13 feet 5 inches by 12 feet 9 inches in the clear and lit by 3 glass windows, and all school requisites in good order. This schoolroom is only temporary, till a schoolhouse now built be fully completed. This new schoolhouse is built of stone and brick, stands 2-storeys high and slated, 40 by 20 feet in the clear, walls 20 inches thick, entrance by 3 different doors. It is a spacious edifice, well finished inside and lit by 14 large oblong windows, heat afforded by a good metal stove, and ventilation by letting down the windows. The lower storey is for the school and the upper storey for the beds and lodging. Cost of the house and furniture, beds etc. when completed is calculated at 300 pounds.

Attached to the school is a commodious thatched house 1-storey high, occupied as the teacher's dwelling, dining room, kitchens, stores, for the accommodation of the school. The school is also kept in it at present. The female pupils will be always lodged and educated in it separate from the boys. The grounds, about 24 English acres, was purchased from a farmer at 348 pounds and is leased from Lord Hertford, annual rent 18s 6d per acre. It is husbanded for the benefit of the school and the chief part of the labour done by the male pupils, who are taught the different branches of agriculture by the teacher of the school, who is also an experienced land steward. The site of the school is eligible and healthy, and has the convenience of spring and river water.

The institution is not only calculated to benefit the aforesaid class of Quaker descendants, who are very numerous in the surrounding neighbourhood, but also to benefit all other classes by their example, who may cause their children to adopt improvement in education, art and farming.

This school has been founded on the suggestion and chiefly on a bequest granted or bestowed by one of the Friends, for establishing an agricultural school in Magheramesk on the principle herein before mentioned. He is a Dr Unthank, residing in Limerick <Limrick>. The bequest given by him was 500 pounds; other Friends gave each 100 pounds, others gave each 10 pounds and others smaller sums according to their circumstances. The school is now and to be supported by donations and subscriptions from Friends only. It stands within 5 miles of Lisburn and within 1 and a half miles of Moira, in an improved part of the neighbourhood, and has the advantage of public and by-roads passing by the farm. Informants Jacob Green and William Shannon. 17th and 18th November 1837.

Emigration

The following are the names, ages, religion and number of persons that have emigrated to America from the above parish during the years 1835 and 1836. It will show the townlands in which they resided and ports to which the different persons have gone, as enumerated from 13th to 30th November 1837. [All emigrated to New York].

1835: James McAreavey, 40, Mary McAreavey, 36, Roman Catholics, from Inisloughlin.

Richard Boyes, 25, Established Church, from Maghaberry.

Francis Graham, 36, Rebecca Graham, 22, Established Church, from Ballynalargy.

Richard Hull, 24, Welsley Hull, 19, Matilda Hull, 21, Margret Hull, 18, Established Church, from Magheramesk.

1836: Edward Feary, 30, Cathrine Feary, 28, Mary Feary, 5, Thomas Feary, 3, William Feary, 1, Roman Catholics, from Maghaberry.

Richard Hull, 20, Established Church, from Maghaberry.

James Dickey, 45, Elizabeth Dickey, 40, Bernard Dickey, 20, Nathaniel Dickey, 18, William Dickey, 16, Robert Dickey, 14, Debby Dickey, 12, Mary Dickey, 10, Norris Dickey, 8, English Dickey, 6, Elizabeth Dickey, 4, Established Church, from Trummery.

The aforesaid emigrants were of the farming class and chiefly in good circumstances. They sold their farms here and calculated on making purchases of land in America, by which they would be enabled to leave free and permanent settlements to their growing families, feeling that such they could not procure in this country for them.

Migration to the Harvest

11 persons only are in the habit of migrating to the Scotch harvest annually from this parish; cause is that many of the working class employ themselves at cotton weaving. Informants James Graham, Adam Hull and many others. Finished 30th November 1837 [signed] Thomas Fagan.

SCHOOL STATISTICS

Table of Schools

[Table contains the following headings: name of townland where held, name and religion of master or mistress, free or pay school, annual income, description and cost of schoolhouse, number of pupils subdivided by religion, sex and by the Protestant and Roman Catholic returns, societies with which connected. All are paying schools].

Maghaberry <Magabary>, master Francis Turner, Protestant, Established Church; income about 30 pounds; schoolhouse good, cost 70 pounds; number of pupils by the Protestant return: 21 Established Church, 17 Presbyterians, 18 other denominations, 1 Roman Catholic, 37 males, 20 females; by the Roman Catholic return: 26 Established Church, 7 Presbyterians, 13 other denominations, 37 males, 17 females; the schoolhouse built by subscription.

Trummery Creenagh, master John Gray, Presbyterian; income about 16 pounds; number of pupils by the Protestant return: 28 Established Church, 6 Roman Catholics, 25 males, 9 females; associations none.

Magheramesk Carinloughrim, master William Forde, Protestant, Established Church; number of pupils by the Protestant return: 12 Established Church, 3 Presbyterians, 5 other denominations, 8 Roman Catholics, 16 males, 12 females; associations none.

Parish of Tullyrusk, County Antrim

Statistical Report by Lieutenant R. Stotherd, March 1833

NATURAL STATE

Name and Derivation

In modern times this parish is commonly known by the name of Tullyrousk or Tullyrusk, as pronounced. In Archdall's *Monasticon Hibernicum*, St Patrick is reported to have founded a church in Tulach and Father Colgan states that it is now called Tulach-ruisc, which no doubt is the present parish of Tullyrusk <Tullyrousk>. Tullagh-riasg, "the moory hill": see *Statistical account* by Revd E. Cupples, L.L.D.

Situation and Union

It was anciently situated in the territory of Killultagh in the south or upper Claneboy and county Down, and now belongs to the manor of Killultagh, barony of Upper Massereene and county of Antrim.

It is one of the united parishes of Glenavy, Camlin and Tullyrusk, in the diocese of Connor, province of Armagh, the reputed patron being the Marquis of Hertford, to whom the rectorial tithes belong. "Tullyrusk is called a grange in the registry of Connor and a chapelry in the terrier and regal visitation book. It was probably either a bishop's mensal or a chapelry dependent on some of the great monasteries. In 1604 the curate paid 2s in synodals and in the year 1622 10s in procurations." See *Statistical survey of the union* by Revd E. Cupples.

Boundaries, Extent and Divisions

It is bounded on the north by the parish of Killead, east by Templepatrick and Shankill <Shankhill>, south by Derryaghy and west by Glenavy and Camlin. The Crumlin river also forms its northern and the Glenavy river its southern boundary. In form it is regular and compact, approaching that of a parallelogram, its greatest length from east to west being 5 miles, from north to south breadth 2 and a half, and contains 4,779 acres 2 roods 16 perches British statute measure. It is divided into 4 townlands viz. Dundrod, Tullyrusk, Budore and Knockairn.

Property and Tenure

The Marquis of Hertford is proprietor and lord of the manor. "The union of which this parish is a part was formerly in possession of the O'Neills. Early in the reign of Elizabeth, Cormack McNeile, called the captain of Killultagh, possessed this country, who, being bribed by Sir Nicholas Bagnall, deserted the standard of O'Neill and submitted to the Queen. Shortly afterwards we find Bryan McArt, in possession of Killultagh, from his impenetrable woods making irruptions against the English. He was, however, attacked in March 1602 by Sir Arthur Chichester, then governor of Carrickfergus, was defeated and driven out of his own territories, into which he had retreated with 500 men. By the act for the attainder of Shane O'Neill, passed in the year 1569, the territories of Killultagh escheated to the Queen, by whom they were granted, with other possessions of the O'Neills, in 1571 to Sir Thomas Smith and son on condition of subduing all rebels therein and planting them with good subjects. Their efforts were rendered abortive by the decided opposition of the O'Neills. The younger Smith lost his life and, the conditions not being fulfilled, the grants in consequence became void and reverted to the Crown. [Insert marginal note: See copy of *Down grand inquisition*, 1623].

In 1604 Con O'Neill, in consideration of a pardon granted to him by the King, consented that these lands, with others, should be conveyed to Sir James Hamilton by letters patent, from whom they passed about the year 1609 to Sir Fulke Conway, at that time an active officer in the English army, who, by the introduction of English and Welsh settlers, greatly contributed towards the civilisation of the inhabitants and the cultivation of the soil.

The family of Sir Fulke Conway enjoyed the territories of Killultagh until the year 1683 when Edward, the last Earl Conway, dying without issue, bequeathed them to Francis Seymour, son of Sir Edward Seymour, speaker of the Long Parliament [insert marginal note: *Lodge's Peerage*] and author of the Habeas Corpus Act. From him the lands of Killultagh have descended in regular succession to the present proprietor, the Marquis of Hertford." See *Statistical account of the union*.

NATURAL FEATURES

Surface

A basaltic ridge bounds the parish on the south, extending from the eastern extremity at 1,003 feet above the level of the sea westwards to the standing stones, the highest point of the parish at 1,059 feet above the sea, thence to the Bochell Stone, 861 feet, and Tullyrusk Fort, 696 feet, to the Glenavy river, the water of which at the Knockairn bridge is 358 feet above low water mark. From this ridge the descent is even and regular northward towards the Crumlin river, its regularity being only interrupted by the round basaltic hill of Budore, the summit of which is 805 feet above the level of the sea.

Soil

The prevailing soil in the lower portion of the parish is a strong loam resting on a substratum of yellow clay. The abundance of stones of trap which appear on first breaking up the soil clearly point out its basaltic origin. As the ground rises the superstratum of vegetable mould is thinner, the yellow till approaching the surface which, in the higher parts of the parish, is in a great measure clothed with a spritty grass and affords excellent pasture for cattle.

PRODUCTIVE ECONOMY

Produce

Barley, oats, flax and potatoes are the usual crops and the mode of agriculture and succession of crops differs little from that practised in the neighbouring parishes. The potato fallow is generally the preparation for a seed crop although the common fallow is sometimes adopted on the stiffer clay soils. The mountain and hilly pasture lands are capable of great improvement, by breaking up and draining and afterwards laying down with grass seed and clover. The coarse spritty bent and grass would by a succession of efforts of this kind be got rid of and the hills be converted into rich and productive downs or sheep farms. In some situations also they would be capable of irrigation, the effect of which in the neighbourhood of so excellent a market as Belfast cannot be foreseen.

Turbary

The turf bogs are nearly exhausted. The little that remains is in the townland of Budore at the eastern extremity of the parish. The principal supply of turbary is from Divis mountain and the Brown moss in the parish Derryaghy.

NATURAL HISTORY

Rocks

Trap rocks appear in various parts of the parish and in sufficient abundance and quality to afford excellent materials for building and for the repair of the roads. On the southern boundary of the parish, in Tullyrusk and Dundrod, a decomposed variolite supplies an admirable sand for mortar and cements; see spec[imen].

MODERN TOPOGRAPHY AND NATURAL FEATURES

Roads

The parish is intersected in every direction with good roads, for the formation of which good materials are abundant on the spot. They lead to Belfast, Antrim, Lisburn, Glenavy and Crumlin.

Rivers

The 2 boundary rivers, the Glenavy and Crumlin, the latter of which has its source at the foot of Divis, are the only rivers. Into this latter innumerable small tributary streams flow, fertilising the soil in their progress down the hills. These 2 rivers in the winter season are subject to very sudden and great floods, but in summer afford but a scanty supply of water. The fall is sufficient, however, to admit of the establishment of mills on both rivers, at almost any point of their course through this parish.

Houses and Villages

There is neither town nor village in the parish. The houses are few and at considerable intervals, being occupied by the farmers who combine a little linen and cotton with their agricultural pursuits.

Places of Worship

There is neither church or chapel in the parish. An old graveyard points out the site of the ruins of an ancient church said to have been founded by St Patrick, the foundation walls of which are now scarcely perceptible. As far as they can be traced, its length appears to have been 66 feet, its breadth 26 feet. The style or quality of the architecture cannot now be distinguished.

A large commodious Presbyterian meeting house was built in 1826 in the townland of Dundrod, the inhabitants of the parish being principally of that persuasion.

Schools

There are 3 schools in the parish, 1 in Dundrod and 2 in Budore, supported by the parents of the children and assisted by the Dublin societies.

Parish of Tullyrusk

Mills

On the Crumlin river near Dundrod bridge is a corn mill, and the ruin of a flax mill without a roof or a wheel in the same townland, on the stream bounding it and Budore.

Woods and Planting

From the ancient records of the country relating to this district, it would appear that it was in 1600 covered with dense woods [insert marginal note: Boate's *Natural history of Ireland*], not a vestige of which now remains. There is a little young planting about the cottage of William Gregg Esquire at Knockairn bridge and scarcely a tree in the parish.

ANCIENT TOPOGRAPHY

Antiquities

See Places of Worship for a short account of the old church of Tullyrusk. There is nothing further of interest with the exception of a number of old forts or raths which, to the number of 20, are scattered over the sides of the hills and in the valley. It is worthy of remark that towards the highest parts of this parish there is not one to be found. This fact is much in favour of the supposition that they were originally used as places of refuge and defence, for in all probability the woods were more dense at the foot than at the summit of the hills, where the soil is more scanty and therefore less subject to discovery in their seclusion. [Signed] R. Stotherd, Lieutenant Royal Engineers, 1st March 1833.

Memoir by James Boyle, September 1836, with additions from Office Copy by G. Scott, T.C. Hannyngton and Another

NATURAL FEATURES

Hills

A basaltic ridge, forming a portion of the western side of the Divis range of mountain, extends westward along the southern side of this parish, declining rapidly near its western side and terminating in an almost level tract in the more westerly parish of Camlin. The highest point in the parish is at its eastern side, where it is 1,059 feet above the sea, and from this there is a very rapid though unbroken fall southward to the Glenavy river, the average height of which in this parish is 370 feet above the sea. The fall northward is also rapid and regular, being alone interrupted by the round basaltic hill of Budore, 805 feet above the sea. These hills are mostly smooth and kept as pasture. The principal point in this parish is Bouchell <Bochell> Stone, 864 feet above the sea.

Rivers

The small streams known by the names of the Crumlin and Glenavy rivers bound this parish, the former on the north and the latter on the south. The Crumlin water takes its rise on the western side of Divis mountain in the adjoining and easterly parish of Shankill, at an elevation of about 1,058 feet above the level of the sea and 1,010 feet above Lough Neagh, into which it discharges itself. After a short distance it enters on the northern boundary of this parish, along which it flows westward for 4 miles, separating it from the parish of Killead and also forming the boundary between the baronies of Upper and Lower Massereene.

On quitting this parish it descends to a level of 228 feet above the sea and, after a total course of 12 and three-quarter miles and passing through the town of Crumlin, discharges itself into Lough Neagh, 2 and three-quarter miles west of that town. Its average fall is 1 foot in 37 feet, its average breadth 10 feet. Its depth is very variable but does not exceed 3 feet in ordinary weather. Its bed is partly gravelly but occasionally crossed by a stony ford. Its floods are frequent, rapid and harmless, subsiding quickly from its inclination and the drained state of the country through which it flows. There are some flat holmes <hoames> which it inundates and rather fertilises. The supply of water is scanty in summer but sufficient for the moderate machinery of the country. It is also applicable to irrigation. Its banks are very low.

The Glenavy river is a stream which takes its rise in the south western side of Divis mountain in the adjoining and more southerly parish of Derryaghy and at an elevation of about 950 feet above the sea. From this it pursues a westerly course for a short distance and, descending to a level of 590 feet, enters the south side of this parish and flows along its southern boundary for 1 and a quarter miles. It then pursues a north west course along the south west boundary of the parish for 3 and a quarter miles and descends to a level of 302 feet above the sea. After this it pursues a more westerly course between the parishes of Glenavy and Camlin, and discharges itself into Lough Neagh after an entire course of 9 and a half miles. Its average fall in this parish is 1 foot in 64 feet and breadth 9 feet. It is secured by steep clay banks averaging 20 feet in height, which confine it in its rapid though harmless floods. Its bed is gravelly. It is applicable to and usefully situated for the purpose of machinery and is also applicable to drainage. The parish is sufficiently supplied with spring and river water for domestic uses.

Bogs

In Budore townland at the east of the parish, and at an elevation of from 800 to 1,000 feet above the sea, is a small tract of turf bog now nearly exhausted from being used for firing. Its depth does not exceed 6 feet. The subsoil is a reddish-coloured clay. A very little fir timber, principally stumps, is found in this bog. The stumps stand, broken and sometimes burnt, at the same height. The trunks lie scattered indiscriminately.

Woods

[Insert addition: There is scarcely a tree in the parish, with the exception of a few small plantations round the better description of farmhouses].

Climate

There is much difference in the climate of this parish, the seasons in the lower grounds along its western side being from a week to 10 days earlier than in the hilly grounds along its eastern side. Throughout the parish the air is pure and healthy. It is, however, in the higher grounds much exposed to the south west wind which here prevails, and also to rains, the vapours being either attracted by or wafted to the hills and then condensed. The soil, being stiff, requires moisture and the climate in that respect is suitable. Potatoes and oats constitute the crops mostly cultivated here. In the lower districts the former are planted generally during the beginning of May and raised early in November. The latter is sown mostly during the month of March and cut down in the early part of September. In the more hilly parts the crops, though sown about the same time, require from a week to 10 days longer to ripen.

MODERN TOPOGRAPHY

Towns

There is no town in the parish. The hamlet of Dundrod is the only thing approaching to a village. It is situated at the north side of the parish, at the junction of 3 roads with that leading from Antrim to Lisburn and contiguous to the bridge over the Crumlin water. It is situated in the townland from which it takes its name and 4 miles east of Crumlin. It is merely a collection of 12 dirty-looking thatched cottages and one 2-storey house occupied as a whiskey shop. The cottages are built irregularly and it is an uninteresting spot unworthy of further notice.

The only public building in the parish is the Presbyterian meeting house in the townland of Dundrod, near its northern side and on the road from Antrim to Lisburn. It is a plain but neat roughcast house measuring 60 feet long and 40 feet wide, rather lofty and having a high pitched, hipped roof. It is very neatly and comfortably fitted up internally, having a good gallery and containing accommodation for 800 persons. It was erected by subscription in 1827 and cost 1,100 pounds.

Gentlemen's Seats

Knockcairn Cottage, the seat of Fortescue Gregg Esquire, is pleasantly situated in the townland of the same name and at the eastern side of the parish.

Mills

In the townland of Dundrod, and on the Crumlin water, is a corn mill propelled by an undershot water wheel 4 feet 4 inches broad and 14 feet in diameter. It has a fall of water of 13 feet.

[Insert addition: On the Crumlin river near Dundrod bridge is a corn mill and the ruin of a flax mill. The diameter of the wheel belonging to the corn mill is 14 feet, breadth of buckets 4 feet 4 inches, fall of water 13 feet, an undershot wheel].

Communications

This parish is amply supplied with roads which are kept in repair at the expense of the barony of Upper Massereene. The main roads are that from Antrim to Lisburn, which passes through the centre of the parish from north to south for 2 and a third miles. It is a pretty good hard road but very hilly. It might be rendered much less so and nearly level. Its average breadth is 24 feet.

There are not any other roads which can properly be termed main roads but there are several roads passing through the parish and communicating with the neighbouring towns. The principal of these are that from Glenavy to Belfast, which passes along the north side of the parish for 2 and three-quarter miles. The part of this road west of the village of Dundrod is level and kept in tolerable repair. That part of it east of Dundrod is very hilly and rough. Its average breadth is 32

Parish of Tullyrusk

feet. This road forms one of the principal communications with Belfast.

There is another road traversing the eastern side of the parish for 1 and a half miles and forming another means of communication with Belfast. It is very hilly and mountainous and is in indifferent repair.

There is 1 mile of a good level road from Dundrod to Crumlin passing along the northern side of the parish. Its average breadth is 23 feet. There are numerous other crossroads connecting those already mentioned and affording to the people every facility of intercourse with the neighbouring districts. They are all kept in repair at the expense of the barony of Lower Massereene. The material used is whinstone, trap and the common field stones broken. These materials are everywhere abundant.

There are 4 bridges in the parish, namely Dundrod and Lathemstown bridges, on the road from Antrim to Lisburn, the former over the Crumlin and the latter over the Glenavy water; Thompson's bridge over the Crumlin water, on a road to Belfast; and Knockcairn bridge over the Glenavy water, connecting this parish with that of Glenavy. These bridges are all plain, substantial old structures and sufficient in every respect.

General Appearance and Scenery

Though the surface of the ground presents a considerable diversity, still the absence of planting gives the parish an uninteresting appearance, particularly in its more eastern districts where, though the country is hilly, still the features are not bold and the large pasture fields enclosed with stone fences have rather a dreary aspect.

From the higher grounds the prospect is wide and magnificent, embracing Lough Neagh from its southern to its northern extremity, portions of the counties of Down, Armagh, Tyrone and Derry, and the western side of Antrim. On the south the view is bounded by the serrated ridge of the Mourne Mountains, on which Slieve Donard stands conspicuous. Towards the west the noble chain of the Derry mountains may be seen from the northerly extremity of that county, traversing to its southern and finally disppearing in Tyrone, while underneath, and more near, Lough Neagh, with its low and wooded shores and the rich country extending along its eastern side, combine to present a landscape of extraordinary variety, richness and beauty.

[Insert addition: The parish of Tullyrusk has nothing picturesque in itself. It is well fenced with ditches of earth and stone. There are not many thorn hedges. It is a good hunting country but from the Bouchell Stone, on a hill of the same name, a wide and beautiful view may be obtained on a clear day: Slieve Donard in county Down may be seen with the town and spire of Lurgan and Mournes or Newry mountains rising in the distance. The counties of Armagh, Tyrone and Derry are also visible and have a fine effect, contrasted with Lough Neagh and its rich shores. Looking north, Slemish and Slieve Nane are visible, also Shane's Castle and Randalstown rising on the opposite side of Antrim bay.

Any view to the eastward is entirely shut out by Divis mountain. The Bouchell is a small green mountain 864 feet above the level of the sea. On the top there is a standing stone 3 feet high. It stands on a small platform of mason work. It is not of any antiquity, at least the building at the base. The mountain derives its name I think from the stone having the appearance of a boy on the top from a distance. Bouchell in Irish, I think, means "a boy."

On this mountain, 40 yards from the standing stone, there is a mound in the form of a cross. It is a cross at right angles so: [drawing, cross shape], 49 feet each way. The tradition is that it was used as a place of worship previous to the erection of Tullyrusk <Tullyrousk> chapel, which stood about half a mile to the westward of the Bouchell. The mark of the foundation of the chapel is all that now remains [initialled] T.C. Hannyngton].

SOCIAL ECONOMY

Early Improvements

The improvements which [have] taken place in this parish are probably to be attributed to its colonisation by the English settlers who came over in the reign of Elizabeth under the Seymours or Conways, the ancestors of the present Marquis of Hertford, who then obtained possession of their vast estates in this county, of which this parish forms a portion. There is also a considerable mixture of Scots, probably the descendants of the settlers during the reign of James I and also some Roman Catholics, who would seem, if not the aborigines, the descendants of some very early settlers, as the difference is perceivable in their manners from those of the other inhabitants. No name can be said to be prevalent, but those of McClure, White, Strachan, McLernon (the last Roman Catholic) are commonly met with.

Improvements: Situation and Farms

To their proximity to Belfast, which is 9 miles

distant, the people are almost entirely indebted for their independence and support, as to it they take their milk, butter and grain but particularly the former articles, this parish from its hilly nature being chiefly a pasture district in which large flocks are kept. The cultivation of the ground is, however, increasing rapidly and much more grain is now sown for the market. A good deal of pork and some cheese are also sent from this parish to the Belfast market.

The parish is exclusively an agricultural one. The usual size of the farms is from 30 to 40 acres but there are some of from 130 to 150 acres. The latter, however, are in the more hilly districts and are chiefly laid down in pasture. The leases on this estate are for 3 lives and the system of fining down the rent one-fourth at each renewal is strictly practised, the reduction made in the rent being considered equivalent to 6 and a half per cent on the purchase paid. The lands are reasonably let, the system of subletting does not exist and the people live under a good landlord. Their proximity to lime, which is within between 5 and 6 miles, is another benefit which they enjoy.

These circumstances, and the fact of the labouring class not being more numerous than necessary (and therefore never out of employment), have rendered the people easy in their circumstances and comparatively comfortable in their mode of living.

Progress of Improvement

The causes which have affected their habits and morals have sprung from the same source, as even to this day a difference exists between the Roman Catholics and Protestants as to their habits and dispositions, the former, though improving daily, being still less enlightened, less civilised in their tastes, less neat in their manner of dressing and less comfortable in their style of living, both as to comfort and cleanliness. They are not so independent in their circumstances, their holdings being generally much smaller than those of the Protestants. Still they are intermixed with them, not inhabiting any one particular district nor the more remote parts of the parish, as is so frequently the case in similar cases. But they are scattered over its surface and have within memory improved much in every respect owing to their intercourse with and the example of their neighbours. Schools, particularly Sunday schools, have done much good in this parish.

A Presbyterian congregation (in connection with the Synod of Ulster) was established here and a meeting house erected by subscription at a cost of 1,100 pounds in 1827, and this event has produced a most perceptible change in the moral habits of the people as, from its retired situation and distance from a place of worship, the people had been very much neglected; and no greater proof of this can be adduced than the fact of many Episcopalians having since then become Presbyterians and many improper practices being since then discontinued such as drinking at wakes, cock-fighting (now confined to the Roman Catholics).

Sunday schools have been kept up and Sunday much better observed. Previous to this period there had been a laxity of morality owing to the neglected state of the people, but they have since been much improved and are now on a par with their neighbours.

Obstructions to Improvement

There are not any obstructions to improvement, but the improvement of the country would be much facilitated by improved means of communicating and intercourse with Belfast and Lisburn, the present roads being hilly and badly laid out.

Local Government

There is one local magistrate, Fortescue Gregg of Knockcairn, Esquire, who generally resides in this parish. His residence is conveniently situated and he is respected by the people. This parish is included in the Crumlin district, at which town petty sessions are held on every alternative Tuesday. This parish, however, furnishes but little business for sessions or assizes.

It is included in the manor of Killultagh, in which town manor courts are held once in 3 weeks and courts leet once in 6 months, William Gregg Esquire, seneschal. Sums not exceeding 20 pounds are recoverable by civil bill process and sums not exceeding 100 pounds by attachment at these courts.

There is neither outrage nor illicit distillation in the parish. There are not any insurances.

Dispensary

This parish is included in the district of the Crumlin dispensary, which was established in 1832 and has been of much use here in cases of fever which occasionally visit this parish and, should it commence with the hilly districts, seldom omits visiting almost every family in that part of the parish, not confining itself to the poorer people as is usually the case. No disease is, however, particularly prevalent. For details as to the support of this

Parish of Tullyrusk

Schools

The advantages of education are, from the number of schools and the cheapness of instruction, within the reach of all. The system of education has much improved of late years and schools, particularly sabbath schools, have done much good and produced a perceptible change on the habits of the rising generation. The people seem anxious for instruction and all the rising generation are being or have been instructed. Reading, writing, arithmetic, a little English grammar and occasionally a little book-keeping or mensuration complete the education of the children.

Poor

There are very few poor, perhaps not more than 10 actual paupers in the parish. The collection on Sundays and the voluntary charity of the people is their only support and it is quite adequate.

Religion

This parish is episcopally united to those of Camlin and Glenavy, which union is better known in the country by the name of Glenavy. The union forms a vicarage of which the Revd Edward Cupples, the vicar-general of the diocese, is vicar. The vicarial tithes of the union amount to 380 pounds per annum and the lay tithes (payable to the Marquis of Hertford) to 101 pounds per annum. The vicar resides in Lisburn but keeps a curate who resides in the adjoining parish of Glenavy and to whom he pays a salary of 75 pounds per annum. A curate would be required for this parish alone. The church is also in Glenavy parish.

A Presbyterian congregation was established here and a meeting house erected in 1827. It is in connection with the Synod of Ulster. The clergyman receives 100 pounds per annum regium donum and [blank] per annum stipend.

The Roman Catholics worship at the chapel in Derryaghy which, in their church, is united to this. They support their priest in the usual manner.

By the revised census of 1834 there are in this parish 184 Episcopalians, 785 Presbyterians and 294 Roman Catholics.

Habits of the People: Farms and Houses

This is quite an agricultural district, very few being engaged in weaving, and spinning being carried on by the females merely as an alternative to idleness rather than from anything they can earn by it. There are some farms of from 100 to 200 acres. These, however, are chiefly pasture and the general size of the farms being from 30 to 40 acres. The largest farms are in the more easterly and hilly districts of the parish, where the ground is better adapted for pasture, but cultivation is rapidly creeping up the hills. The fields are in general large and the country open and well suited for hunting, which is kept up here, the hounds coming from Lisburn.

There is a shade of difference between the inhabitants of this parish and those of Camlin, the latter being the more wealthy and, from their being more exposed to intercourse with strangers, rather the more civilised. Their houses and farms bear a greater air of substance and comfort about them and those of the lower class are much more cleanly and neat than in this parish. The situation of this parish is retired and rather out of the way but still, in some of its most remote districts, very snug farmhouses with neat gardens are to be found. Gardens, indeed, are general throughout the neighbourhood and are a strong proof of the English descent of the people.

The farmers' houses are in general snug, comfortable and neat, retired from the road and surrounded by trees. There are few of them more than 1-storey. They are mostly thatched, roughcast and whitened, and pretty roomy and well furnished. Clocks are numerous as are also watches. The houses of the smaller farmers and labouring class are not so neat or cleanly as in Killead but they have improved greatly of late years and some of them are pretty snug.

The people are now getting into the habit of slating their houses. They usually consist of 2 apartments, are built of stone and lime but seldom roughcast. Generally speaking they are not cleanly. These houses have neat little gardens attached to them.

Food and Employment

The farmers are a decent class of persons, generally educated and living rather comfortably. They make a good deal of cheese for domestic use and some little for the market. Bacon, meal, potatoes, some baker's bread and milk constitutes their food. The food of the lower class is rather inferior, chiefly consisting of potatoes and milk, very little animal food being used.

The agricultural labourers are in constant employment and generally live on the land of the farmer, paying their rent by their labour.

Amusements

All classes are industrious, peaceable, honest and obliging, frugal and charitable. They are rather given to whiskey drinking and, generally, on quitting their places of worship resort to the alehouse, an establishment which is always to be found in the immediate vicinity of meeting houses and chapels. Though wakes are not now attended by the Presbyterians for amusement, the practice of serving whiskey at them is kept up. The Roman Catholic wakes are usually scenes of mirth and joviality. There is a great deal of immorality in this parish, particularly among the sons and servant women of farmers.

Their amusements are not so numerous as formerly. Dancing is now the only one, with the exception of a little cock-fighting said to be confined to the Roman Catholics. They attend the summer fairs for amusement and the men generally get drunk at them. They dress well and neatly, there being no difference between them and the people of Camlin in this respect.

Fuel

Fuel is scarce, the nearest being 4 and a half miles distant. This is in Divis mountains. In a few years the bog there will be exhausted and they will be obliged to go at least 9 miles for their firing.

Longevity

They are rather shorter lived than the people in Killead, persons above 75 being rather rarely met with. They do not marry early. The usual number in a family is 5.

Orangemen are numerous but all parties live on good terms.

Physical Features

There is nothing peculiar to them except that they are free from the Scottish accent so prevalent in this county, and speak pretty well. Their high and broad foreheads distinguish them as a different race from the inhabitants of the more northern parishes. They have generally light hair and fair complexions, and lightish grey or blue eyes. Their tastes for gardens is another distinguishing peculiarity.

Roman Catholic Population

The foregoing remarks apply generally to the people of this parish but it may be stated with impartiality that the Roman Catholics are inferior in civilisation to the rest of the population. They do not dress so neatly or well or with the same taste. They are less cleanly in their habitations and live more poorly. They attend wakes for amusement and keep up cock-fighting. They are not so generally educated and they are inferior in their circumstances, their farms being small and a greater proportion of them engaged as labourers or servants. But at the same time they are fully more hospitable and generous, open and frank in their manners than their neighbours and possess most of the good traits of character peculiar to Irishmen, still, among aliens, retaining much of their native natural love of fun, their hospitality, pugnacity and improvidence.

Emigration

Though emigration does not prevail to the same extent as formerly, still it exists to a greater degree than in many neighbouring parishes. About 12 individuals still annually emigrate to Canada from this small parish and only one has returned during the last 6 years. Some of those who emigrate are farmers who, having sold their farms, take with them their price and many go from this parish who take a capital of from 100 pounds to 500 pounds with them. Few of the poorer class and scarcely any Roman Catholics emigrate. One or perhaps 2 individuals go annually to the Scottish harvests.

Remarkable Events

There is no record of this parish having been the scene of any remarkable event or of its having given birth to any remarkable person.

Education

[Table contains the following headings: name, situation and description, when established, income and expenditure, physical, intellectual and moral education, number of pupils subdivided by sex, age and religion, name and religious persuasion of master or mistress].

In a suitable house (somewhat out of repair) built for the purpose by local subscription and situated in the townland of Dundrod; it is more than 40 years since it was originally established; income from pupils 16 pounds; intellectual education: spelling, reading, writing, arithmetic, books of the Kildare Place Society, *Bonnycastle's Algebra*, mensuration, *Jackson's Book-keeping*; moral education: Sunday school, visited by the Presbyterian minister, Authorised Version of Scriptures daily, Protestant and Presbyterian catechisms on Saturday after school hours; number of pupils:

Parish of Tullyrusk

males, 9 under 10 years of age, 11 from 10 to 15, 2 above 15, 22 total males; females, 7 under 10 years of age, 5 from 10 to 15, 12 total females; 34 total pupils, 6 Protestants, 26 Presbyterians, 2 Roman Catholics; master Richard Hood, Protestant.

In a suitable house built for the purpose by subscription and situated in the townland of Budore; established under the Kildare Place Society in 1831 and under the Synod of Ulster in 1836; income: the Synod of Ulster will grant it annually the sum of 3 pounds, from pupils 20 pounds; intellectual education: spelling, reading, writing, arithmetic, books of the Kildare Place Society, *Bonnycastle's Algebra*, mensuration, *Jackson's Book-keeping*; moral education: visited by the Presbyterian minister, Authorised Version of Scriptures daily, all catechisms on Saturday after school hours; number of pupils: males, 11 under 10 years of age, 12 from 10 to 15, 23 total males; females, 9 under 10 years of age, 8 from 10 to 15, 17 total females; 40 total pupils, 5 Protestants, 23 Presbyterians, 12 Roman Catholics; master John MacHenry, Presbyterian.

[Totals]: income from benevolent individuals or public societies 3 pounds, from pupils 36 pounds; number of pupils: males, 20 under 10 years of age, 23 from 10 to 15, 2 above 15, 45 total males; females, 16 under 10 years of age, 13 from 10 to 15, 29 total females; 74 total pupils, 11 Protestants, 49 Presbyterians, 14 Roman Catholics.

Memo relating to schools: I have taken the average attendance during the past year derived from the books of the school or, when such are not kept, from the authority of the teacher. Signed James Boyle, 4th February 1837.

Table of Schools

[Table contains the following headings: name of townland where held, name and religion of master or mistress, free or pay school, annual income of master or mistress, description and cost of schoolhouse, number of pupils subdivided by religion, sex and the Protestant and Roman Catholic returns, societies with which connected].

Dundrod, master Wallace Ireland, Presbyterian; pay school, annual income about 12 pounds; schoolhouse: good slated house, cost 35 pounds, built by subscription; Marquis of Hertford 5 pounds 13s 9d and aided by the lord lieutenant's school fund; number of pupils by the Protestant return: 3 Established Church, 31 Presbyterians, 2 Roman Catholics, 21 males, 15 females; by the Roman Catholic return: 3 Established Church, 31 Presbyterians, 2 Roman Catholics, 21 males, 15 females; the schoolhouse was built by subscription aided by the lord lieutenant's school fund; the Marquis of Hertford gave 5 pounds 13s 9d.

Budor, master Thomas Atkinson, Protestant; pay school, annual income about 6 pounds; schoolhouse: thatched cabin, cost 6 pounds; number of pupils by the Protestant return: 5 Established Church, 10 Presbyterians, 2 Roman Catholics, 9 males, 8 females; by the Roman Catholic return: 5 Established Church, 10 Presbyterians, 2 Roman Catholics, 9 males, 8 females; associations none.

Drawings

Sketches of Antiquities

[By James Boyle?].
    Draft ground plan of fort [?].
    Drawing of object [stone axehead].
    Draft drawing of metal spearhead with dimensions, 15 inches long.
    Plans of 13 forts in Tullyrusk, 1 in Knockcairn showing 3 associated forts; 2 and 3 in Dundrod.
    Plans and sections of 3 forts in Tullyrusk.

www.ingramcontent.com/pod-product-compliance
Lightning Source LLC
Chambersburg PA
CBHW051211290426
44109CB00021B/2420